ENGLISH SYNTAX

ENGLISH SYNTAX

From Word to Discourse

Lynn M. Berk

New York   Oxford

OXFORD UNIVERSITY PRESS

1999

Oxford University Press

Oxford New York
Athens Auckland Bangkok Bogotá Buenos Aires Calcutta
Cape Town Chennai Dar es Salaam Delhi Florence Hong Kong Istanbul
Karachi Kuala Lumpur Madrid Melbourne Mexico City Mumbai
Nairobi Paris São Paulo Singapore Taipei Tokyo Toronto Warsaw

and associated companies in
Berlin Ibadan

Published by Oxford University Press, Inc.
198 Madison Avenue, New York, New York 10016

Oxford is a registered trademark of Oxford University Press, Inc.

Library of Congress Cataloging-in-Publication Data
Berk, Lynn M., 1943–
    English syntax : from word to discourse / Lynn M. Berk.
      p. cm.
    Includes bibliographical references.
    ISBN 0-19-512352-2. — ISBN 0-19-512353-0 (pbk.)
    1. English language—Syntax. I. Title.
PE1361.B47 1999
425-dc21   98-23348
                                               CIP

Printing (last digit): 9 8 7 6 5 4 3 2 1

Printed in the United States of America
on acid-free paper

For Toby
and
In memory of
my father

Contents

Preface

Although *English Syntax: From Word to Discourse* has been influenced by a number of syntactic theories, my overall goal is to provide a descriptive grammar of English and my overall approach is loosely discourse/functional. This book presumes no theoretical background on the part of the student and the material should be completely accessible to anyone with a rudimentary knowledge of English grammar. Grammatical constructions are discussed in terms of their form, meaning, and function in discourse. I have tried to ensure that students learn the basics of English grammar but that at the same time they come to understand the richness and complexity of the system.

English Syntax: From Word to Discourse is filled with examples; some are my own creation, many come from literary and other print sources, and others from actual conversations. Most sections also conclude with a summary chart containing at least one example of each structure discussed. Whenever a new term is introduced, it appears in boldface. Most boldface terms also appear in the extensive glossary at the end of the book.

Sometimes the nature of a particular construction can be illuminated by a look at its linguistic history. This text includes some very brief forays into the history of the English language, especially in cases where constructions have been influenced by language contact between the English and the Norman French.

I field-tested earlier drafts of this book in a number of sections of English Syntax at Florida International University. This introductory M.A.-level course serves Linguistics majors, TESOL students, and a few English majors. The examples, ideas, and critical comments provided by these students were invaluable in shaping this textbook.

Acknowledgments

I am grateful to all the English Syntax students who used various versions of this book. Their ideas were invaluable and they proved to be astute reviewers, excellent editors, and a wonderful source of examples and counter-examples.

I would like to thank Florida International University and the United Faculty of Florida for the sabbatical that allowed me to finish the final draft of the book. I also benefitted from the hospitality of the Linguistics Department at the University of Colorado, where I spent two sabbatical years (1989–90 and 1996–97). Special thanks to University of Colorado faculty members Barbara Fox and Susanna Cumming (now of University of California, Santa Barbara), who taught me the value of discourse-functional syntax, and to my FIU colleague Kemp Williams, who read pieces of the manuscript and listened patiently as I bounced ideas around.

Many thanks to the all the Tunas in my life (especially those in Boulder and Miami) for not letting me take myself too seriously.

Above all, I am deeply grateful to my husband Toby, who offered constant encouragement and unqualified support, as well as significant technical and editorial assistance. I know that there were many months when his work load doubled because I was too busy with this project to do my share.

ENGLISH SYNTAX

Introduction

What Does *Grammar* Mean?

To most nonlinguists, the term *grammar* refers to set of **prescriptive rules,** i.e., rules that dictate which forms and structures are "correct" and which are not. The following are classic examples:

Don't say *ain't*.

Never end a sentence with a preposition.

Don't split an infinitive.

Never use a double negative.

School children often learn such rules about the same time that they learn the basic rules of table etiquette:

Never chew with your mouth open.

Don't put your elbows on the table.

Don't slurp your soup.

Don't eat with your fingers.

It's no accident that these two sets of rules have a similar ring. Both were established to outline the parameters for socially acceptable behavior. Neither traditional rules of grammar nor table manners are essential to life; they are simply aesthetic flourishes. The teenager who eats with her elbows on the table will not jeopardize her digestion by doing so, just as the child who says *I don't want no cookies* doesn't really impede communication by using the double negative.

But this prescriptive approach to English grammar is ubiquitous and its origins are centuries old. Speakers of Germanic languages came to literacy late. The various Germanic speaking groups that came to Roman Britain in 449 had only the most rudimentary writing system and it was used primarily for casting magic spells. By the time English had established itself as a separate Germanic language in Britain, Latin had long been the language of religion and diplomacy in Western Europe. During much of the medieval period, when English speakers read at all, they read Latin. But of course classical Latin was not a living language and it had to be taught in formal and artificial ways to those who wished to learn it. The first dictionaries and grammars used in Britain were designed to teach Latin to native speakers of Irish Gaelic and English and for centuries the word "grammar" meant "Latin grammar."

Very early on then grammars were associated with the study of Latin; medieval students never studied the structures of their native languages. During the Renaissance, an intense interest in all things classical gave new impetus to the status of Latin. Latin was seen as the language of a golden age; it was beautiful and pure. Jonathon Swift (1667–1745), the author of *Gulliver's Travels*, expressed a view widely held among the English intelligentsia when he wrote to the Lord High-Treasurer of Great Britain:

> I believe your Lordship will agree with me in the Reason why our Language is less refined that those of *Italy, Spain,* or *France.* It is plain, that the *Latin* Tongue in its Purity was never in this Island. (1957, p. 6)[1]

But of course Latin was an artifact, a fossil. Spoken languages evolve and change much like organisms. Classical Latin no longer had native speakers; it existed only in ancient texts. Its very immutability made it seem far purer than contemporary languages. This fact, combined with the long tradition of scholarship in Latin, conspired to enshrine Latin grammar as the standard for all European grammars.

The whole notion of a grammar designed to instruct speakers in how to use their native language would have seemed preposterous to a twelfth-century citizen of England. One was born in a dialect region and into a social class and these constraints shaped both social and linguistic behavior. But by the fifteenth century, social structures began to crumble due to internal political and economic forces, including the bubonic plague, which greatly increased social mobility. (A serious labor shortage in the cities meant that serfs were no longer tied to the land.) By the seventeenth and eighteenth centuries, a new and socially insecure middle class had emerged. Suddenly individuals were not sure how to speak, how to act, how to dress. The result was a spate of how-to manuals. It is no accident that the first serious dictionary of English, the first comprehensive grammar of English, and the first etiquette books were all published in the middle of the eighteenth century.

Bishop Robert Lowth's *A Short Introduction to English Grammar with Critical Notes*, first published in 1761, was the most important English grammar of its time and was to become a model for most future English grammars. Its influence can be felt even today. Given the history of language study in Britain, it is not surprising that Bishop Lowth's grammar was based heavily on Latin models. In the Preface to his grammar Lowth responds to Jonathon Swift's complaints.

Does [Swift's charge] mean, that the English Language, as it is spoken by the politest part of the nation, and as it stands in the writings of our most approved authors, often offends against every part of Grammar? Thus far, I am afraid, the charge is true. Or does it farther imply, that our language is in its nature irregular and capricious; not hitherto subject, nor easily reducible, to a System of rules? In this respect, I am persuaded, the charge is wholly without foundation. (1767, iv)

Lowth then proceeded to set out a system of grammatical rules. His goal was to root out "inaccuracy" and teach us "to express ourselves with propriety in that Language, and to enable us to judge of every phrase and form of construction, whether it be right or not" (viii). Lowth believed that teaching "correctness" should be the primary goal of English grammar and, like most of his contemporaries, his view of correctness was shaped in large part by the forms and structures of classical Latin. Unfortunately, English and Latin are only remotely related and the two languages are very different structurally. Many of the "rules" put forth by Lowth and his followers simply did not reflect the English usage of his time or any other.

In the nineteenth and twentieth centuries, Western scholars began to study languages that were hitherto unfamiliar to Europeans and most North Americans. Indigenous American languages, sub-Saharan African languages, and the languages of the Pacific contained forms and structures that were new to language scholars. **Description,** not prescription, became the goal of those who were seeking to write grammars for these previously unrecorded languages. The data from which these grammars were constructed were actual language as it was spoken in a particular place at a particular time. In the process of describing these languages, linguists revolutionized the study of English as well. They began to analyze the English language as it was actually spoken with all its *ain'ts*, double negatives, and split infinitives. By the 1930s, a strong tradition of descriptive linguistics stood in opposition to the traditional prescriptive approach to English grammar.

In 1957, linguist Noam Chomsky published *Syntactic Structures,* a book that launched another revolution in the study of grammar. Chomsky called his approach **generative grammar** and his goal was to provide the structural descriptions necessary to generate all the grammatical sentences and only the grammatical sentences in a given language. Chomsky's approach went well beyond description; he hoped to formalize the system of unconscious rules that we all exploit in speaking our native languages. Chomsky's work has had a profound impact on the study of syntax and today there are a number of formal theoretical models which owe some debt to Chomsky's generative grammars.

In the push to create formal syntactic models, however, one important dimension of language was lost. Generative models tend to examine individual sentences in isolation and often these sentences are created by the syntactician. But language is primarily a social tool; its function is communication among human beings and rarely do human beings utter single, isolated sentences in

---

the absence of a hearer. In the late 1970s and 1980s, **functional grammars** were developed in order to explore the rules that govern language use in a communicative context. Functional grammarians often focus on **discourse,** i.e., chunks of language larger than the individual sentence (conversations, narratives, letters, etc.).

To contemporary linguists, whatever their theoretical orientation, a grammar is, at the very least, a systematic description of the structure of a language. Their goal is to explain the relationships among parts of the sentence, to understand how form and meaning are related, and in some cases to describe how sentences flow into larger pieces of discourse. A sentence like *I ain't got no cookies* is as worthy of study as *I don't have any cookies;* the dialect of an Appalachian coal miner is as worthy of analysis as that of a member of Britain's royal family.

Grammaticality (Acceptability) Judgments

Linguists study what speakers actually <u>do</u>, not what some rule-maker says they <u>should</u> do. Linguists carry out such studies by (1) examining actual spoken conversations and written texts and (2) using their own judgments and those of others as to what is *acceptable* or *grammatical.* (I use the two terms interchangeably.) This textbook employs both techniques. It is filled with examples of actual language use, most of which are from written texts but some of which are fragments of recorded conversations; it also exploits **grammaticality judgments,** for the most part my own and those of my friends, family, and colleagues. A sentence will be considered acceptable or grammatical if it might reasonably be uttered by a native or fluent speaker of English under ordinary circumstances. Thus, even a sentence like *I don't want no trouble* is an acceptable utterance to any English speaker who routinely uses double negative constructions, and *I might could help you* is perfectly grammatical for many American Southerners. However, no native English speaker would say *We shot herself* or *Addie couldn't have being mad.* Sentences that are grammatical in one historical period may not be grammatical in another. A character in a seventeenth century play might say "Go you to London?" but no modern English speaker would say this even though we all understand what it means.

The standard convention for indicating that a sentence is ungrammatical is a preceding asterisk.

*We shot herself.

*Addie couldn't have being mad.

*Go you to London?

*Down barn the burned night last.

If a sentence is marginally acceptable, i.e., it might be used by speakers under limited circumstances, I have marked it with two preceding question marks *??.*

??She has been going to finish that project for years.

??Into the cave the hikers didn't venture.

If a sentence is merely odd, I have marked it with one question mark.

?This land is possessed by the Jones family.

?She was waving me goodbye.

There is no hard and fast rule for making such grammaticality judgments. Grammaticality is a continuum. *Addie couldn't have being mad* is completely uninterpretable; *Down barn the burned night last* can be interpreted only by rearranging all the words; *Go you to London?* is immediately understandable but we also know that no modern speaker of English would say this. *Into the cave the hiker's didn't venture* sounds very strange but it might be possible in a highly literary context. "She was waving me goodbye" sounds a bit odd but is in fact a line from an old Chuck Berry song (Berry, 1959).

Clearly, making grammaticality judgments is a tricky business. Every linguist depends heavily on his/her own dialect and intuitions in making such judgments. There may be a few sentences in this textbook that I have marked ?? or even * that you may find completely acceptable. Conversely, you may find some of the sentences I consider grammatical to be very strange. Don't worry about these small differences of opinion. Overall, you will find that grammaticality judgments are a valuable, even an essential, tool in the study of syntax.[2]

Historical Periods

Sometimes knowing the historical origins of a grammatical form or construction helps in understanding it. On occasion, I will provide you with a brief history of the syntactic construction under discussion. When I refer to **Old English,** I am speaking of the language spoken in Anglo-Saxon England from the sixth century to about 1100. Old English looks far more like modern Icelandic than it does modern English.

Ðū ūre fæder, þe eart on heofonum, sy þin nama gehālgod.

Cume þin rice. Sy þin willa on eorþan swāswā on heofonum.

Syle ūs tōdæg ūrene dæghwāmlīcan hlāf. And forgyf ūs ūre gyltas swāswā

wē forgyfaþ þæm þe wiþ ūs āgyltaþ. (Hussey, 1995, p. 1)

Both the grammatical structure and the spelling conventions of Old English raise impediments to the modern reader. The symbol þ is pronounced like the *th* in *thigh.* The symbol æ is pronounced like the *a* in *cat* (at least as *cat* is pronounced in my midwestern American dialect). The lines over some vowels indicate that these vowels were long. (These lines are a modern convention and don't actually appear in the original Old English texts.)

Middle English was spoken from 1100–1500. This period begins shortly after the Norman invasion of England in 1066. Language contact with Norman French speakers accelerated some significant linguistic changes that were already underway in English and precipitated others. Middle English is somewhat more accessible to the modern speaker. Here is the same passage in Middle English and those of you familiar with Christian liturgy will probably recognize it now.

> Oure fadir þat art in heuenys, halewid be þi name. Ði kyngdom come to. Be þi wille don as in heuene and in erþe. ȝive to us þis day oure breed ouer oþer substaunse. And forȝiue to us oure dettes, as we forȝiuen to oure dettouris. (Hussey, pp. 1–2)

(In Middle English *u* is used to stand for the *v* sound as well as the *u* sound and ȝ represents the sound of the *g* in *give*.)

The **Early Modern English** period spans 1500–1800. While the English of this period still contains a few constructions and forms that are unfamiliar to modern speakers, the language is almost completely accessible. The version of the *Lord's Prayer* which was routinely used by most Christian congregations until the middle of the twentieth century was actually written in 1611.

> Our Father which art in heaven, hallowed be thy name. Thy kingdom come. Thy will be done in earth, as it is in heaven. Give us this day our daily bread. And forgive us our debts, as we forgive our debtors. (Hussey, p. 2)

It is the linguistic conservatism of religious liturgy that has made forms like *art, thy, goest,* and *maketh* familiar to many modern English speakers.

Something that prescriptive grammarians fail to recognize is that language changes. It is an utterly natural phenomenon and no amount of intervention on the part of English teachers and newspaper columnists can change that. Many of the "oddities" of modern English syntax are remnants of old forms and systems that have changed more slowly than other parts of the grammar. Some of the constructions we will explore in this book are still in an active state of flux and this creates an interesting challenge for the grammarian.

Edited English

In the popular imagination the term *grammar* is often associated with writing. But writing is merely an attempt to capture speech; it is a secondary, not a primary phenomenon. All human beings are biologically equipped for language. Except for the most profoundly retarded individuals, any child who hears human language will acquire it. (Deaf children who are exposed to sign language acquire it just as hearing children acquire spoken language, and while some autistic children do not speak, they typically understand.) Writing, on the other hand, is a learned activity, a cultural artifact. While all societies have spoken language, some still lack writing systems. Linguists do recognize that in literate societies there are aesthetic standards and accepted techniques for writing just as there are standards and techniques for painting and sculpture. In the case of English, the rules for formal writing are often called **edited English.** This book will address issues of edited English only on those occasions when there are interesting syntactic issues involved.

It's All in Your Head

Remember that when you study English syntax, you are not studying some exotic phenomenon in nature; you are in effect studying yourself. You have used most if not all of the syntactic structures discussed in this book. If you are a native speaker of English, you learned these forms and constructions without even being aware that you were doing it. If you are a native or fluent non-native speaker, you undoubtedly construct English sentences automatically, with little premeditation. The study of syntax allows us to make conscious a complex range of activities that fluent speakers engage in unconsciously. Just as we don't need to know how neurons fire in order to feel pain, we don't need to know what a modal auxiliary is in order to use one in a sentence.

Syntax is intrinsically interesting stuff. The world is full of linguistic data— classroom lectures, a conversation between teenagers on the phone, the labels on shampoo bottles, e-mail messages, comic strips, talk shows, etc. Test the generalizations contained in this textbook against your own real world experience. Your data may lead you to conclusions that are different from mine. At that point you cease to be a student of syntax and become a syntactician in your own right.

1

Basic Sentence Structure

Linguists often divide their enterprise into more or less separate fields of study:

a) phonology—sounds
b) morphology—the shape of words and affixes
c) syntax—the ways words are combined into larger structures including sentences
d) semantics—meaning
e) pragmatics—language in a social context
f) discourse—chunks of language larger than a sentence

This textbook will focus primarily on syntax, semantics, and discourse, with brief forays into morphology and pragmatics. As you will see, it's not always easy to separate these different levels of analysis. Structure and meaning are always inextricably bound; *The Chihuahua ate the cockroach* means something very different from *The cockroach ate the Chihuahua,* even though the two sentences contain exactly the same words. *Father is cooking* probably means that father is cooking food, but in the unlikely event that father has fallen into the hands of cannibals, *Father is cooking* means something quite different and requires a different grammatical analysis. The social context in which a sentence is uttered will affect its form and its interpretation. A student who is seeking a favor from a professor is far more likely to say "Can you give me an extension?" than "Give me an extension." And only the most socially inept hearer will interpret "Can you pass the ketchup?" as a question requiring nothing more than a "yes" or "no" answer.

Before we explore the structure of English sentences in detail, it is important to understand the overall structure of the simple sentence. In this chapter we will examine the internal structure of some short, simple sentences. What these sentences will dramatically illustrate is that English speakers exploit a very small number of basic sentence-making structures. As you will see throughout this textbook, these basic structures are used over and over again to create increasingly long and complex utterances.

It takes a fairly small inventory of words and phrases to generate a significant number of sentences. The 27 sentences listed below can all be produced by rearranging just 10 words or phrases. Some sentences omit words or phrases, but in no case have words or phrases beyond these ten been included.

Words and phrases

the bear, Goldy, my porridge, ate, eaten, gave, given, was, to, by

---

Goldy ate.

Goldy ate my porridge.

The bear ate.

The bear ate my porridge.

My porridge was eaten.

My porridge was eaten by Goldy.

My porridge was eaten by the bear.

The bear ate Goldy.

Goldy was eaten.

Goldy was eaten by the bear.

Goldy ate the bear.

The bear was eaten.

The bear was eaten by Goldy.

Goldy gave the bear my porridge.

Goldy gave my porridge to the bear.

The bear was given my porridge.

My porridge was given to the bear.

The bear gave Goldy my porridge.

The bear gave my porridge to Goldy.

Goldy was given my porridge.

My porridge was given to Goldy.

My porridge was given to Goldy by the bear.

My porridge was given to the bear by Goldy.

Goldy was given the bear.

The bear was given to Goldy.

The bear was given Goldy.

Goldy was given to the bear.

Although many of these sentences are closely related, careful scrutiny should convince you that no two are identical in form. And this is the key to the efficiency of language—the same words can be combined into different structures and different words can be put into the same structures. Theoretically, the speakers of any language can produce an infinite number of sentences with a finite number of words and structures.

Authors of syntax textbooks face one significant problem. The structure of any language is immensely complex; every structure seems to be connected to every other structure. Grammar is a bit like cooked spaghetti; when you pick up one strand, you find that ten others are wrapped around it. I will try hard to address issues one at a time so that you are not forced to grapple with structures to which you have not been properly introduced. But sometimes, especially in these early stages, it will be necessary to allude to structures that we have not yet discussed in any detail. But each of these structures will be revisited later and any lingering questions you might have should be cleared up at that point.

The Subject

The difference between the subject and predicate is probably the first fact of English grammar that any school child learns, and it is a significant fact. The very terms "subject" and "predicate" provide some clue as to the distinction being made. The grammatical subject of the sentence is often the conversational subject, i.e., the person or thing that the sentence is about. The predicate often makes a comment about that subject, i.e., it "predicates."

In most languages a sentence does not require a word or phrase that functions as subject; a Spanish speaker, for example, can say "No hablo Ingles" ("I don't speak English"). This English translation is misleading, however, because where English requires the pronoun *I*, Spanish does not; the meaning of *I* is simply encoded in the verb *hablo*. This option is not available in English, because, with the exception of the imperative (*Sit down*), subjects must be expressed. For this reason English is often called a **subject dominant language.** According to one researcher, there are only seven languages in the world in which the main verb is <u>required</u> to have a subject and English is one of them (Gilligan [1987], cited in Lambrecht, 1994, p. 191).

SYNTAX OF THE SUBJECT

The distinction between the subject and predicate is the basic division within the sentence. Grammarians have been aware of this distinction for millennia and in modern times a number of different graphic devices have been employed to capture this division. Early twentieth century school grammars drew a line between the subject and the predicate.

<u>Children|love animals.</u>

The generative grammars of the 1970s exploited tree diagrams in which the subject (called the NP for noun phrase) branches left and the predicate (called VP for verb phrase) branches right. S stands for sentence. The following graphic says that every sentence contains an NP and a VP, in other words, a subject and a predicate.

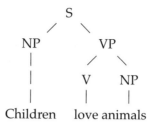

The construction grammars of the 1990s use the term predicate and exploit boxes to illustrate the division between the subject and the predicate.

Predication

Children	love animals

Each of these graphic devices underscores the same insight—that all English sentences can be divided into two basic structures (subject and predicate) and the subject is (typically) first.

But what do subjects look like; what shape do they take? A simple subject is always a **noun phrase** and a noun phrase is a proper name, a pronoun, a noun, or a noun plus its modifiers. We will discuss all of these forms in detail in Chapter 2, but for now let me give you a brief and simplified introduction.

The basic structure of a noun phrase

noun	rice	music	boys		hatred
noun + modifiers	a book some books	this bike these bikes	that idiot those idiots		the dog two dogs
proper name	Jane Smith Lassie	Chicago Maxine	George Washington the Mississippi River		
pronouns	I / me you	he / him she / her	they / them we / us		it

---

Pronouns differ from other noun phrases in that they are used only after the noun to which they refer, i.e., the **referent**, has already been introduced into the narrative or conversation.

*I can't eat **clams**.* **They** give me a rash.

*I like **Danny Glover**.* **He** is a fine actor.

The dog is upset. **She** doesn't want to go to the kennel.

In many European languages (e.g., Russian, Greek, and Lithuanian), the subject receives a special suffix to mark its subject (or nominative) status. Modern English subjects carry no special endings, but they are usually the first structure in the sentence.

Subject	Predicate
Josephine	danced all night.
Your kids	ate all the candy.
The flood	destroyed their new condo.
Skill	is essential.
It	isn't important.
She	offered me her new bike.

Putting the predicate first in any one of these sentences produces an ungrammatical utterance—*danced all night Josephine; *Ate all the candy your kids, *Isn't important it.*

A subject is a far simpler structure than a predicate. In a simple sentence, a subject is a single structure, while a predicate can have internal structure, i.e., structures within structures.

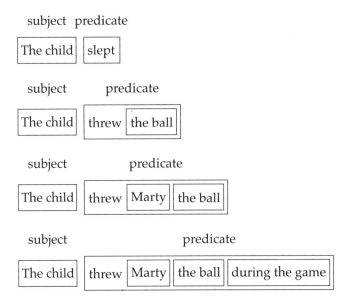

English subjects have a profound effect on other grammatical categories in the sentence. In some instances the subject controls the form of the verb. If a subject is singular (and third person) and the verb is in the present tense, that verb must carry a special singular marker {-s} as in *Sue smokes* and *My brother lies.*

The subject also has a special role in the creation of questions that are typically answered "yes" or "no." Notice what happens when the following statements are turned into yes/no questions. (In these examples the verbs are in boldface and the subject is double underlined.)

<u>Lars</u> **can attend** the party.   **Can** <u>Lars</u> **attend** the party?

<u>Kate</u> **is repairing** your computer.   **Is** <u>Kate</u> **repairing** your computer?

<u>Your teacher</u> **was fired.**   **Was** <u>your teacher</u> **fired?**

<u>Erin</u> **has finished** her homework.   **Has** <u>Erin</u> **finished** her homework?

In each case, when the question is produced, the first verb (i.e., the auxiliary verb) is moved to a position in front of the subject, leaving the second verb behind. As a result, the subject of the question is surrounded by verbs. Of course native or fluent speakers of English never have to think about all this in constructing a question; they unconsciously identify the subject and place the auxiliary verb in front of it.

The subject also controls the structure of so-called tag questions, those little questions speakers put at the end of a statement in order to seek confirmation—*Ben likes Carla,* **doesn't he**? *Sue left,* **didn't she**? Note that *he* reflects the male status of the subject *Ben,* and *she* reflects the female status of Sue. Speakers of English couldn't perform any of these operations unless they could intuitively identify the subject of the sentence.

Number agreement and the creation of a question or tag question are true diagnostics for subjecthood. Only subjects stand in these relationships to the verb. While word order is not a definitive diagnostic, it is extremely useful. All of the graphic devices displayed above indicate a subject followed by a predicate. These graphics reflect prototypical word order. While there are certainly exceptions, e.g., *A Corvette he wants now,* the first NP in an English sentence is typically the subject. When speakers choose to put an NP other than the subject first in the sentence it is almost always because they want to signal something special like surprise or annoyance.

All of the constructions discussed in this section on the syntax of the subject will be taken up in detail later on, but these simplified examples should give you some sense of how important the grammatical category **subject** is in English.

SEMANTIC ROLES OF THE SUBJECT

It is of course the semantic component of the subject that is most salient to speakers. Even small children intuitively recognize some sort of division between a "doer" and an "action." In *Jack yelled, Bonnie studied all night,* and *The child put the candy in her pocket,* Jack, Bonnie, and the child are all "doers" engaging in some activity. This division between the doer and the action is often what people point to when they distinguish between the subject and the predicate. But to <u>define</u> the subject as a doer and the predicate as an action would be misleading. In the following sentences, the subject is in no way doing anything—*Susan is tall; The wall looked dirty; My mother was mugged last night.* If the subject is not necessarily a doer, what is it?

Subjects play a number of different **semantic roles** in English and "doer of the action" is only one of them. (These roles are also called **thematic** or **theta** roles in some syntactic models.) I've identified below some of the most common semantic roles played by subjects in English sentences. While this list is not exhaustive, it will give you a good sense of the semantic variety.

Agent Subjects

The agent subject is the classic doer of the action. An agent subject is an animate being that acts deliberately, with intent. Most speakers consider the agent the most typical subject. If you ask someone to construct a sentence out of thin air, it is likely that s/he will utter one with an agent subject. All of the agentive subjects below are engaging in willful, deliberate action:

(a)	(b)
Catherine's boss *fired her.*	**The little boy** *yelled.*
Fred *threw the frisbee.*	**Those kids** *are whispering.*
Joan *built a birdhouse.*	**My niece** *smiled.*
My sisters *washed the car.*	**Mom** *sat down.*
The dog *tore up the newspaper.*	**The choir** *sang.*
The mare *devoured her oats.*	**The bulldog** *growled.*

The agents in column (a) are acting on someone or something, i.e., the direct object, while the agents in column (b) are not acting on anyone or anything else. In other words, an agent subject can occur with or without a direct object. (Direct objects will be discussed shortly.)

Whether or not amoebas, slugs, and other lower creatures actually have agency is probably a biological question and not a linguistic one. They certainly don't do things deliberately but they do engage in some of the same activities that higher creatures do—crawling, eating, swimming, etc. It is probably reasonable to treat them as agents even though they are acting instinctively rather than deliberately.

Of course we often anthropomorphize machines and treat them as agents, even though they are technically inanimate—*The ATM machine refuses to return my card; My computer ate my term paper; The engine threw a rod.*

Causer Subjects

A causer is either an animate being who acts without volition or an inanimate entity. We distinguish causers from agents because the semantics of the two roles are quite different. A sentence like *Rob tripped Roy* is potentially ambiguous; if *Rob tripped Roy* just to see Roy fall, *Rob* is an agent, but if *Rob tripped Roy accidentally*, then *Rob* is a causer.

All the sentences below contain animate causer subjects.

Mavis *inadvertently touched the wet paint.*

Benjamin *accidently cut his finger.*

Susanna *bumped her head.*

Sometimes animate causers inadvertently affect another person's psychological state.

The clown *(accidentally) frightened my daughter.*

Betsy *hurt Rene's feelings inadvertently.*

Michael Jordan *amazes me.*

Nan *depresses her mother.*

Michael Jordan certainly doesn't know that he amazes me, but he has that effect, nevertheless. Nan may depress her mother because her mother is worried about her lifestyle, in which case Nan might be totally unaware of the effect she is having.

It's not always easy to tell whether an animate subject is an agent or a causer. Out of context, we don't know whether the following subjects are acting deliberately or not.

Butch disgusts everyone.

The child amused the adults.

Professor Smith intimidates her students.

Of course inanimate entities lack intention or volition by their very nature. Causers can be things like rocks, forces like tornadoes, or abstract qualities like love.

Hail *cracked our windshield.*

Oil *stained the carpet.*

A hurricane *damaged the village.*

The wind *broke the window.*

The revolution *terrified the king.*

Determination *saved the family.*

Hate *destroyed her.*

Unlike agents, causers always act on something or somebody else; in other words, they are always followed by a direct object.

Instrument Subjects

An instrument subject, as the label implies, is an inanimate entity which acts on someone or something else because it is being used as an instrument. In a sentence like *The key opened the safe,* we can assume that some unnamed agent is wielding the key because keys don't operate by themselves; in *The tweezers removed the splinter,* an unspecified agent is using the tweezers.

Sometimes an instrument subject allows a speaker to avoid taking responsibility. A child might say "My ball broke your window" rather than "I broke your window with my ball." Here the ball is the instrument used by the child in the breaking of the window. On the other hand, in *The hail broke your window, the hail* is clearly a causer, not an instrument.

Instrument subjects are fairly unusual in English. We most often find instruments in (adverbial) prepositional phrases—*Meredith opened the safe **with a key**; The nurse removed the splinter **with the tweezers**; I broke the window **with my ball***. I will discuss these constructions at some length in Chapter 4.

Experiencer Subjects

Experiencer subjects are always animate, usually human. An experiencer experiences a sensory perception or a psychological state. In other words, the experiencer is not <u>doing</u> anything but is instead experiencing something through the senses or the mental faculties. The verbs that co-occur with experiencer subjects relate to consciousness; they are verbs that reflect "private" internal states.

Each of our five senses allows for an agent subject and an experiencer subject. When an agent engages in a sensory activity, the agent actively employs the sense in question. An experiencer, however, has a sensory experience that was unsought. An agent looks at or listens to something on purpose. An experiencer sees because an event passes before the eyes and hears because a sound occurs within earshot. When *Mary tastes the sauce,* she does so by putting her spoon in the bowl and then to her lips. But when *Mary tastes mold on the bread,* her taste buds simply register a sensation; she has taken no direct action to engage that sense.

Sensory verb with agent subject	Sensory verb with experiencer subject
Joan looked at the scar. [She examined it carefully.]	**Joan** saw some blood. [She didn't want to see it.]
Alex listened to the argument. [He put his ear to the wall.]	**Alex** heard the argument. [He couldn't help it; they were screaming.]
Maria smelled the tulips. [She leaned over to do so.]	**Maria** smelled smoke. [It wafted in through the open window.]
Tony tasted the wine. [He put the glass to his lips.]	**Tony** could taste pepper in the soup. [Too much had been added.]
Margaret felt the cloth. [She ran her fingers over it.]	**Margaret** felt some pain. [It came on her suddenly.]

A sentence like *Gene smelled the perfume* is ambiguous out of context.

As you can see, sometimes the semantic difference between an experiencer subject and an agent subject is reflected in the verb and sometimes it's not. In the case of *look at* versus *see* and *listen to* versus *hear,* this semantic difference is **lexicalized**; in other words, the difference in meaning is signaled by different words. In the case of agentive *smell* and experiencer *smell,* the semantic difference is not lexicalized; the verbs take the same form.

Mental state verbs, more often called **psych-verbs,** also take experiencer subjects. These subjects are not really engaging in action. Normally, when an agent acts, the direct object is directly affected by that action. But none of the experiencer subjects below has a <u>direct</u> effect upon the direct object.

Joan *wants a raise.*	**Susan** *loves stamp collecting.*
Brad *thinks about food constantly.*	**Ted** *adores Sally.*
Mary *can't tolerate liver.*	*I believe them.*
Rich *doesn't believe in love.*	**Eric** *is dreaming.*
She *admires her mother.*	**Sheila** *trusts her son.*

The fact that Ted adores Sally and that Sheila trusts her son might theoretically affect both Sally and the son in many ways, but the sentences above are silent on that issue. In fact, Sally may not even know that Ted exists and Sheila's son may be totally unaware of her feelings.

Later we will examine experiencers that are functioning as direct objects and prepositional phrases.

Patient Subjects (and Patient Direct Objects)

I'll approach the issue of patient subjects indirectly, by first previewing an-other category—the direct object. It is probably apparent to you that a noun phrase which follows a verb is often affected by the action of the verb. A noun phrase which follows the verb and is affected by the action of that verb is typ-ically a **direct object.** Direct objects are structures inside predicates.

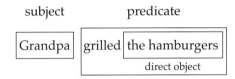

In *Jack dropped* **the vase,** *Keisha opened* **the door,** and *The insects killed* **the plants,** the vase, the plants, and the door are the affected parties; they are also direct objects. In each of these sentences, an agent or causer subject has caused something to happen to the direct object. An event can also be expressed by eliminating the agent/causer and making the affected party the subject of the sentence. In **The vase** *fell,* the vase is not doing anything but rather is being acted upon by another unnamed force—somebody dropped it, the wind knocked it over, somebody kicked the table it was sitting on, etc. In **The plants** *died,* something killed the plants—insects, frost, the lawn mower, old age. In **The door** *opened,* someone or something caused this to happen—Keisha, the wind, a ghost. The traditional semantic label for an affected subject or an af-fected direct object is **patient.** (This label derives from the adjective *patient* which historically described one who "bears or endures.") A patient is never volitional; a patient never exercises control; a patient is an entity to which things happen. You will find that most patient subjects co-occur with verbs that de-scribe a change of state—*The water boiled; The chair broke; The water heater ex-ploded; Rosa fell; The mirror shattered.*

In the examples below, you will find that none of the sentences with pa-tient subjects contain direct objects.

Patient direct objects	Patient subjects
He laid **the book** on the table.	**The book** lay on the table.
The intruder opened **the door.**	**The door** opened.
Maria broke **the vase.**	**The vase** broke.
Dad thickened **the sauce.**	**The sauce** thickened.
We emptied **the pool.**	**The pool** emptied.
The soldier detonated **the bomb.**	**The bomb** exploded.

Patient direct objects (cont.)	Patient subjects (cont.)
The earthquake shook **the house.**	**The house** collapsed.
The frost froze **my garden.**	**My garden** froze.
Alan darkens **his hair.**	**His hair** darkened.
Tom hung **the clothes** outside.	**The clothes** hung on the line.
The baby bounced **the ball.**	**The ball** bounced.

Semantically, a sentence like *Lance jumped* or *The woman rolled down the hill* is ambiguous out of context. Lance may be a agent subject who deliberately jumps or a patient subject who jumps involuntarily because something startles him. Similarly, *The woman rolled down the hill* can be interpreted as having an agent subject (she rolled on purpose) or a patient subject (something tripped her and she rolled). Usually when a sentence contains an animate subject which acts involuntarily, the agent/instrument can be found elsewhere in the discourse, e.g., Lance jumped because someone set off a firecracker.

There can be only one patient in a simple sentence and if there is a direct object, it, not the subject, will carry that semantic role. In *Susan tripped **the professor,*** *Susan* must be an agent or a causer. Patient subjects occur only in intransitive or passive constructions. (Intransitivity will be explained shortly and the passive will be explained in Chapter 3.) In the sentence ***Susan** tripped* there is no direct object; Susan is clearly the affected party and thus a patient.

In his mystery novel *The Little Sister,* Raymond Chandler (1971) uses a series of patient subjects to underscore the fact that the hero has been knocked to the floor and cannot see his assailant, although he can hear the results of her activities. "The door opened. A key rattled. The door closed. The key turned" (p. 54).

Described and Located Subjects

Some subjects are simply being characterized or described by the information in the predicate. These subjects always co-occur with copulas, verbs that have little independent meaning but relate the information in the predicate back to the subject. (Copulas will be discussed in detail later.)

Michael is tall.	[*Tall* describes Michael]
Marty seems pleasant.	[*Pleasant* describes Marty]
This food is French.	[*French* characterizes the food]
The bread was stale.	[*Stale* describes the bread]

Other subjects are simply located in space. In the following sentences the location is double underlined.

Samson is <u>*in his doghouse*</u>.

The pots are <u>*in the bottom cupboard*</u>.

Tomi is <u>*on the porch*</u>.

The Centrust Building stands <u>*on Miami Avenue*</u>.[1]

Empty It

The normal function of the pronoun *it* is to refer to something that has already been mentioned in the discourse—*Natalie bought **a new car**. **It** is a red convertible*. Whenever a pronoun refers back to an item that has already been introduced into the discourse, the pronoun is making **anaphoric reference**. (The Greek prefix *ana-* means "back or backwards.") There are, however, contexts in which *it* does not have anaphoric reference.

Many languages have odd ways of commenting on the weather or the ambient environment and English is no exception. In the sentences *It is raining* and *It's sunny out today*, the subject *it* doesn't refer to any previously introduced noun; in fact, it doesn't really refer to anything at all. But except for the imperative construction, all English sentences demand subjects and *it* is acceptably neutral in those cases where there isn't a semantically meaningful subject.

It *is hot!*

It's *foggy in Seattle.*

It *is cold in Alaska.*

It *was smoky in that restaurant.*

Empty *it* is sometimes called **expletive it,** a rather unfortunate traditional label.

Cataphoric It

When a complex clause functions as the semantic subject of a sentence, a speaker will often put that clause at the end of the sentence and replace it with the pronoun *it*. In this case *it* is not semantically empty; its semantic content is the subsequent clause.

That my daughter had lied *bothered me.* / **It** *bothered me* **that my daughter had lied.**

That Megan would win *was predictable.* / **It** *was predictable* **that Megan would win.**

That Sam was mad *was obvious.* / **It** *was obvious* **that Sam was mad.**

This *it* is called cataphoric because it refers to something that comes after; the Greek prefix *cata-* means "away." We'll discuss cataphoric *it* in detail in Chapter 5. For now, simply be aware that subject *it* can have three very different functions—anaphoric reference, cataphoric reference, and empty place-holder.

Some Other Semantic Roles

Subjects play other semantic roles in the sentence and linguists don't always agree on how far to go in categorizing these. For example, some of the empty *it* subjects above can also be paraphrased with subjects that express place.

Seattle *is foggy.*

Alaska *is cold.*

This bar *is smoky.*

These are usually called **locative subjects** because they simply name a location. (Don't confuse locative subjects with <u>located</u> subjects.)

Subjects that express time are sometimes categorized semantically as **temporal subjects.**

Wednesday *is the baby's birthday.*

Tomorrow *is our anniversary.*

Weekends *are lonely.*

Subjects like these have an adverbial quality and can in fact be paraphrased with adverb constructions—*It is rainy in Seattle; The baby's birthday is on Wednesday.* (We will discuss adverbs in Chapter 4.) Some grammarians (e.g., Quirk, Greenbaum, Leech, and Svartvik, 1972, p. 42) also establish an **event** category for subjects—*The party is at 9 P.M; The concert is over.*

It isn't clear just how far we should go in creating semantic categories for subjects or any other grammatical construction. Meaning is a continuum and we could go on forever creating ever finer semantic distinctions, but such an exercise has limited utility. You will find that different grammarians sometimes employ different labels and grammarians don't always agree on just what should be included in a given category, but the roles agent, instrument, experiencer, and patient are quite standard. The semantic categories discussed above can encompass a large number of English sentences and, as you will see later, most of these categories have important grammatical implications.

Summary of subject semantic roles	
Agent subject	**Tom** threw his socks on the floor.
	My dog ate my term paper.

Summary of subject semantic roles (cont.)	
Causer subject	**Walter** stubbed his toe.
	The water damaged the furniture.
Instrument subject	**The key** opened the door.
	The chain saw felled the tree.
Experiencer subject	**Benny** wants a new sports car.
	I smell smoke.
Patient subject	**Our pipes** froze last night.
	The chair broke.
Described subject	**That hairdo** is hideous.
	The room grew dark.
Located subject	**Marlene** is in the yard.
	Terry was on the boat.
Empty *it*	**It** is cold outside.
Cataphoric *it*	**It** is sad that Juliet can't date Romeo.

DISCOURSE FUNCTIONS OF THE SUBJECT

For many decades modern syntacticians explored individual sentences in isolation, rarely if ever examining them in a larger context. But language is most often used in chunks, whether in a conversation, a monologue, or a written text. Furthermore, language is a social tool. We string sentences together to chat with others, to give orders, and to elicit information. We engage in banter, write letters and e-mail messages, give lectures, tell jokes, and yell at our kids. All of this is **discourse** and discourse can have a profound effect on the structure of a given sentence. To put it another way, we often manipulate structures to serve our discourse goals.

One of the important functions of the subject is to reflect the **topic** (or **theme**) of a discourse. The topic is what the discourse is about. Topics represent **given information** (sometimes called **old information**). Given information, as the term suggests, refers to information that the speaker assumes the hearer already knows. If you and I are discussing Malcolm and I say "He drives me crazy," there is no confusion; but if I suddenly walk up to you on the street and yell, "He drives me crazy," you will probably conclude that I'm crazy. In a few languages, the topic of a sentence actually takes a special form or carries a special marker. English has no such special forms but the topic is often (but not always) expressed by the subject of the sentence.

A topic is not the topic until it is introduced into the discourse, and the first mention of a potential topic often occurs in the predicate. Once something has been introduced, it becomes "topicalized" and typically occupies subject position. In the following examples, first mentions are double underlined and topics are in boldface.

> *I met <u>the ambassador from Viet Nam</u> yesterday.* **He** *was very charming.*
>   [first mention]   [topic]

Consider this fictional passage from a Ross Macdonald novel (1996). It concerns promotional photographs of an aspiring young actress. (Underlining and boldface added.)

> Four of them were pictures of <u>Kitty</u>. . . .**She** stood and gazed romantically out to sea. **She** reclined erotically on a chaise lounge. **She** posed dry on the diving board. **Kitty** had been a beautiful girl, but all four pictures were spoiled by her awkward staginess. (p. 85)

Once Kitty is introduced to us in the predicate of the first sentence, she becomes the topic of the discourse and occupies the subject position in subsequent sentences. The predicate in each of these sentences is the **comment** on the topic. In the first three sentences the comment tells us what Kitty did and in the last sentence the comment tells us what Kitty looked like.

Here is a another passage, this one from a Robert Parker thriller (1996). (Underlining and boldface added.)

> "Here's <u>Woody</u>". . . . **Woody** was sitting on a bench, at a chest press machine catching his breath. **He** had on rainbow striped spandex shorts and a spaghetti strap black tank top. **His thick blond hair** was perfectly cut. . . . **He** was tanned so evenly that he must have worked on it very carefully. **He** was lean and muscular. **His teeth** were expensively capped. And **he** had a small diamond in **his left ear lobe.** (p. 143)

Once Woody is presented to us in the first sentence, he becomes the topic of the discourse and he or some part of his body is the subject of every subsequent sentence.

In both these fictional passages you will notice that once a character has been introduced, the subsequent mentions are made by means of pronouns like *she, he,* and *his.* As was noted early in this chapter, this is one of the primary functions of personal pronouns. They provide a convenient shorthand for referring to individuals who have already been introduced into the discourse. It is no accident that we often find pronouns in subject position, since subject position is also topic position. We'll discuss pronouns at length in Chapter 2.

Because subjects often express the topic of a discourse, it should not surprise you that human subjects are more common than nonhuman subjects. We are egocentric creatures and we like to talk about ourselves. In conversation, *I* and *you* are the most frequent topic/subjects. But different kinds of topics (and thus subjects) emerge in different kinds of discourse. Locative subjects are not very common as a rule but they occur frequently in travel brochures and guide books—*Miami is humid most of the year; The Riviera is crowded in August.* Temporal subjects crop up frequently in a conversation in which a group of people are trying to schedule a meeting—*Tuesday is bad; Thursday looks good though.*

The Predicate

The predicate is typically the structure that follows the subject. If the subject is an agent, causer, or instrument, the predicate will express the action carried out by that subject; if the subject is something which is being described, the predicate will provide the description; if the subject is a patient, the predicate will indicate what happened to the subject. For most speakers the notion of a predicate that is separate from the subject is fairly intuitive.

The English predicate must contain a verb; it can contain other structures—a direct object, an indirect object, various complement structures, and adverbs—but it must contain a verb. While most imperative utterances omit the subject (*Sit down; Drink your milk*), there are no English sentences in which the verb is omitted. In many ways the verb controls what happens grammatically in a sentence. Certain verbs require or at least allow a direct object; other verbs require two objects, a direct objects <u>plus</u> an indirect object; some verbs can be followed by adjectives; others must be followed by adverbs. For example, the verb *like* must be followed by a direct object—*Diana likes the woods.* The verb *put* must be followed by both a direct object and an adverb of location—*She put the book on the shelf*; **She put the book* and **She put on the shelf* are both ungrammatical sentences. On the other hand, the verb *laugh* can stand alone in the predicate—*Elaine laughed.*

Verbs also constrain the semantic roles of subjects; some verbs require agentive or causer subjects—*She punched a hole in the door; The flood damaged the golf course*; others require experiencer subjects—*She heard the siren; Tom smelled smoke.* A discussion of verbs cannot be separated from a discussion of what can be found in the rest of the sentence.

Transitive Verbs and Direct Objects

The direct object is a structure contained within the predicate. It is typically the noun phrase that follows the verb, although indirect objects and subject complements can also occupy this position, as you will see shortly.

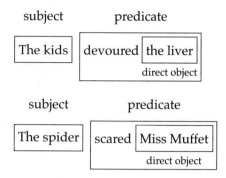

Most speakers would probably regard a *subject + verb + direct object* sentence as the prototypical English sentence. Verbs that can be followed by direct objects are considered **transitive** because, in most cases, an action taken by the subject is transmitted to the object. (The Latin prefix *trans-* means "across.") As a rule, only transitive verbs can be followed by direct objects. As you saw above, a direct object is a noun phrase that follows a verb and is often (but not always) affected by the action of verb.

*Lisa wrecked **her bike.***

*The fire damaged **the bedroom.***

*Bob washed **the dishes.***

*Eugene read **a novel.***

*The baby likes **those cookies.***

The direct object has a special role in the construction of passive sentences. Without even knowing what a passive sentence is, any relatively fluent English speaker can readily return an active sentence into a passive sentence after hearing just a few illustrative examples.

(a)	(b)
Bruce ate the pizza.	*The pizza was eaten by Bruce.*
The snails destroyed my garden.	*My garden was destroyed by the snails.*
Flossie slugged Bert.	*Bert was slugged by Flossie.*
Gloria sang the anthem.	*The anthem was sung by Gloria.*

Successful completion of this exercise depends on an individual's ability to identify the direct object of each of the sentences in column (a). That direct object then becomes the subject of the corresponding sentence in column (b). Of course, fluent speakers do all of this unconsciously.

SEMANTIC ROLES OF THE DIRECT OBJECT

Like subjects, direct objects reflect various semantic roles. Traditional school grammars often describe the direct object as the "receiver of the action," and, loosely speaking, that is one of its primary roles. But the direct object reflects a variety of other semantic relationships as well. In each of the following sentences the direct object *the monster* has a different relationship with the verb,

Dr. Frankenstein slapped the monster.

Dr. Frankenstein created the monster.

Dr. Frankenstein scared the monster.

The semantic roles of direct objects are less varied than those of subjects and lines between semantic types are often muddier. Nevertheless, the semantic distinctions among direct objects are important in understanding the overall semantics of the sentence.

Patient Direct Objects

You were first introduced to **patient direct objects** in the section on subjects. Patients are always affected by the action of the verb (to a greater or lesser degree). In fact, direct objects are so named because they are in a sense the direct target or object of the verb's action.

*Jill smashed **my car**.*

*Dorothy threw **her coat** on the floor.*

*Timothy folded **the clothes**.*

*The plaintiff destroyed **the evidence**.*

*Maezel lifted **the box**.*

As you saw earlier, subjects can also take the semantic role of patient. Remember that in a given simple sentence there can be only one patient role. If the sentence contains a direct object, it, not the subject, will be the patient.

Patient will also be our **default** (garbage can) category. We will consider any direct object that cannot be comfortably placed in another semantic category a patient. This means that even relatively unaffected direct objects as in *Kim read the novel* will be considered patients. The one exception to this will be the direct objects of psych-verbs, as you will see in the next section.

Experiencer Direct Objects

You've already seen that the subjects of psych-verbs (mental state verbs) are experiencers—*I like pizza; Stephanie wants a new computer*. Direct objects can be experiencers as well if the verb causes the direct object to achieve a new psychological state. It doesn't matter whether the subject is an agent (volitional and animate) or a causer (nonvolitional and animate or inanimate). In a sense, experiencer is a subcategory of patient in that the direct object is affected by the action of the verb in a very particular way.

*Annie annoyed **her siblings**.* [It doesn't matter whether she did it deliberately or not.]

*Dad calmed **the baby**.*

*Lester frightened **me**.*

*That novel bothered **my students**.*

*The vandalism saddened **everyone**.*

A direct object can be an experiencer only when the subject is not. There can be only one experiencer in a simple sentence. When the <u>subject</u> of a verb is an experiencer, the direct object is relatively unaffected by the action of the verb.

*I love **movies**.*

*Libby believed **their lies**.*

*Captain Ahab fears **that whale**.*

*We abhor **violence**.*

*Carmen craves **chocolate**.*

*I smell **smoke**.*

The movies are indifferent to the fact that I like them and lies are unaffected by the fact that Libby believes them. The whale may be affected in some way by the fact that Ahab fears him, but there is nothing in the sentence that indicates this. In a sentence like *Captain Ahab harpooned the whale,* the affectedness is communicated directly.

Created Direct Objects

Occasionally a transitive verb actually creates a direct object, rather than affecting an already existing entity. In a sentence like *Bell invented **the telephone*** or *My daughter built **a tree house**,* the direct object is actually brought into existence by the action of the verb. Such direct objects are **created** direct objects. The difference between a patient direct object and a created direct object explains the ambiguity in a sentence like *Maria paints barns.* If Maria paints pictures of barns, the direct object is created; if she paints barn walls, the direct object is a patient.

Patient direct object	Created direct object
Agatha lost **my novel**.	Agatha has written **a novel**.
Margaret tore **her blouse**.	Margaret made **a blouse**.
Lynn is painting **the ceiling**.	Lynn is painting **a landscape**.
The kids broke **the statue**.	The kids are carving **a statue**.
Teddy fixed **the bike**.	Teddy fixed **lunch**.

One can of course quibble about the status of some direct objects. If *Martha sang a Jimmy Buffet song,* did she create something or affect something already in existence? If *Ali baked a cake,* did he create something or merely cook a pre-existing entity? These are clearly gray areas. But the fact that not all direct objects can be neatly categorized doesn't diminish the value of these semantic distinctions.

Locative Direct Objects

Sometimes noun phrases expressing location are used as direct objects.

Sir Edmund climbed **Mt. Everest.**

Diana swam **the English Channel.**

I have hiked **the Grand Canyon.**

As you will see in Chapter 4, location expressions are usually prepositional phrases functioning as adverbs—*Sir Edmund climbed* **up Mt. Everest**; *I have hiked* **in the Grand Canyon**. What makes locative direct objects interesting is that they express a quality of completeness which is lacking in the prepositional phrases. *Sir Edmund climbed Mt. Everest* suggests that Sir Edmund climbed all the way up to the top and *I have hiked the Grand Canyon* suggests that I have walked its entire length. I will take up this issue again in Chapter 4.

Some Other Semantic Roles

In some highly idiomatic expressions, empty *it* occurs as a direct object. In utterances like *Let's call* **it** *a day, Sue has* **it** *made, and They are living* **it** *up, it* has no anaphoric or cataphoric referent. Such expressions are rare, however.

Occasionally a normally intransitive weather verb will take an object—*It was hailing* **golf balls**; *It was raining* **buckets**. These constructions, too, are very idiomatic.

Summary of Direct Object Semantic Roles

Patient direct object	The kids are smashing **the furniture**.
	Becky fixed **my car**.
Experiencer direct object	Isabella scared **me**.
	That movie disgusted **my parents**.
Created direct object	That firm manufactures **computers**.
	My aunt made **a pie**.
Locative direct object	Michelle swam **Lake Powell**.
	He walks **the streets** [when he is depressed].
Empty *it* direct object	Maggie is living **it** up.

Other semantic categories for direct objects have been suggested, but this set should give you an adequate sense of the semantic variation.

COVERT DIRECT OBJECTS

The term *transitive* really refers to a verb's potential. Any verb that can potentially take a direct object can be considered transitive. Transitive verbs can sometimes occur without an overt direct object, although there is almost always an unexpressed, **covert** direct object, one that is somehow understood. (I will routinely use the term *covert* for a structure that is not explicitly articulated but can be determined by the sentence grammar or the discourse context.) In *Fred ate* the presumption is that he ate food, not rat poison; in *Martha is studying* the presumption is that she is studying some academic subject, not her navel; and in *The children are reading,* the presumption is that the kids are reading books or magazines, not shopping lists.

The verbs *bake, hunt,* and *iron* can all occur with unexpressed but commonly understood direct objects. When someone hunts something other than wild game, a direct object is required and *for* typically follows the verb—*Wayne is hunting* versus *Wayne is hunting for his shoes*. When *drink* occurs without a direct object, it usually implies the consumption of alcohol—*Tina drinks*. Curiously, transitive verbs that are closely related semantically often behave differently in terms of their need to express an overt direct object. Unlike *eat,* the verbs *devour* and *gobble* require an overt direct object; **Fred devoured* and **The child gobbled* are ungrammatical.

"LIGHT" TRANSITIVE VERBS

There are a few transitive verbs in English that carry little information and depend on the rest of the predicate to provide meaning. Like light beer, these verbs have little content, but they are, nevertheless, quite productive, i.e., they appear in a variety of constructions. The verb *do* is an especially interesting example of this. In sentences like *Lana did her homework, Alan did the dishes,* and *My sister does my taxes*, the verb *to do* has meaning only in the context of the direct object. In fact, *to do* constitutes a kind of shorthand in these contexts; in the first sentence, it includes all the activities that might be involved in working on homework; in the second sentence it probably involves the acts of both washing and drying, and in the third it includes a variety of accounting activities. Such expressions tend to be fairly idiomatic. One has to know that when a woman "does her nails," she is filing and painting them and when a couple "does the tango," they are dancing. We *do the dishes* when we wash and dry them but we don't **do the clothes* under the same circumstances. Speakers can use *do* to create novel expressions. The expression *Let's do lunch* has become a part of the lexicon, even though many speakers only use it facetiously.

Take and *have* also occur in contexts in which the verb depends on the direct object for meaning.

The baby took a nap.	*Judy had a nap.*
Asher is taking a walk.	*They had a fight.*
He took his leave.	*We had dinner at eight.*
She is taking a shower.	*They had a chat.*
Let's take a swim.	*They are having a meeting.*
Nan took a drink of water.	*The child had a good cry.*
He took a glance at the note.	*Michael had a smoke.*
Holyfield took a swing at Tyson.	*Maxine had a look at the results.*

In British and Australian English the *have* construction is even more productive than in American English, e.g., *He is having a lie-down* or *She is having a read*. (For a detailed discussion of *have* in such constructions, see Wierzbicka, 1988c.)

Each of the verb plus direct object constructions cited above can be paraphrased to some extent by a single verb—*The baby napped; Asher is walking; They are fighting; They chatted*. The single-verb paraphrases, however, lack a semantic dimension shared by the transitive sentences; in each case the transitive version suggests that the event is time-bounded, that it has a clear-cut beginning and end. *Michael had a smoke* suggests one cigarette, while *Michael smoked* does not. *Having a chat* is a single event, while *chatting* is an ongoing activity. This is underscored by the fact that we can easily say *Pete and Lynn chatted for hours,* but *??Pete and Lynn had a chat for hours* is odd. The presence of the article *a* in most of these direct object constructions undoubtedly contributes to the sense that these are single, time-bounded events.

The *take* and *have* constructions discussed above represent a only a subset of the possibilities. There are many complications. In some cases, the use of *have* suggests that the subject of the sentence is not an agent. For example, if I say that *Doug is shaving,* you will assume that Doug is doing the job himself; however, if I say that *Doug is having a shave,* you will probably assume that the barber is doing the shaving. Similarly, *Jane is having a shampoo* and *Timmy is having a haircut* both relegate the subject to nonagent status.

DEGREES OF TRANSITIVITY

Transitive verbs co-occur with agent, instrument, causer, and experiencer subjects, but not with patient subjects and empty *it.* The traditional definition of transitivity requires that any verb that takes a direct object be considered transitive. However, linguists Paul Hopper and Sandra Thompson (1980) have argued that transitivity is a continuum and that the degree of transitivity includes a number of factors, including the "agentiveness" of the subject and the "affectedness" of the direct object. All of the sentences below are technically transitive but the degree of transitivity diminishes with each successive sentence.

Cameron smashed the truck.

Nikki read a comic book.

The baby likes cookies.

In the first example *Cameron* is an agent and *the truck* is a highly affected patient. In the second sentence *Nikki* is an agent but *a comic book* is a relatively unaffected patient. In the third sentence *the baby* is an experiencer and *cookies* is a totally unaffected patient. The fact there are degrees of transitivity will have implications in Chapter 3 when we discuss the passive construction. As you will see then, completely unaffected direct objects are the least likely to become subjects of passives, e.g., *??Cookies are liked by the baby,* and highly affected patients are the most likely to become the subjects of passives, e.g., *The truck was smashed by Cameron.*

Intransitive Verbs

The intransitive verb is not followed by a direct object (or an indirect object), although it is often followed by adverbs that express time or place.

*Lisa **fell**.*   *Mindy **is fishing**.*

Tom **is sleeping.**	*All the relatives* **sat** *in the parlor.*
They **traveled** *for days.*	*Scott* **sneezed.**

Some verbs that are normally intransitive will take a direct object if that direct object restates the verb—*She dreamed a wonderful dream; He slept the sleep of the dead; They talk the talk.* Such direct objects are called **cognate direct objects**, since the verb and the object derive from the same root word. Such constructions are somewhat unusual and it's still legitimate to consider *sleep, dream,* and *talk* intransitive verbs. Even a sentence like *She talked a blue streak* does not change the fact that *talk* is typically intransitive. The direct objects in *Les sang a song* and *They did the deed* are also cognates, since they are simply a variation of the verb, i.e., *song* derives from *sing* and *deed* derives from *do.*

There are a few intransitive verbs that can take a direct object, if that object is very narrowly construed. *Run* (meaning to move the legs rapidly) is normally intransitive, but it can take the noun *race* as an object—*Florence ran a race.* Not surprisingly then, *run* can also take as its direct object any noun phrase that refers to a particular race or type of race—*Florence ran a marathon/the 500 meter/the Bay to Breakers.* Similarly, *sing* takes as its object any noun phrase that refers to a particular type of song—*Matt sang a ballad/a blues number/a spiritual/an aria.*

Categories like transitive and intransitive are important because whether or not a verb is transitive will have implications, not only for the rest of predicate, but for the subject as well. Except for the case of passives, patient subjects always have intransitive verbs, because patient subjects are not acting on someone or something else but are themselves being acted upon. Agent subjects on the other hand can co-occur with either transitive or intransitive verbs—*Mary threw the ball; Mary yelled.* Instrument subjects and causers will always take transitive verbs because, in order to carry out these roles, they must be acting on something else.

Often a transitive verb with an agentive subject will have an identical intransitive counterpart that of necessity takes a patient subject.

Yoko emptied the bathtub.	*The bathtub emptied.*
The alarm cleared the room.	*The room cleared.*
Hester dimmed the lights.	*The lights dimmed.*
The cook thickened the soup.	*The soup thickened.*
Orson opened the door.	*The door opened.*

A few very old transitive verbs have a separate intransitive form which is related to the transitive form but is not identical to it—*to fell/to fall; to set/to sit; to lay/to lie.* These verb forms pose problems even for native English speakers. In comparing the forms in the following chart, ignore the {-s} ending on the present tense verb forms.

	Transitive		Intransitive
Present tense		**Present tense**	
Marsha **lays** the book on the table.		The book **lies** on the table.	
Merle **sets** the glass on the shelf.		The glass **sits** on the shelf.	
The woodsman **fells** the tree.		The tree **falls.**	
Past tense		**Past tense**	
Marsha **laid** the book on the table.		The book **lay** on the table.	
Merle **set** the glass on a shelf.		The glass **sat** on the shelf.	
The woodsman **felled** the tree.		The tree **fell.**	

Note that the past tense of intransitive *fall* is identical to the present tense of transitive *fell*. The present and past tense forms of transitive *set* are identical, while intransitive *sit* has a distinct past tense form. The past tense of intransitive *lie* is *lay*, making it identical to the present tense of transitive *lay*. It's no wonder that many people don't know whether to say "I'm going to lay down" or "I'm going to lie down" and for many speakers the distinction between *lay* and *lie* has simply disappeared.

Ditransitive Verbs and Indirect Objects

There is a relatively small set of verbs in English that can be followed by two objects; these two objects traditionally have been called the indirect object and the direct object, although some grammarians simply call them object$_1$ and object$_2$. I will use the traditional terminology. The direct object and the indirect object are both structures within the predicate.

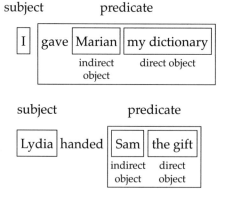

```
        subject          predicate
      ┌──────┬─────┬┌──────────┬────────────┐
      │ Gene │sold ││ a friend │ his condo  │
      └──────┴─────┴└──────────┴────────────┘
                      indirect      direct
                      object        object
```

Ditransitive verbs (*di-* is the Greek root for two) always involve a transference of possession of the direct object to a **recipient**, the **indirect object**. The transference is often literal—*I handed Mike the report,* although sometimes the transference is figurative or metaphorical—*She read me a fairy tale.* Occasionally the transference is pending—*I offered her chicken soup.* Semantically, the **indirect object** carries only the recipient semantic role. In a few cases that role is a negative one, i.e., the fact that the indirect object does not receive is underscored— *The boss denied **her** a raise; They spared **my aunt** unnecessary pain; She refused **the beggar** a meal.*

Literal transference	Metaphorical transference	Transfer pending
I gave **Joanie** the book.	I read **the kids** a story.	Max offered **the kids** candy.
She handed **me** the shovel.	She told **her employees** a lie.	My sister owes **me** $500.
I loaned **my friend** money.	Opera gives **me** a headache.	I guaranteed **Lara** a raise.
He passed **Max** the potatoes.	Mary taught **the newcomers** English.	I promised **Sue** a bicycle.
We fed **the dogs** salami.	I showed **her** my computer.	I wrote **her** a letter.
Mark sold **her** his bike.	The rain brought **us** relief.	He baked **his dad** a cake.
I brought **Tania** a sandwich.	She asked **the teacher** a question.	I bought **the kids** a gift.
Vi served **the patrons** lunch.	She sent **Jake** her best wishes.	The boss assigned **me** an office.
The child slipped **her friend** a note.	The politicians fed **us** lies.	I granted **her** an interview.
Bill took **his wife** some lunch.		They extended **me** credit.

Negative transference

| The agency denied **us** aid. | They refused **the patient** water. | They spared **him** the details. |

(There is sometimes a fine line between transference categories. Your judgments may not match mine in every case. This is not a problem.)

Note that in the examples above, all the recipients (i.e., indirect objects) are animate, in most cases human. This isn't surprising since these constructions all involve a transfer of possession (actual or potential) and inanimate entities don't "possess" in the way living things do. Sometimes, however, institutions or places are treated as collections of people—*I faxed* ***the White House*** *my letter; I owe* ***the University*** *a lot of money; The Marlins gave* ***Miami*** *their best.* There are a few contexts in which we appear to use *give* with truly inanimate recipients—*I gave the furnace a kick; I gave my computer a whack.* But in these constructions there is no real transference; in fact the direct object expresses the action and the verb itself is "light." These sentences can be paraphrased as *I kicked the furnace* and *I whacked my computer.*

While all ditransitive verbs express transfer or potential transfer of possession, there is tremendous variation in just how that transfer is effected. You can *bring/give/throw/slip/serve* or *feed Sally a sandwich* and with each verb the nature of the transfer changes. Similarly, you can *hand/send/e-mail* or *fax Stuart a letter. Bring* entails motion toward the speaker, while *take* entails motion away from the speaker—*Bring me a glass of water* versus *Take Richard this sandwich.*

Many ditransitive verbs are very old. *Give, feed, bring, teach, tell, sell, ask,* and *take* all date back to Old English. But we do occasionally create new ones, e.g., *Azra* **faxed** *me the report; We* **telexed** *Trish the proposal; They* **UPSed** *us the package.*

Grammatically, a recipient can occupy one of two positions. It can appear after the verb but before the direct object—*I gave* ***my brother*** *some money,* or it can appear after the direct object as a prepositional phrase—*I gave some money* ***to my brother.*** I will call the first type an NP (noun phrase) indirect object and the second type a PP (prepositional phrase) indirect object. Instead of marking the indirect object with a suffix, which is the strategy exploited by many other European languages, English signals indirect object status with word order or with a preposition. When an indirect object occurs as a prepositional phrase, the preposition is usually *to—I gave the book to Joanie; I read a story to the kids* and sometimes *for—I made a shirt for my son; I fixed lunch for my girlfriend.*

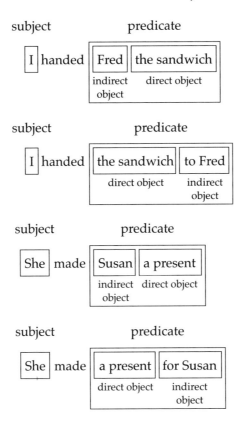

The preposition *for* is used in cases where the subject has <u>created</u> something to give the indirect object.

*Ron baked a cake **for Mary**.*

*I knitted a sweater **for Bill**.*

*Giovanni cooked dinner **for the family**.*

*My cousin fixed a bottle **for the baby**.*

All of these sentences can be paraphrased by placing the indirect object directly after the verb—*Ron baked **Mary** a cake, I knitted **Bill** a sweater*, etc. When indirect objects co-occur with created direct objects, transference is always pending. In *Ron baked a cake for Mary*, we do not know whether the intended recipient actually came into possession of the cake.

Write is one ditransitive verb that creates a direct object, yet exploits *to* as the preposition in the indirect object construction—*Suzy wrote a letter to Santa Claus*.

While created direct objects almost always require *for* rather than *to* in a PP indirect object, not all *for* indirect objects co-occur with created direct objects. In each of the sentences below, the indirect object can be expressed as a *for* prepositional phrase, but the direct object is a patient.

*I saved **Jill** a seat.*	*I saved a seat **for Jill.***
*Betty poured **Bert** some milk.*	*Betty poured some milk **for Bert.***
*She ordered **Talia** some software.*	*She ordered some software **for Talia.***
*I found **you** a sweater.*	*I found a sweater **for you.***
*Mickey fried **Minnie** an egg.*	*Mickey fried an egg **for Minnie.***

There are a few indirect objects that can be expressed by *of* prepositional phrases, e.g., *Vivian asked **the Dean** a question* versus *Vivian asked a question **of the Dean.***

Most truly ditransitive verbs require both a direct object and an indirect object for grammaticality. While *I handed Paulette the shovel* is a perfectly grammatical sentence, **I handed Paulette* and **I handed the shovel* are ungrammatical. However, in many cases the indirect object need not be explicitly stated. Many ditransitive verbs can occur without an **overt**, explicitly stated indirect object. In each of the following sentences there is a covert indirect object which can be determined by looking at the discourse context. In the following examples, the discourse context appears in nonitalicized brackets, while the covert indirect object is indicated by empty brackets within the sentence itself.

[My boss wanted a reference.]	*The Dean wrote [ ] a letter.*
[Donald needed a mechanic.]	*I offered [ ] my services.*
[Alicia went to the Red Cross.]	*She gave [ ] blood.*
[I wanted some potato chips.]	*Melissa passed [ ] the bag.*

In each of the above examples the covert indirect object is "recoverable" from the discourse context, e.g., *The Dean wrote **my boss** a letter; I offered **Donald** my services.* Since a recipient is always animate (usually human), it is not surprising that indirect objects are sometimes a covert, indefinite *someone* or *everyone*. In *Ana sold her house,* we may not know or care who the specific buyer was but we do know that there was one. In *That child tells lies* we understand that the child in question tells lies to everyone.

It is rare for an indirect object to occur without an overt direct object. **Anne gave the kids* is an unacceptable sentence because it does not specify what the kids received. The direct object can be omitted only in those few cases where there is a conventionally understood, covert direct object. This direct object is rarely if ever indefinite. In *George read to the kids,* both speaker and hearer assume that George is reading a story or a poem to the kids, not the tax code or the telephone directory. In *Carrie wrote to her boyfriend,* we assume that Carrie is writing a letter, not a prescription or an examination. In *I give to the United*

Way, most of us know that the covert direct object is *money.* However, an individual who did not recognize *United Way* as a charitable organization might have trouble processing this sentence. In cases in which the direct object is omitted, the indirect object is usually expressed as a prepositional phrase rather than an NP; **George read the kids* and **I give the United Way* are ungrammatical, although many speakers can say *Carrie wrote her boyfriend.*

DEGREES OF DITRANSITIVITY

It is somewhat misleading to label all the verbs discussed in this section as ditransitive. As you saw above, some verbs are truly ditransitive, i.e., they <u>require</u> either an overt or covert indirect object. But fundamentally monotransitive verbs sometimes take on a ditransitive role. While *kick* can be ditransitive— *Rachel kicked Carole the ball,* there is no evidence that *kick* <u>requires</u> a recipient; *Rachel kicked the ball* is perfectly grammatical. Verbs of "ballistic motion" like *throw, toss,* and *kick* are in general **monotransitive**, but they <u>can</u> take indirect objects. (Monotransitive means that the verb requires only a direct object; the Greek root *mono-* means "single.") Verbs that can express their indirect objects as *for* prepositional phrases are also fundamentally monotransitive. A speaker can say *I baked a cake* or *I built a birdhouse* without suggesting that there is some unexpressed recipient.

Monotransitive	Ditransitive
Klaus tossed the bag into the trash can.	Klaus tossed Frances the bag.
Hillary threw the ball over the wall.	Hillary threw George the ball.
Igor slid the box down the hall.	Igor slid Irene the box.
I made an afghan.	I made my uncle an afghan.
My grandad knits sweaters.	My grandad knits me sweaters.

NOT ALL RECIPIENTS ALTERNATE

All of the recipients discussed above can alternate between an NP indirect object construction and a PP indirect object construction. But there are a few indirect objects that become problematic when paraphrased as prepositional phrases. While *I promised Luis a job* is fine for all speakers, *?I promised a job to Luis* is odd for some. *We refused the kids service* and *We charged them a fee* are fine but *?We refused service to the kids* and *??We charged a fee to them* sound odd, if not downright ungrammatical. There are a number of indirect objects that resist appearing as prepositional phrases, including most "negative" recipients.

I wished my opponent luck.	*?I wished luck to my opponent.*
The Dean accorded Al a hearing.	**The Dean accorded a hearing to Al.*
They refused the refugees aid.	*?They refused aid to the refugees.*
I spared Meg the details.	**I spared the details to Meg.*
We charged the vendor a lot.	*??We charged a lot to the vendor.*

There are also a significant number of recipients that can be comfortably expressed only by means of a prepositional phrase. (Some grammarians insist that structures like these are not true indirect objects.)

She donated some money to the museum.	*?? She donated the museum some money.*
Jackie whispered the answer to Raimund.	*??Jackie whispered Raimund the answer.*
Al contributed some money to the poor.	**Al contributed the poor some money.*
Penny returned the bicycle to Kyle.	**Penny returned Kyle the bicycle.*
The boy surrendered the gun to the police.	**The boy surrendered the police the gun.*
The shop delivered the lamps to my mother.	*??The shop delivered my mother the lamps.*
I explained the problem to the Dean.	**I explained the Dean the problem.*

The variability of these alternation patterns creates problems for both first and second language learners. Non-native speakers of English and native-speaking children often produce sentences like **He explained me the answer.*

The problem here is that the grammatical category indirect object is not an altogether coherent one in Modern English grammar. The confusion goes back to the medieval period. In Old English, the recipient of the direct object was usually in the **dative case**. This means that the indirect object noun carried a set of suffixes that clearly distinguished it from the direct object. In addition, the position of the indirect object in the sentence was fairly predictable; pronoun indirect objects almost always preceded the direct object and noun indirect objects usually did. In 1066, the Norman French invaded England and, at least among the members of the ruling class, there was a great deal of language contact between French and English speakers. This contact affected English in a variety of ways. For one thing, French nouns had no dative case; French exploited the preposition *à* ("to") in indirect object constructions and English speakers gradually adopted this strategy without abandoning the old dative forms. Eventually the special dative endings disappeared[2] but Old English word order persisted; in other words, the indirect object continued to precede the direct object. But when the recipient was marked with a preposition, it reflected French word order, i.e., it followed the direct object.

Not surprisingly, most of the verbs that take only prepositional indirect objects came into the language after the Norman invasion, e.g., *donate, report, explain,* and most of the verbs that take NP indirect objects date back to Old English, e.g., *give, feed, sell, bring, tell, buy.* Often verbs that are semantically related will have different indirect object constructions. *Give, donate,* and *contribute* share many semantic features, yet, only *give* takes an NP indirect object and has Anglo Saxon roots. *Contribute* and *donate* came into the language in the sixteenth and nineteenth centuries, respectively. This does not mean, however, that all verbs that entered the language after the Norman invasion take only prepositional indirect objects. Consider *She guaranteed Nick a spot, He bequeathed us a fortune,* and *Carmela faxed Alex a memo.* Both *guarantee* and *bequeath* are French loan words and *fax* is obviously a very recent creation derived from the noun *facsimile.* Conversely, there are a few very old verbs that require that the "recipient" appear in a prepositional phrase. *Say,* which dates back to Old English, has always required that the recipient follow the preposition *to—I said something to Jerome.*

Because of these complications, grammarians don't always agree on how to characterize the semantic category recipient grammatically. Some consider only those recipients that occur directly after the verb to be indirect objects, e.g., *I gave **Clarice** some candy.* Others categorize as an indirect object any recipient that can even potentially occur as NP after the verb, e.g., *I handed the book **to Sean**,* which can be paraphrased as *I handed **Sean** the book.* Still others accept as indirect objects even those prepositional recipients that never appear as NPs, e.g., *I surrendered the gun **to the police.***

DISCOURSE FUNCTIONS OF THE INDIRECT OBJECT

Most grammarians subscribe to the **no-synonymy rule** in language. There is a general assumption among linguists that no true synonyms exist among words or structures. Why then do we have two ways to express recipients in English? While *I threw Signe the ball* seems on the surface to mean the same thing as *I threw the ball to Signe,* these two sentences are not quite synonymous. Speakers who find *I threw the ball to Signe but she couldn't catch it* a perfectly acceptable sentence often balk at *?I threw Signe the ball but she couldn't catch it.* A number of grammarians have pointed out that with certain verbs an NP indirect object reflects <u>successful</u> completion of the transfer while a PP indirect object is silent on the issue. (For example, see Lakoff and Johnson, 1980, p. 130.) Thus, *I taught my students Swedish* indicates the students actually learned Swedish, while *I taught Swedish to my students* expresses only the attempt. The explanation for this phenomenon is to be found in a general tendency in grammar—the closer an object is to the verb, the more likely it is to be affected by the action of that verb. Thus, when the indirect object follows the verb directly, the sense of a successful transfer is stronger than when the indirect object appears later in the sentence.

Another piece of evidence in support of the no-synonymy rule is found in discourse. We have already discussed the fact that topics are usually first introduced in the predicate. A corollary to this generalization is that the newest information in the sentence goes after all the given information. Where we find the indirect object often depends on whether the recipient is new or given information. If the indirect object represents new information in a discourse and the direct object represents given information, the indirect object will appear after the direct object in a prepositional phrase. For example, assume that you're engaged in a conversation with friends. You have already established that Marcy owns a motorcycle and isn't riding it today. Someone says "She loaned it to Jack." *Jack* is the new information here; *she* (Marcy) and *it* (the motorcycle) have already been mentioned. As newly introduced information, *Jack* follows the pronoun *it; ??I loaned Jack it* sounds very strange. On the other hand, if the direct object is the new information, it will appear after the indirect object. Assume that your friends are wondering how Candace obtained her new stereo. You clear up the mystery with "I gave her the money." *I* and *her* (Candace) are given information and *the money* is new information. As new information, *the money* follows the given information.

We see the same phenomenon in question and answer sequences. In response to "What did you do with the report?" a secretary might say, "I handed it to the boss." Here *the report* is given information (it was mentioned in the preceding question) so *it* precedes *the boss* who hasn't been mentioned yet. If the question had been "What did you hand the boss?" the answer might be "I handed her the report." Here *the boss* is the given information, so *her* precedes *the report*, which is new information. And of course when an indirect object precedes a direct object, it always appears in NP, not prepositional, form. We've already discussed the fact that personal pronouns always encode given information. Not surprisingly then, when an indirect object is pronoun and the direct object is a full noun phrase, the indirect object (given information) precedes the direct object (new information.)

In the following chart, given information is single underlined and new information is double underlined.

(a) Indirect object is new information. Direct object is given information.	(b) Indirect object is given information. Direct object is new information.
I loaned <u>it</u> <u>to Jack.</u>	I loaned <u>him</u> <u>the car.</u>
Eileen gave <u>it</u> <u>to the boss.</u>	Eileen gave <u>her</u> <u>the report.</u>
I bought <u>them</u> <u>for Debbie.</u>	I bought <u>her</u> <u>some marbles.</u>
He sold <u>it</u> <u>to my parents.</u>	He sold <u>them</u> <u>a policy.</u>

Note that it is the <u>final</u> structure in each sentence that encodes new information; note, too, that the new information is expressed by a full noun phrase, not a pronoun. In column (a), the last structures are all indirect objects; in column (b), the last structures are all direct objects. Pronouns can occur in sentence final position as prepositional indirect objects—*I loaned the car to him; I gave the report to her.* But while such sentences are perfectly grammatical, they are less common in discourse than sentences in which a pronoun indirect object <u>precedes</u> the direct object. The following passages from Raymond Chandler's novel *The Little Sister* reflect the typical position of a pronoun indirect object. (Boldface added.)

They gave **me** his phone number at home. (p. 229)

"I paid **you** twenty dollars, Mr. Marlowe," she said coldly. (p. 39)

Then she comes in and takes the twenty away from me gives **me** a kiss. (p. 89)

I handed **him** . . . the registration card. (p. 50)

Sentence final indirect object pronouns occur most often when a speaker wishes to articulate some sort of contrast and the pronoun is stressed—*I bought a car for <u>them</u>, not for <u>him</u>.* However, <u>direct object</u> pronouns seldom appear last in the sentence; while *I handed Karen the book* and *I handed her the book* are fine, *?I handed Karen it* and *?I handed her it* are somewhat less acceptable. (In British English a sentence like *I gave it him* is perfectly grammatical, but in this case the preposition *to* has been omitted in the indirect object construction.)

BENEFACTIVES

There is another construction containing the preposition *for* which is similar but not identical to an indirect object. Consider the following sentences.

*Leah raked the yard **for the neighbors.***	*Jorge changed the sheets **for the guests.***
*I mailed a package **for Helen.***	*Fritz hung the picture **for his father.***
*Kirby cleaned the car **for Bert.***	*I trimmed the trees **for Yvette.***

In none of these sentences can the object of the preposition *for* be moved to occupy the position before the direct object. **Kirby cleaned Bert the car* and **Fritz hung his father the picture* are absolutely ungrammatical. *I mailed Helen a package* is grammatical but it means something quite different from the original sentence. In a similar vein, *Martha wrote a letter to her boss* means something very different from *Martha wrote a letter for her boss.*

In each of these cases the *for* prepositional phrase represents, not a recipient indirect object, but a **benefactive**; (*ben-* is the Latin root for "good"). In other words, *Leah raked the yard on the neighbors' behalf.* In a benefactive construction, the beneficiary doesn't receive the direct object, but rather benefits from some action involving the direct object. Only ditransitive verbs can take indirect objects and only verbs that take a created direct object and few other verb types can take an indirect object of the *for* variety. Benefactives, however, can follow any number of transitive verbs. In fact, almost any transitive sentence with an agentive subject can be turned into a benefactive. *Benefactive* is a semantic label; there is no separate grammatical label for such constructions.

Occasionally speakers make threats using a benefactive construction—*I'll break your arm for you [if you don't let go of me].* (These are sometimes called **malefactives**, *mal-* being the Latin root for "bad.")

Recipients	Benefactives
Lourdes fixed lunch **for the kids.**	Lourdes fixed the computer **for Jay.**
Stuart made a sandwich **for Joyce.**	He made the bed **for my mother**.
I built a birdhouse **for Samantha.**	I painted the birdhouse **for Samantha.**
I crocheted a scarf **for Shirley.**	I mended a scarf **for Shirley.**
Teresa drew a tree **for Trevor.**	Teresa trimmed the tree **for Trevor.**
She wrote a script **for the actor.**	She edited a script **for the actor.**
I got the book **for Deb.**	I destroyed the book **for Deb.**

Copulas and Subject Complements

A copula (also called a **linking verb**) is neither transitive nor intransitive; it represents a separate syntactic category. *Be, seem,* and *become* are just a few of the copulas in English.

A copula can never stand alone in the predicate; it must be followed by another structure. One cannot say **Betty seems, *Those buildings are,* or **That man became.* Linguists routinely use the term **complement** to refer to any structure that is required in a predicate for grammaticality. The obligatory structure after a copula is called a **subject complement**. When the subject complement is an NP, it is a **predicate nominative** (or **predicate nominal**). Since predicate nominatives are NPs that follow verbs in the predicate, they look at great deal like direct objects.

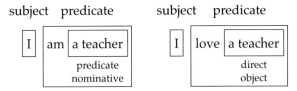

The difference here is that a copula does not transfer an action to a direct object the way a transitive verb does. Unlike a direct object, a predicate nominative NP refers to the same entity as the subject NP. In the sentence *I am a teacher,* *I* and *a teacher* are noun phrases that refer to the same individual. If a speaker uses a transitive verb, e.g., *I love a teacher,* the hearer will assume that *I* and *a teacher* refer to different people.

Subject complements can also be adjectives. When an adjective follows a copula, it refers back to the subject of the sentence. In *Some politicians are corrupt,* the adjective *corrupt,* which occurs in the predicate, describes the subject *some politicians.* Such adjectives are called **predicate adjectives**, but despite this label they never modify nouns in the predicate.

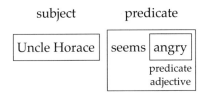

Be is the only copula that can take an adverb of location as its complement—*Stu is in the basement; Tilly is on the golf course. *Stu seems in the basement* is ungrammatical. Other copulas can co-occur with an adverb of location only when the adverb is preceded by a predicate adjective or predicate nominative—*Tommy seems unhappy in that school.* As you will see shortly, copulas involving sensory perception can take as a subject complement a prepositional phrase headed by the preposition *like—This liquid smells **like turpentine**; That cloth looks **like silk**.*

There are a very limited number of copulas in English and they fall into just a few general semantic categories.

SENSORY COPULAS

Each sensory perception has a copula associated with it. (Remember that each sense also has a verb form that takes an agent subject and one that takes an experiencer subject.) Interestingly, in the case of copulas, the sensory perception is not that of the subject of the sentence, but rather that of the speaker. These copulas must be followed by an adjective, a prepositional phrase with the preposition *like,* or, on rare occasions, a noun phrase.

*The record **sounds** scratched. / That animal **sounds** like an elk.*

*Margie **looks** terrible. / She **looks** a mess. / That cloth **looks** like silk.*

*Your cabin **smells** musty. / This room **smells** like a barn.*

*This meat **tastes** rancid. / This squid **tastes** like rubber.*

*This cloth **feels** rough. / This lump **feels** like a cyst.*

You can say *This room smells* without an overt adjective following the copula, but your hearer will presume the adjective *bad*. If you want to suggest any other quality, you must include an adjective.

We have already seen that certain transitive sensory verbs have experiencer subjects, e.g., *Roger smelled smoke*. In the examples listed above, the experiencer of the sensory perception is unexpressed but is assumed to be that of the speaker—*That record sounds scratched [to me]*. However, it's possible to override the presumption that the sensory perception is that of the speaker by specifying someone else—*The room smelled musty **to Richard**; The meat tasted rancid **to the cook**; Becky sounded sick **to her mother***. In these cases the experiencer is contained in a prepositional phrase. *Miriam* has the same semantic role in each of the following sentences—***Miriam** could taste the spices in the soup; The soup tasted spicy to **Miriam***. While transitive verbs can have experiencer subjects, copulas cannot; when the verb is a copula, the experiencer must be expressed by an overt or covert prepositional phrase.

STATIVE COPULAS

There are two copulas, *seem* and *appear,* each of which suggests that a subject has a particular quality or is in a particular state—*Joyce **seems** happy; Tom **appears** satisfied*. These copulas underscore the fact that the state is apparent, but not necessarily real. Here, too, the perception is assumed to be that of the speaker—*Joyce seems happy [to me]*, unless that assumption is explicitly canceled—*Joyce seems happy to Bill*. Don't confuse copula *appear* with intransitive *appear,* which has a very different meaning—*A ghost appeared suddenly before us*. *Seem* and *appear* are usually followed by adjectives, although *seem* can also be followed by the preposition *like*—*She seems like a nice person; This seems like the only alternative*. (The construction *seems to be*, as in *She seems to be nice* will be discussed in Chapter 3.)

Copula *remain* is closely related to intransitive verb *remain*. In a sentence like *Jorgen **remained** angry*, the copula indicates that a state persists. In a sentence like *Jeff remained in the room*, the intransitive verb indicates that subject persists in a particular location.

CHANGE OF STATE COPULAS

Some copulas suggest a change in the state of the subject. Most change of state copulas are followed by adjectives which express the result of the change. *Become* can be followed by an adjective or an noun phrase.

*The milk **turned** sour yesterday.*	*My husband is **going** bald.*
*Michelle **became** an architect.*	*My grandparents **grew** old last year.*
*She **became** irate.*	*Henry **gets** angry easily.*

Turn constrains its predicate adjective more than other resultative copulas do. Since it usually suggests a relatively rapid change of state, sentences like **He turned tall* or **The baby turned fat* are unacceptable.

While copula *turn* cannot be followed by a noun phrase, *turn into* can— *The frog turned into a prince; She turned into a lovely woman.* Since the second NP in each of these sentences has the same referent as the subject, it makes sense to treat *turn into* as a two-word copula. (Multiword verbs will be taken up in some detail in Chapter 3.)

COPULA *BE*

The most ubiquitous copula is *be*. *Be* in its various forms is the only copula that need not be followed by an adjective or a noun phrase. However, if there is no adjective or noun phrase in the predicate, *be* must be followed by an adverb of location.

*I **am** angry.*	*Mary **was** in the garden.*
*Gene **is** an engineer.*	*Her shoes **were** on the floor.*
*Those buildings **are** ugly.*	*I **am** at the store.*

Occasionally *be* is used to mean *arrive* and in these cases, *be* can co-occur with adverbs of time, e.g., *Becky was an hour late; Maxwell was on time.*

Unlike the other copulas, *be* has little semantic content of its own. When it is followed by an adjective, it acts as a signpost, directing the hearer to the quality described by the adjective; when it is followed by a noun phrase, it acts almost as an equal sign (*Gene = engineer*); and when it is followed by an adverb, it acts as a locator. When *be* is followed by an adjective, it normally communicates a state—*The Sears Tower is tall; Donald Trump is rich; Rosalind is kind.* It resembles *seem* and *appear* in this regard.

RESTRICTED COPULAS—STATIVE AND CHANGE OF STATE

There is a small class of highly restricted copulas that co-occur with a very limited number of subject complements.

*The problems **loomed** large.*

*The children **fell** silent/asleep/ill.*

*The task **proved** difficult/impossible/insurmountable.*

*The kids **ran** wild.*

These verbs are **homophonous** with other intransitive or transitive verbs, i.e., they are pronounced in the same way. But the meanings of the copulas are rather different from those of their transitive or intransitive counterparts. Clearly, copula *fall* does not mean to topple but to *become,* and like *become* it communicates a change of state. But *fall* often has negative or ominous overtones. *He fell sick* is fine but **He fell well* is impossible. Downward motion is frequently used in English to suggest negative states or events—*She fell into despair; His spirits sank; I feel down*—and copula *fall* often exploits this same metaphor.

Intransitive *loom* can refer to physical objects or abstractions—*A freighter loomed in the fog; Disaster loomed*—but copula *loom* is usually associated with abstractions and is almost always followed by *large.* Copula *run* does not necessarily mean "run" in a literal sense, but rather suggests lack of supervision. *The children ran wild* is closer to *The children were wild* than *The children ran wildly.* Copula *prove* is closely related to its transitive counterpart. In the transitive sentence *The prosecution proved Jeffrey guilty, prove* indicates that the prosecutors somehow demonstrated Jeffrey's guilt, while in *The job proved impossible,* something demonstrates that the job is impossible.

Sensory copulas	Stative copulas	Change of state copulas
The wind **sounds** loud.	Maggie **seems** content.	It **turned** cold last night.
This **tastes** awful.	Your mom **appears** upset.	Wally **got** mad.
The task **looked** impossible to Joseph.	The world **is** flat.	She **became** an attorney.
This plaster **feels** cracked.	**(Restrictive)**	They **grew** old.
The fish **smelled** rotten to the customer.	This problem **looms** large.	The prince **turned into** a frog.
	The disease **proved** incurable.	**(Restrictive)**
		The passengers **fell** ill.

The copula in a sentence dictates the semantics of the subject complement. The subject complement following a stative copula will reflect a state—*The baby is fat; This milk smells sour.* A subject complement that follows a change of state copula expresses the resultant state—*The baby became fat; The milk turned sour.*

Subject complement—stative	Subject complement—resultative
Helena sounds **angry**.	Helena grew **angry**.
Vera was **a doctor**.	Vera became **a doctor**.
That music seems **loud**.	The music got **loud**.
The weather looks **bad**.	The weather turned **bad**.

Complex Transitive Verbs and Object Complements

There is a small set of verbs in English that can be followed by both a direct object and an object complement. **Object complements** are adjectives or noun phrases that describe or refer back to the direct object. The relationship of an object complement to the direct object is very much like the relationship of a subject complement to the subject.

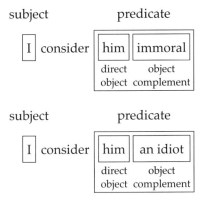

Like subject complements, object complements can be stative or resultative. Those that are stative describe an existing state (or at least a state that the subject of the sentence presumes to exist)—*Gisela found the conversation **dull***; *Wayne considered my candidate **a loser***. In sentences containing resultative object complements, the subject actually causes the direct object to undergo a change, the result of which is then reflected in the object complement—*Pierre painted his room **purple***; *They appointed Sarah **treasurer***.

Resultative object complements always co-occur with agent, instrument, or causer subjects—*Tracy's agent made her **a star***; *The back hoe made the job **easier***; *Becky makes Sidney **mad***. Stative object complements typically occur with either agentive or experiencer subjects—*I called his paintings **ugly***; *I consider his paintings **ugly***.

Object complements—stative	Object complements—resultative
Dale called her boss **a fool**.	Annie colored the sky **orange**.
The kids considered Lena **crabby**.	They spoil their kids **rotten**.
I like my coffee **black**.	She made Lionel **a supervisor**.
He wanted his steak **rare**.	He tied the rope **tighter**.
I prefer my eggs **sunny side up**.	They elected her **president**.
She found the concert **tedious**.	My sister named her baby **Hrothgar**.
The boss rated her performance **excellent**.	They christened the ship **the Titanic**.
They deemed the school **suitable**.	The citizens proclaimed him **king**.
The detective proved Dick **innocent**.	I now pronounce you **husband and wife**.
	She hammered the metal **flat**.

DEGREES OF COMPLEX TRANSITIVITY

Many of the verbs listed above are truly complex transitive in that they require either an overt or covert object complement to maintain their original meaning. *The citizens proclaimed him,* *I now pronounce you,* *They deemed the school,* and *The detective proved Dick* all require object complements to restore grammaticality. *Consider* means something very different in *The kids considered Lena* and *The kids considered Lena crabby; found* means something different in *She found the concert* and *She found the concert tedious.* In each of these examples, the object complement is required to retain the original meaning of the complex transitive verb. In sentences like *They christened the ship, They elected her,* and *The teacher appointed Sarah,* there must be a covert object complement that can be understood from the context.

On the other hand, some of the verbs in the chart above are basically monotransitive verbs that can be used in complex transitive constructions. *They spoil their kids* and *He tied the rope* are perfectly grammatical without object complements. This pattern is especially common when the object complement describes a result—*He wiped the table clean; She drained the glass dry; We painted the barn green; He beat his opponent bloody.* The object complement can be omitted in any one of these sentences without doing violence to meaning or grammar. On a scale with monotransitive verbs at one end and complex transitive verbs at the other, these verbs fall in the middle, behaving like monotransitive verbs in some contexts and complex transitive verbs in others.

True complex transitive verbs (those that <u>require</u> an object complement) tend to fall into a few general semantic categories:

appoint verbs—{*crown, elect, ordain, proclaim, designate*}

dub verbs—{*anoint, baptize, call, christen, crown, dub, label, pronounce*}

declare verbs—{*find, judge, prove, think, declare, brand, rate, deem*}

(These categories are based on Levin [1993, p. 47], although she does not use the term *complex transitive.*)

Since both complex transitive verbs and ditransitive verbs allow the verb to be followed by two noun phrases, there is potential for ambiguity. A number of classic bad jokes exploit this potential:

"Make me a milkshake." "Zap, you're a milkshake!"

"Call me a cab." "Okay. You're a cab."

Marked and Unmarked Word Order

This chapter has been devoted to basic sentence types. Most of the sentences discussed above can be reduced to a few basic patterns:

Transitive	Subject + Verb + Direct Object
Intransitive	Subject + Verb
Ditransitive	Subject + Verb + Indirect Object + Direct Object
Copula	Subject + Verb + Subject Complement
Complex Transitive	Subject + Verb + Direct Object + Object Complement

Note the consistency of word order in these sentences. The subject always precedes the verb; the direct object follows the verb unless there is an intervening indirect object. The vast majority of sentences in English reflect this word order. Linguists call this word order "unmarked." There is nothing weird about it, nothing about it that might attract a hearer's attention.

But sometimes speakers deliberately alter this standard word order to do something special in the discourse. In other words, they "mark" their utterance by employing nonstandard word order. **Markedness** plays an important role in language in general. An **unmarked** structure is one that is usual or typical. A **marked** structure, on the other hand, is noteworthy. Edwin L. Battistella (1990) provides this real world example of markedness.

The unmarked style of dress for everyday affairs . . . is casual dress. To adopt a formal style of dress for everyday affairs—to go to the supermarket in a tuxedo or to teach a class in an evening gown, for example—would be unusual behavior (the marked case) that would cause one to be singled out against the background of unmarked casualness. (p. 5)

Since markedness stands in contrast to our normal expectations, a sentence that exhibits marked word order signals to a hearer that this sentence is doing something special in the discourse. As we have already seen, prototypical sentences with normal word order are often used to make comments about topics. But English is full of structures that do not make comments about topics. We use language to solicit information, to exclaim about surprising events, to point things out, to command.

Can you speak Urdu?

Here comes trouble!

There is a strange man sitting in my bathtub.

Be quiet.

Significantly, none of these sentences has "normal" **subject** + **verb** + **object** word order. Every one is marked in some way.

As you work your way through this textbook, keep this notion of markedness in mind. While many of the sentences we encounter will have unmarked word order, some will not, and those are the ones that pose the most interesting problems for students of grammar. This issue of markedness will come up time and time again.

Summing Up

As you can see from the above discussion, it is sometimes difficult to separate structure from meaning. While we can define *subject* in grammatical terms, it is clear that there are a number of semantic roles that are closely associated with this grammatical category. We can also talk about the *transitive verb* in strictly grammatical terms, e.g., takes a direct object, but certain semantic fallout is inevitable, e.g., transitive verbs never have patient subjects. Form and meaning are inextricably bound.

We can identify a very limited number of basic sentence structures for English and these structures provide the basis for most English sentences, no matter how complex. The five basic sentence types listed above provide the scaffolding. In Chapter 2, you will explore the internal workings of the noun phrase. In Chapter 3, you will see how the basic verb types can be expanded through the use of aspect, passive voice, auxiliaries, and mood markers. In Chapter 4, you will see how these basic sentence patterns can be expanded by a variety of adjective and adverb constructions. In Chapter 5, you will learn how each of the basic grammatical categories described above—subject, direct object, indirect object, subject complement, and object complement—can be expressed by a number of different, sometimes highly complex clause constructions. But the basic structure is always there, holding up the edifice.

2

The Noun Phrase

In the last section we examined the overall structure of the basic English sentence. Apart from the verb, most of the structures discussed in that chapter were **noun phrases** (NPs). As you saw, noun phrases typically function as subjects, direct objects, indirect objects, subject complements, and object complements. (NPs also function as the objects of prepositions, but this will be taken up later.) In Chapter 1, I defined a noun phrase very simply as a pronoun or a noun plus its modifiers. But this definition glosses over some important questions, the biggest of which is "What exactly is a noun?"

This is not an altogether easy question to answer and there are a number of ways we might go about it. The first is to identify a noun in terms of its characteristic endings. In many languages nouns can be identified exclusively in terms of their **inflections.** An inflection is any prefix or suffix that carries grammatical information. Modern languages like Lithuanian and Russian and ancient languages like Classical Latin and Sanskrit use inflections to indicate the grammatical function of a noun (i.e., subjects take one set of endings, direct objects another, and indirect objects yet another). These endings also reflect singular or plural status. Old English nouns also carried this kind of information, although most of these endings were lost by Chaucer's time in the late fourteenth century.

Take a look at the endings for the Old English word for *stone.*

Grammatical function	Singular	Plural
Subject (nominative case)	stān	stānas
Possessive (genitive case)	stānes	stāna
Indirect object (dative case)	stāne	stānum
Direct object (accusative case)	stān	stānas

As you can see, nouns performing different grammatical functions had different endings; only subjects and direct objects share the same forms. Note, too, that the plural forms were <u>different</u> from one another, e.g., a plural subject looks different from a plural indirect object, which looks different from a plural possessive.

In a language like Old English, form and function are inseparable. The form of a noun dictates its grammatical function; the grammatical function of a noun is reflected in its form. But this isn't true in modern English. With the exception of the possessive, you can't tell the function of a noun by its grammatical form, since only the singular possessive {-s} ending and the plural subject/object {-s} ending have survived into Modern English. But our modern possessive and plural endings do help us identify nouns as a general category.

When new nouns enter the language, we routinely inflect them with the plural {-s} ending—*geeks, snafus, modems,* etc. When an old noun takes on a new function, confusion can arise. English speakers are still unsure about the plural of *computer mouse*; computer types usually opt for *mice,* but lay people sometimes exploit *mouses.*

While not all nouns can be pluralized (e.g., *music, rice, furniture*), most can. Some very old English nouns are pluralized by internal vowel change—*goose/geese, man/men, tooth/teeth* or by an {-en} suffix—*children, oxen;* but these plural forms are no longer **productive.** This means that contemporary speakers don't create new plurals by changing the vowel or adding {-en}. In a small number of cases, the plural of a noun is identical to the singular—*deer, sheep,* and these forms, too, are very old.

We can also attempt to identify nouns in terms of their meaning. For many decades linguists rejected the old "a noun is a person, place, or thing" definition, arguing that it was too subjective and too limited. And there are certainly problems with this characterization; it excludes abstractions like *theology* and *responsibility* and references to internal mental states like *thought* and *belief.* But in fact this old saw, repeated by generations of schoolchildren, contains more than a grain of truth; nouns most often do refer to entities that have physical reality. Consider this paragraph from *Pigs in Heaven* by Barbara Kingsolver (1994). All of the nouns (excluding pronouns) are in boldface. (Boldface added.)

> At a **table** nearby, a **wife** and **husband** are having a **fight.** They have on matching **outfits, jeans** and fringed **shirts** that **cowboys** might wear, or **people** in a cowboy-related **industry.** The **woman** has colorless flippy **hair** molded together with **hairspray** so that it all comes along when she turns her **head.** The **man** looks very old. (p. 132)

Out of the 15 nouns highlighted, 13 refer to concrete entities. Only *fight* and *industry* can't be characterized as people or things.

This pattern is widespread. One of the primary uses of nouns in everyday discourse is to code "thing-like" entities. Our world is filled with people, creatures, and objects and we use nouns to talk about them. It is no accident that the first words toddlers learn are those that refer to physical things in their environment—*mommy, cup, juice, doggie.* This is not to say that words like *hatred, joy,* and *respect* are not nouns; they certainly are. But more often than not the nouns we use in everyday discourse refer to entities that have physical reality. Significantly, the more thing-like a noun's referent is, the more likely it is that the noun can accept the characteristic noun inflections, especially the plural marker. A table, a pencil, and a wagon have clear-cut physical reality and each of these nouns can be pluralized. Music, respect, and insanity, however, are not thing-like and they cannot be pluralized. This reflects only a tendency in English, not a hard and fast rule. There are nouns that refer to non-things that readily pluralize—*thoughts, beliefs, ideas* and there are concrete nouns that don't—*oil, rice, gold*. The point here is that nouns tend to share a common semantics; they often do refer to things (animate and inanimate) that have a physical reality. The more thing-like a referent is, the more likely it is that its noun will take nominal inflectional endings. (See Langacker [1987], Givón [1979], and Hopper and Thompson [1984, 1985].)

Unfortunately, inflectional endings aren't a foolproof way of identifying nouns. Some English nouns can't be pluralized and some rarely if ever carry a possessive ending. Furthermore, there are many languages like Chinese and Vietnamese in which nouns carry no affixes whatsoever. Semantic criteria are problematic, too. But there is another way of determining noun status and we spent most of Chapter 1 discussing it, albeit indirectly. Nouns participate in structures that have specific grammatical functions in a sentence.

*An **idiot** scratched my car last night.*	**Subject**
*They arrested **an idiot** in the parking lot.*	**Direct object**
*She offered **an idiot** her car.*	**Indirect object**
*She is **an idiot**.*	**Subject complement**
*Tom considers his boss **an idiot**.*	**Object complement**

In a simple sentence, the **head** (i.e., central element) of any structure, which can function as a subject, direct object, or indirect object, will be a noun. (Subject and object complements aren't really diagnostic, since adjectives can also take on these functions.)

The Determiner

Nouns rarely stand alone; they are usually accompanied by modifiers. But since the noun stands at the head of the noun phrase, it dictates which modifiers may be used and it carries a heavy semantic load. If a noun phrase is stripped of all its modifiers, it still has meaning:

> *All the beautiful trees were destroyed* → ***Trees** were destroyed.*

But if a noun phrase is stripped of its noun head, it will probably be impossible to interpret.

All the beautiful trees were destroyed → ***All the beautiful** were destroyed.*

The most common noun modifiers in English are the determiners. While an adjective is never required for grammaticality in an NP, determiners often are. **Child put book on shelf* is an understandable English sentence, but no native speaker would ever say it in normal conversation.

The determiner is a grammatical category that includes a number of rather different kinds of words, all of which date back to Old English. The determiners constitute a **closed class**; i.e., a class of words that will not admit new members. Articles, possessive (genitive), and demonstrative forms are all considered determiners. These words constitute a single grammatical category because they always occupy the same position in the NP; they always precede both the noun and any adjectives. Furthermore, the noun can be modified by only one item from this class. While *this book, our house,* and *the motorcycle* are all acceptable NPs, an English speaker cannot say **the this book* or **our a house.* The words in the determiner category are mutually exclusive. Whereas possessive determiners and *the* can precede either singular or plural nouns, *a, this, that,* and stressed *sóme* modify only singular nouns, and unstressed *some, these,* and *those* modify only plural nouns.

Determiners that modify singular nouns		Determiners that modify plural nouns	
a	house	some	houses
the	potato	the	potatoes
this	child	these	children
that	plate	those	plates
his/her/its/their	son	his/her/its/their	sons
my/our	cap	my/our	caps
your	doctor	your	doctors
sóme	kid		

The determiner category is fairly rich in meaning. These little function words communicate a great deal of fairly complex information. We'll examine the semantics and the discourse uses of determiners below.

ARTICLES

You are probably familiar with the category **article,** and you may have been taught that *a* is an **indefinite article** and *the* a **definite article.** But what do these terms mean? It turns out that they are very misleading. Most students assume that the term "indefinite" means that the article and subsequent noun don't refer to anyone or anything in particular. But that is seldom the case. In *There is **a snake** in my bathroom,* the speaker is referring to a very specific reptile; in *I know **a fellow** who always wears six ties,* the speaker is referring to a particular man with particular taste in clothes. There are, however, times when the article *a* does not have specific reference, as in *A **robbery** is committed everyday in this neighborhood* or *I hate **a crabby clerk***. The grammatical context will usually reveal if the reference is specific or nonspecific.

Article *a* with **specific** reference	Article *a* with **nonspecific** reference
(a) Becky is dating a nice doctor.	(b) Becky is looking for a nice doctor.
(c) She is slicing a juicy mango.	(d) I enjoy a juicy mango.
(e) I see a red Porsche.	(f) I want a red Porsche.
(g) I witnessed a bad crash.	(h) I fear a bad crash.

In sentence (a) we assume that Becky is dating a particular nice doctor but in (b) it seems that Becky is looking for any nice doctor. In (c) and (e) the speaker is referring to specific entities and in (g) to a specific event. In (d) any juicy mango will do, as will any red Porsche in (f). In (h) the speaker fears something that can't have specific reference because it has not occurred yet. An utterance like "I was searching for a sweater" is potentially ambiguous. If the speaker continues with "and I found it," the NP *a sweater* has specific reference; the speaker found the one s/he was looking for. But if the speaker continues with "and I found one," the NP has nonspecific reference; the speaker found some sweater or other (Lambrecht, 1994, p. 80).

What then is the function of the article *a*? Its primary function is simply to introduce a noun phrase into the discourse. Not surprisingly then, *a* is one of the ways speakers introduce <u>new information</u> into a discourse. Once a noun phrase is introduced with *a*, a speaker (or writer) can use *the* or an appropriate pronoun to refer to this entity.

*Melinda bought **a** new house last week. **The** house is white with green trim.*

***A** little brown puppy wandered into our yard last night. **It** was obviously lost.*

*There is **a** new student in my class. **She** seems rather shy.*

Some is usually considered the plural indefinite article—***Some** puppies wandered into our yard*. In this context, the discourse function of *some* is identical to that of *a*. As you will see later, however, *some* is also used with non-count nouns, many of which never have a plural ending. Here, too, it is used to introduce a noun into discourse but it does not suggest plurality in any way—*I spilled **some** milk; Let's listen to **some** music.*

Stressed *some* can be used with singular nouns when a speaker wishes to underscore the fact that the identity of the noun is unimportant—*Sóme sopho-*

*more got hurt during football practice; My older sister is dating **sóme** boy*. In both these cases, the noun modified by *some* has specific reference, but the identity of the referent is irrelevant to the speaker. Stressed *some* also serves to express annoyance or contempt—***Sóme** idiot left gum on this seat*.

In most cases, *the* cannot be used unless the person or object has already been introduced into the discourse. In other words, the article *the* typically refers back to something. This is another case of **anaphoric reference.** You would find it baffling if, out of the blue, a friend said "The woman stole your calculator." You would undoubtedly respond, "What woman?"

The article *the* can be used without first introducing the item into discourse if there is only one such item in the immediate world of the speakers and they share knowledge of its existence. We refer to ***the** sun* and ***the** moon* because we all recognize their existence and there is only one of each in our sky. Future space settlers living on Jupiter won't be able to refer to ***the** moon*. In a given household, family members will put on ***the** kettle*, open ***the** refrigerator*, and read ***the** paper* while lying in ***the** hammock*, because, as a rule, there is only one such item in the house. If the family includes one infant, "The baby is crying" is an appropriate observation, but if there are quintuplets, it is not. If you routinely go to the same grocery store and financial institution, you probably refer to them as ***the** store* and ***the** bank*. On the other hand, if you are shopping for a mortgage, you may go *a bank* that you don't usually patronize. The use of *the* signals that the referent should be identifiable to the hearer as well as the speaker.

Sometimes the discourse itself will contain the information that allows the hearer to identify the referent of the noun, even though the noun itself hasn't been used. In the case of *We could see Mt. Everest in the distance; **the** peak was covered with snow*, the hearer is expected to deduce that mountains have peaks. By introducing Mt. Everest into the discourse, the speaker has indirectly introduced its peak as well. If an acquaintance says "My wife was hit by a car last night," he could go on to say, "The driver was arrested." The driver is introduced into the discourse by inference; we assume that moving cars have drivers.

In general, singular nouns cannot occur without a determiner. **Dog is in the garden* and **House is brick* are ungrammatical. There are, however, some exceptions to this rule. Singular nouns that refer to abstract institutions rather than physical structures can occur without determiners—*I am going to **school** now; She was sent to **prison** for three years; He has left for **church**; Olympia is attending **college***. Which school, prison, church, or college is immaterial. British and Canadian speakers exploit this construction even more often than Americans do; for example they *go to hospital* and *attend university*. On the other hand, when any English speaker wishes to refer to a particular building, determiners are required—*We drove by **the school**; **That prison** needs repair; **My temple** is on this street*.

When a singular noun refers to the means by which an act is carried out, it, too, occurs without a determiner. In *Sally went by car* or *My parents travel by train*, the speaker is referring, not to a specific vehicle, but to an abstraction, i.e., a means of transportation. We also send things *by mail* and make things *by machine.* Even the noun *bed* exhibits this behavior. We go to *bed* but we buy *a bed* and *make **the** bed.* In the first example, bed is an abstraction, not an entity; in fact, we can go to bed on the floor or on the couch. Note, too, that when such nouns are used in this abstract way, they cannot be pluralized. **I am going to beds* and **My parents travel by trains* are both ungrammatical. You will find that there are a number of abstract nouns that do not co-occur with *the* or the plural marker—**He is in the trouble; *The sincerity shows; *Isn't loves wonderful?*

Earlier, I noted the fact that nouns that refer to concrete entities are more likely to carry nominal inflectional endings (possessive and plural) than nouns that are abstract. We see the same pattern with articles. When words like *school, train,* and *machine* refer to concrete entities, they occur with the appropriate article. But when those same words are used to refer to an abstract institution as opposed to a particular place, a means of transportation rather than a particular vehicle, or a means rather than a particular piece of equipment, the article is often omitted. Like inflectional endings, articles tend to attach themselves to nouns that refer to physical entities. But remember that this is only a tendency, not a hard and fast rule.

DEMONSTRATIVES (AND DEIXIS)

Demonstratives represent another type of determiner. The demonstrative determiners and the article *the* all derive from the same Old English part of speech. It seems quite likely that the original function of this form was demonstrative and that the definite article eventually evolved from this usage. The function of demonstratives is to point items out—***this** book, **that** child, **these** boots, **those** trees.* Demonstratives reflect a quality called **deixis.** Normally a word's meaning does not depend on who utters the word or on when or where it was uttered. However, **deictic** forms change reference when circumstances change. Some pronouns and some adverbs share the quality of deixis with demonstratives. If I say *I,* I am referring to a different person than you are when you say *I.* This is **person deixis.** If I say "Mable is arriving tomorrow" on a Tuesday, you know that *tomorrow* refers to Wednesday. But if I utter the same words on Saturday, *tomorrow* refers to Sunday. This is **temporal** (time) **deixis.** The spot where I am standing is *here* and, from my point of view, where you are standing is *there.* But if I go to where you are standing, that spot becomes *here* to me and the spot I have vacated becomes *there.* This is **spatial** (place) **deixis.**

Demonstratives typically reflect spatial deixis. When I am pointing out someone or something close to me, I choose *this* as my determiner; if the person or thing is not so close, I choose *that.* To me, the book I am holding is *this book,* while the one you're holding is *that* book. But of course to you, the book you are holding is *this book,* while mine is *that book.* The plural forms *these* and *those* work in exactly the same way. Some languages have three or more different deictic forms to express relative distance. Japanese for example has one form for "near the speaker," one for "near the hearer," and one for "distant from both" (Crystal, 1997b, p. 99).

Because deictic determiners locate entities in space, they are often used in conjunction with physical gestures, e.g., a pointing motion or a turn of the head—*This desk is mine; That car over there is Sid's; The robber ran that way.* If I pick up a kitten and say "This cat is my favorite," I give the kitten proximity by singling it out from the others. We often use deictics when we are demonstrating how to do something—*You adjust the fuel mixture this way* or when we critique another's actions—*Don't try to remove the cork that way.* In these cases the deictic refers to a series of actions and in general speakers will use *this* to refer to their own actions and *that* to refer to the actions of another.

Demonstratives also express temporal deixis. We often use *this/these* to refer to recent events or ideas and *that/those* to refer to those more remote in time. Your current vacation is *this vacation,* while last year's is *that vacation;* your most recent proposal is *this proposal,* while the one you made an hour ago is *that proposal.* The item that is most proximate in time or space will co-occur with *this* and *these.*

It is often the case, however, that demonstrative determiners are more anaphoric than deictic—*I've signed up for an advanced linguistics course next term.* **This** *class is going to keep me very busy.* An anaphoric demonstrative will sometimes refer back, not to an individual NP, but to a series of actions or events. We see this pattern in the following passage from Kinky Friedman's novel *God Bless John Wayne* (1996).

> I made some coffee, putting a small bit of eggshell in with the grinds as was the habit of my old pal Tom Baker. **This** little ritual . . . enriched the flavor of the coffee. (p. 114)

INDEFINITE *THIS*

English speakers sometimes use *this* and *these* in non-deictic, non-anaphoric ways. When someone says, "This guy walked up to me and slugged me," s/he is simply using *this* to introduce the noun into discourse. When *this* is used in this fairly specialized way, it is called **indefinite** *this*. (This is another case in which "indefinite" is used inappropriately.) Indefinite *this* has roughly the same function as the indefinite article, except that it always has *specific* reference; a sentence like **Marcy wants to marry this Australian, any Australian* is ungrammatical.

Indefinite *this* seems to be a relatively new phenomenon. There is no known record of it occurring before the 1930s (Ward, 1983, p. 94) and it is still very rare in written discourse. It crops up a lot in casual conversation, however. The following is from an actual interview with a 12-year-old boy.

> . . . **these** two girls, they were like playing hide-n-go-seek, [and] **this** little boy [and] **this** girl, they . . . came (Ward, p. 96).

This speaker uses both *this* and *these* to introduce new NPs into the discourse. A speaker is especially likely to use indefinite *this* or *these* (as opposed to *a* or *some*) in cases where the speaker intends to continue speaking about the referent of the NP at some length (Prince, 1981).

QUANTIFYING DETERMINERS

Most determiners express quantity, whatever their other functions in the discourse. While *a* and *some* are used to introduce entities into discourse, they also express the quantities "one" and "more than one," respectively. *This* and *these* express deictic relationships but at the same time encode number. But there are some determiners whose sole function is to express quantity.

Each, every, and *no* indicate how many individuals in a particular set are relevant to the discourse—*Hortense gave* **each** *child a pencil; They expelled* **every** *student;* **No** *contraband was found on the ship. Each* and *every* have specific reference. Loosely speaking, you should be able to identify the children who received pencils and the students who were expelled. *No,* of course, does not have specific reference; it's impossible to refer to something that does not exist. *Any* is used when a speaker wants to underscore <u>nonspecific</u> reference—*Geoff will go to* **any** *movie; Those kids will eat* **any** *kind of fruit.* Because *any* has nonspecific reference, it is often used in questions and negatives—*Do you know* **any** *mechanics? I haven't seen* **any** *dolphins; I don't want* **any** *coffee; Did the miners find* **any** *gold?*

Either and *neither* are interesting determiners because the quantity they express has historically reflected the number two. *Either,* in cooperation with the conjunction *or,* often refers to one out of two; *neither* in cooperation with *nor* refers to none out of two—*You can have either tea or coffee; Neither Charles nor Maggie was there.* Many speakers do, however, use these forms to express numbers larger than two—*Either Bill, Cathy, or Bertha will finish the project.*

GENITIVE DETERMINERS

The forms *my, our, his, her, its, your,* and *their* constitute a class of determiners called **genitives.** (Up until now I have used the more familiar label "possessive" for these determiners, but this term is misleading, as you will see shortly.) Like the other determiners, these constitute a closed class of small function words. These forms are considered determiners only when they precede a noun head—*I dislike* **his** *brother;* **Our** *pizza is here.* The forms that follow copulas as subject complements (*mine, ours, his, hers, theirs*) are not considered determiners, since they do not precede nouns—*The book is* **mine***; This hammer is* **hers***; That car is* **his***. His* is the only form that can be found in both positions; in the other cases the genitive determiner is turned into a genitive subject complement by marking it with a genitive {-s}, e.g., *their* becomes *theirs* and *her* becomes *hers.* Genitives will be discussed in some detail later.

My, your, and *our* are deictic determiners. *My* always refers to the speaker, *our* refers to the speaker and someone else, and *your* always refers to the hearer(s). The third person genitives, on the other hand, have anaphoric reference. They cannot be used unless the entity to which they refer has already been introduced into the discourse. (In the following examples the genitive determiner appears in boldface and its referent is double underlined.)

*<u>Dorothy</u> is upset because **her** children are moving back into the house.*

*I really dislike <u>Ned</u>. **His** insincerity bothers me.*

*<u>This typewriter</u> is missing one of **its** keys.*

INTERROGATIVE DETERMINERS

Like other question words in English, interrogative determiners typically begin with the letters *wh* in written texts—***Which** child ate all the candy? **Whose** car was stolen? **What** subjects do you teach?* In each case the *wh* word stands for one of the determiners discussed above.

*I choose **this** book.*	***Which** book do you choose?*
*This is **my** cat.*	***Whose** cat is that?*
*I know **the** time.*	***What** time is it?*

Which and *what* have slightly different uses. If the possible noun referents are constrained in some way, *which* is the appropriate determiner. For example, if you and your sister are looking at five cars on a showroom floor, you might ask "Which car should we buy?" In other words, *which* is used when the options are clear. When the options are not constrained, *what* is the appropriate determiner.

Which dress should I wear?	*What kind of shoes should I buy?*
Which folder did you bring?	*What projects have you started lately?*
Which book did she borrow?	*What books have you read this year?*
Which child is yours?	*What sort of person would do that?*

Whose functions as a genitive and an interrogative determiner simultaneously.

Like all interrogative *wh* words, the interrogative determiner appears first in the sentence. This will be discussed in more detail later.

Summary of determiners

Articles	I own **a** tractor.
	Some windows were broken.
	The house is dirty.
	Sóme woman took my parking place.
Demonstratives	I don't like **this** movie.
	Hand me **that** hammer.

	Summary of determiners (cont.)
	These cookies are delicious.
	I can't stand **those** people.
Quantifiers	**No** dogs are allowed.
	I gave **each** student a grade.
	Every photograph was scratched.
	Did you find **any** chocolate?
Genitives	**Whose** hat are you wearing?
	Our loss is **your** gain.
Interrogatives	**Which** bicycle do you want?
	Whose coat did you borrow?
	What color do you prefer?

Predeterminers and Postdeterminers

Occasionally, determiners will be preceded by **predeterminers.** All the words in this category express quantity—*all, both,* all multiples, and all fractions.

All the players left the field.

Half the students missed the bus.

Both my daughters like science.

*This was **one third** the cost.*

*This car will give you **twice** the power.*

The determiner can sometimes be omitted in such constructions—*Both kids like science; All jurors must report now.*

Technically, *all, half,* and *both* are predeterminers only if they directly precede the determiner or the noun. Constructions containing the preposition *of* as in *all of the players* or *both of my daughters* don't contain predeterminers; in these cases *all* and *both* are considered pronouns, which are then modified by prepositional phrases. However, despite the difference in structure, it is clear that the phrases *all the players* and *all of the players* are virtually synonymous. This is one of the few instances in English when different grammatical forms seem to yield the same meaning.

Some predeterminers can move into the verb phrase. Compare *All the kids have had the measles* and *The kids have **all** had the measles.* Here *all* still modifies *kids* even though it no longer precedes it. *Both* can behave in exactly the same way—***Both*** *my nephews are attending MIT; My nephews are* ***both*** *attending MIT.* This phenomenon is sometimes called **quantifier float,** since the predeterminer, which normally occurs before the subject noun head, can "float" to the right of the subject or to the right of an auxiliary verb (if there is one).

| All | his employees | | quit. |

------------------------↑

| Both | my sisters have | | been to Paris. |

------------------------↑

There is also a group of words that can follow the determiner but must precede all adjectives. Not surprisingly, these are called **postdeterminers.** Like predeterminers, all postdeterminers are quantifying terms. Cardinal and ordinal numerals fall into this category.

*Those **five** administrators are in trouble.*

*The **two** women on the horse were yelling.*

*He just made his **second** big mistake.*

*Every **tenth** person will be chosen.*

Cardinal numbers often occur without a preceding determiner—*There are two buzzards on the roof; Sixteen candidates are running for mayor.*

Cardinal and ordinal numbers express specific quantities, while postdeterminers like *many, little,* and *few* express nonspecific quantities

*Her **many** friends deserted her.*

*I'd like a **little** butter.*

*The program has a **few** bugs.*

Be sure to distinguish between postdeterminer *little,* which is clearly a quantifying term, and adjective *little* which refers to size—*a little butter* versus *a little girl.* Postdeterminers *little* and *few* express rather different meanings, depending on whether or not they are preceded by a determiner. *Joe has little faith in the system* reduces the amount of faith to almost zero, while *Joe has **a** little faith in the system* projects a more optimistic outlook. *Few* behaves in exactly the same way. *Oscar has few friends* suggests a sadder state of affairs than *Oscar has a few friends.*

A cartoon by Dan Piraro (1997) exploits this difference between adjective *little* and postdeterminer *little.* The single frame shows a young girl sitting at table set for dinner. She is asking someone to pass the mint jelly and the caption reads, "Tired of it following her to school each day, Mary had a little lamb."

Summary of predeterminers	Summary of postdeterminers
All the furniture was damaged.	The **one** room in the basement was flooded.
I dislike **both** those patterns.	My **second** choice is vanilla.
Half her clothes were stolen.	I know the **five** people in that car.
This is **one third** the cost.	A **few** people showed up.
She put in **five times** the effort.	I'm having a **little** trouble with my printer.

The fact that determiners, predeterminers, and postdeterminers are said to modify the noun in some way does not mean that they are peripheral. Traditional school grammars often treat modifiers as somewhat extraneous items. This has led many English teachers to promulgate the notion of the "simple" subject or the "simple" direct object, i.e., the noun without any of its modifiers. This is extremely misleading. All the words in a structure are important; in fact, overlooking modifiers can have serious consequences. Certainly *No children are allowed* means something very different from *Children are allowed. All the kids can come* means something very different from *Half the kids can come.* When we study NPs that are complex clauses, the notion of the simple subject or simple object becomes even more ludicrous.

Determiners, predeterminers, and postdeterminers are an extremely heterogeneous group semantically and you have undoubtedly noticed that there are quantifying terms in all three categories. It is not always easy to pigeonhole these items. But while the boundaries between these categories are muddy at times, together this collection of little function words provides a tremendous amount of crucial linguistic information.

Genitives

You were briefly introduced to genitives in the determiner section. Genitives take various shapes. They can be determiners—*her computer,* **their** *cabin,* **our** *opinion*; they can be proper nouns—***Rosemary's*** *baby,* **Nixon's** *pardon,* **Ms. Trilling's** *book*; or they can be full noun phrases— **the office manager's** *desk, a* **child's** *toy,* **the tall guy's** *shoes.*

Genitives often have internal grammatical structure. With the exception of genitive determiners, genitives are noun phrases and each can contain its own determiner, just like any other noun phrase. In a phrase like *This boy's father, this* modifies *boy* not *father*; the genitive construction modifying *father* is actually the phrase *this boy's.* In *a child's furniture, a* clearly modifies *child*, since *fur-*

niture does not occur with the indefinite article *a*. The entire phrase *a child's* modifies *furniture*.

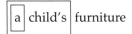

A genitive phrase can contain another genitive phrase and that phrase can contain another genitive phrase, and so on. In *My aunt's boyfriend's mother's car,* the genitive phrase modifying *car* is *My aunt's boyfriend's mother's*; the genitive phrase modifying *mother* is *My aunt's boyfriend*; and the genitive phrase modifying *boyfriend* is *my aunt*. The genitive modifying *aunt* is the determiner *my*. Here we have structure embedded within structure embedded within structure:

Each of these genitive phrases can be paraphrased by a single genitive determiner—**her** *car,* **his** *mother,* **her** *boyfriend,* **my** *aunt.*

GENITIVE SEMANTIC TYPES

You may have been taught to call constructions like those discussed above "possessives," but this label is often incorrect. Only a fraction of genitive constructions actually express a possessive relationship.

I will use the term **possessive genitive** only for those constructions that do indeed describe a possession relationship. These can be paraphrased loosely with the verb *have* or *own*.

Possessive Genitives

The child's bicycle was smashed to bits.   [The child had a bicycle.]

Weifang's pencil fell on the floor.   [Weifang had a pencil.]

Their yacht won't fit in this harbor.   [They own a yacht.]

A bully stole **my kids'** cookies at recess.   [My kids had cookies.]

Hamish's hair is black.   [Hamish has hair.]

My mother is a surgeon.   [I have a mother.]

In some languages (e.g., Chinese and Hawaiian), something that is seen as permanently possessed by the possessor receives a special genitive marker. In these languages body parts and kinship terms are among the nouns that are marked for **inalienable possession.** ("Inalienable" simply means that possession cannot be surrendered or transferred to someone else.) English makes no formal distinction between alienable and inalienable possession, although the semantic difference does have an effect on reflexive and passive constructions, as you will see later.

In the following sentences the relationship between the genitive and the noun is not one of ownership or possession.

Susan's application was denied.

Madonna's performance was outstanding.

Picasso's last painting was stolen from its owner.

Susan did not possess an application; she engaged in an activity by applying. It is even possible that no physical application form was involved. Madonna did not possess a performance; she performed. Picasso did not own the painting; he created it. Such genitives are called **subject genitives** because the relationship of the genitive word to the noun it modifies is rather like the relationship of a subject to its predicate.

Subject genitives

The police didn't believe **Mary's** story.	[Mary told a story.]
Hemingway's novels are exciting.	[Hemingway wrote the novels.]
The government was surprised by **his** defection.	[He defected.]
Carol resented **the child's** refusal.	[The child refused.]
The Dean's lecture was boring.	[The Dean lectured.]
Mozart's quartets are magnificent.	[Mozart composed quartets.]

A sentence like *Marge's new novel is on the table* is potentially ambiguous. Is this a novel Marge owns or one she wrote? The answer of course depends on the real world context.

In some genitive constructions, the relationship of the genitive word to the noun it modifies is like the relationship of a direct object to its verb. In *Max's promotion made him happy,* Max is not doing anything or possessing anything. Here the implication is that someone has promoted Max. The relationship of *Max* to *promotion* is that of direct object to its verb. *Max's* is an **object genitive.**

Object genitives

The city's destruction was total.	[Something destroyed the city.]
She was upset by **that neighbor's** murder.	[Somebody murdered that neighbor.]
Freddie's eviction shocked everyone.	[Someone evicted Freddie.]
I was surprised by **Nixon's** pardon.	[Someone pardoned Nixon].

(In paraphrasing a genitive, be sure to avoid the passive construction. Since the affected party, not the agent, is the subject of a passive, a passive paraphrase will give you the wrong result. If, for example, I paraphrase *the city's destruction* as *the city was destroyed by something, the city* becomes the subject of the paraphrase, not its object. But *the city's* is an object genitive, not a subject genitive.)

Sometimes a genitive can be ambiguous. A phrase like *Sylvia's photograph* is ambiguous in three ways; *Sylvia's* might be possessive genitive (she owns the photo), a subject genitive (she took the photo), or an object genitive (someone photographed her). The sentence *Liz had heard about **Jane's** betrayal* has two potential meanings. If Jane betrayed someone, the genitive is a subject genitive; if someone betrayed Jane, the genitive is an object genitive. The sentence can be "disambiguated" if the genitive construction also includes a prepositional phrase that acts as a patient, as in *Liz had heard about Jane's betrayal **of her friends**.* This is a clear example of how the grammar of a structure and its semantics can diverge. Grammatically *Jane's betrayal of her friends* is an NP containing the noun head *betrayal* which is modified by the genitive *Jane's* and the prepositional phrase *of her friends.* Semantically, however, *Jane('s)* is acting like an agent subject, *betrayal* is acting like a verb, and *of her friends* is acting like a patient direct object. Similarly, if Jane is the one being betrayed, the sentence can be disambiguated by including an agent—*Liz had heard about Jane's betrayal **by her boss.*** (Although you are accustomed to thinking of agents as subjects and of patients as subjects or objects, agents and patients do occur in prepositional phrases. You will see more of this in Chapter 4.)

Nouns that are modified by subject and object genitives are often, but not always, **deverbal nouns,** i.e., nouns derived from verbs. *Betrayal, refusal, eviction,* and *destruction* are all created from verbs by the addition of a suffix; the nouns *murder* and *pardon* derive from identical verb forms. Each of these nouns still carries some verbal force and it's not surprising that their genitive modifiers behave rather like subjects and objects.

Genitive nouns are not always marked by {-s}. In Old English, most genitives were marked with inflectional suffixes but after the Norman invasion that pattern changed somewhat. French genitives have always been prepositional constructions, e.g., *la maison **de Marie*** ("the house of Marie"), and as a result of the language contact between French and English after the eleventh century,

Modern English uses both the inflection and the preposition to mark genitive relationships.

Entities fairly high on the animacy scale, people and higher order creatures, require an inflected possessive genitive—*Teresa's book, the dog's dish, the bird's perch*. Inanimate nouns typically take an *of* genitive—*the shape **of the rock**, the color **of that hat**, the top **of the table***. There are, however, many contexts in which the use of an inflected genitive with an inanimate noun is perfectly acceptable—*The building's design was very functional*. The *of* genitive is almost never used to modify a human possessor. **The coat of Jesse* and **the office of Marilyn* are ungrammatical, but Spanish and French speakers who are learning English as a second language often make this very mistake because such prepositional constructions are required in the Romance languages.

The *of* genitive is called a **periphrastic genitive.** The term *periphrastic* is used to describe a construction that uses extra words rather than an inflectional suffix to communicate grammatical information. *Periphrastic* is a grammatical term; it has nothing to do with the semantics of the genitive construction. A genitive of any semantic type can theoretically be a periphrastic genitive. As you will see later, English has a number of non-genitive, periphrastic constructions as well. (In a nontechnical context, the term *periphrastic* refers to any kind of circumlocution.)

While the periphrastic form of the genitive can be used with any semantic type, it is most often used when the noun being modified is inanimate. For this reason some genitives are more likely to be periphrastic than others. Genitives that reflect **part/whole** relationships and **measurements** are frequently periphrastic.

When a periphrastic genitive expresses a part/whole relationship, the noun phrase being modified is the part and the NP within the prepositional phrase refers to the whole—*the legs of the table, the side of the cabinet*. Of course, inflected genitives can express part/whole relationships, too, and here the inflected noun (or genitive pronoun) refers to the whole—*the book's cover, a car's interior, the dog's tail*.

the top **of the table**	**the dog's** *tail*
[part] [whole]	[whole] [part]

Body parts like *the dog's tail* are sometimes considered part/whole genitives and sometimes (inalienable) possessive genitives. Either analysis can be supported.

Part/whole genitives

The roof **of the house** blew off during the big storm.

That woman scratched the hood **of my car** with her keys.

The tree's branches swayed in the wind.

My car's battery is dead. / **Its** battery is dead.

Genitives of measure have an interesting history. In Old English, the plural genitive marker was not {-s} as it is in Modern English, but rather a vowel, usually -a. (Revisit the Old English word for *stone* at the beginning of this chapter.) Sometime later, vowel suffixes were lost in English and so the plural genitive had no ending at all. Eventually most plural genitives took on the {-s} genitive marker. However, in many regions of the United States, you can still hear speakers say "He lives three mile down the road" or "That ceiling is ten foot tall." And we all use the old genitive of measure in expressions like "I'm five foot four." The lack of a plural marker on *mile* and *foot* is a remnant of this ancient form. We see the same phenomenon in *a nine inch stick* and *a two hour lecture; *a nine inches stick* is completely ungrammatical.

In genitives of measure, the measurement term is the noun head and the entity being measured always takes inflectional or periphrastic genitive form.

the length	*of this room*	*the baby's*	*length*
[measurement term]	[entity being measured]	[entity being measured]	[measurement term]

Genitives of measure

None of my students knows the circumference **of the earth.**

The length **of the trial** surprised the jurors.

She calculated the weight **of the shipment.**

I was intimidated by **the man's** size.

Do you know **Sally's** weight?

There are genitive types that have not been discussed here, many of which are hard to characterize semantically. Consider the semantics of *a winter's day, a girl's school, for pity's sake, an hour's run.* None of these fits comfortably in the categories described above. For example, *a winter's day* and *an hour's run* can be best paraphrased with adverbs—*a day in winter, run for an hour.* As you can see, the semantics of genitives is very complex. Nevertheless, this brief discussion should give you a good sense of the richness of the category.

Summary of genitive semantic types

Possessive	**Carol's** suit was wrinkled.
	The child's face was sunburned.
Subject	**Frank Lloyd Wright's** homes are priceless now.
	The boy's lie outraged his mother.

	Summary of genitive semantic types (cont.)	
Object	**Daphne's** promotion pleased everyone.	
	Victoria was upset about the rejection **of her proposal.**	
Part/whole	**The book's** cover was torn.	
	The roof **of the barn** blew off.	
Measure	The weight **of the cargo** was calculated.	

DOUBLE GENITIVES

English speakers sometimes exploit double genitive constructions, constructions in which the genitive is marked both inflectionally and periphrastically. In *I am reading a novel of Austen's*, Austen is marked by {-s} and at the same time occurs in an *of* prepositional phrase. In other words, *Austen* is marked genitive twice.

Such constructions are highly constrained in terms of form. The noun head is usually indefinite, i.e., preceded by the article *a*. The genitive NP (i.e., the NP carrying the {-s} suffix) must have highly specific reference; it often contains a pronoun or a proper noun.

*A friend **of Bill's** is coming over later.*

*An idea **of yours** has been adopted by the boss.*

*An admirer **of my mother's** sent her a dozen roses.*

*<u>The</u> friend of Bill's is coming over is ungrammatical as is **A friend of <u>a guy's</u> is coming over.*

Normally, double genitives are used when a speaker wishes to refer to one of a class of individuals. Expressions like *a friend of mine, a fan of Reba's,* or *a student of hers* are perfectly acceptable, but *?a husband of mine* and *?a car of Reba's* are odd. The size of the category seems to be a constraining factor here. An individual might have lots of friends, fans, and students, but a woman typically has only one husband and most of us have only one or two cars. Anna Wierzbicka has also argued that the double genitive "is particularly suited to collective categories, where all members can be viewed as equidistanced with respect to the person who provides the point of reference" (Wierzbicka, 1997, p. 43). In other words, the members of the category are undifferentiated. Speakers of English avoid sentences like *A child of mine gave me that necklace* (even if the speaker has many children), precisely because children are not undifferentiated in the way that shirts or fans are.

Surprisingly, demonstrative determiners can appear in the noun head of a double genitive construction.

I can't stand those cats of Susan's.

That music of Stan's is simply awful.

This idea of theirs is great.

In these sentences the NP is highly definite; the speaker knows that the hearer is familiar at some level with the cats, the music, and the idea. Constructions like these are often used emphatically. *I can't stand those cats of Susan's* sounds much stronger than *I can't stand Susan's cats.* In fact, even a noun like *child* can be used in an emphatic double genitive—*That child of mine will drive me insane!* (The noun head in a double genitive construction can sometimes be preceded by the definite article *the* when the genitive is followed by a restrictive relative clause—*The friend of mine **who gave me this dress** wants it back.* Relative clauses will be explained in Chapter 5.)

GROUP GENITIVE

In Old and Middle English the genitive marker was always attached to the noun head being made genitive. *The Queen of England's robe* would have been *the Queen's robe of England.* In the modern version *England* carries the genitive marker, even though it is not England's robe. The Chaucer story which modern readers know as *The Wife of Bath's Tale* was in Chaucer's manuscript *The Wyfes Tale of Bath.* In the seventeenth century, a **group genitive** developed whereby the entire noun phrase receives the genitive marker—*[the Queen of England]'s robe.* Today, complex constructions are often marked with the genitive, especially in casual speech.

> | the dentist who lives around the corner |'s car

A periphrastic paraphrase makes it clear exactly which part of the structure is receiving the genitive marker—*This is the car of **the dentist who lives around the corner**.*

Humorist Dave Barry (1997) pokes fun at this construction in his newspaper column, "Mr. Language on the butchered apostrophe." (Underlining added.)

Q: Recently, did your research assistant Judi Smith make a grammatically interesting statement regarding where her friend, Vickie, parks at *The Miami Herald*?

A: Yes. She said, quote: "She comes and parks in whoever's not here's space that day."

Q: Can that sentence be diagramed?

A: Not without powerful pharmaceuticals. (p. 7)

While group genitives may not be acceptable in most forms of edited English, they are quite common in informal discourse.

Generic Reference

Normally the article *a* refers to one entity but in a sentence like *A manta ray is a dangerous creature,* the speaker is using the indefinite article to refer to the entire class of manta rays. The definite article *the* typically refers to specific entities in discourse, but in *The bear is an omnivore,* the speaker is referring to the species as a whole, not a specific animal. In these sentences the articles *the* and *a* have **generic** reference.

Plural nouns without determiners can also have generic reference—*Boys will be boys; Cobras are beautiful; Italians are very hospitable.* When a determiner is added, such NPs typically cease to have generic reference and the resulting sentence often sounds odd—*The cobras are beautiful; ?The boys will be boys; ?The Italians are very hospitable.*

Not surprisingly, the predeterminer *all* can also be used to refer to all the members of a class but only when it occurs without a determiner—*All camels spit; All two-year-olds are defiant.* When a determiner is added, the generic reference is canceled—*All the camels spit; All the two-year-olds are defiant.*

As you can see, there are four distinct strategies for communicating generic reference—plurality, the indefinite article, the definite article, and the predeterminer *all.* Not all of these strategies work in all situations. We can say *The Bachman's warbler may be extinct* and *Bachman's warblers may be extinct* but not **A Bachman's warbler may be extinct.*

Proper Nouns

Nouns allow us to talk about the people, things, and events in our world. Some things are especially familiar to us, notably the people and places we see every day, and it is not surprising that humans have always assigned special labels to these, i.e., names.

Linguists typically use the term **proper noun** for "names." This term is somewhat problematic, however, because we use it rather differently than do English teachers or other nonlinguists. Traditional grammar books routinely defined a proper noun as a word or words that refer to a specific person, place, or thing. But it is possible to refer to something very specific without ever using a proper noun, e.g., *the woman with blue hair who is standing on a chair in the back row.* Many students define proper nouns in terms of capitalization, but of course we don't speak in capital letters and capitalization rules change from generation to generation and from language to language. In modern German, for example, all nouns are capitalized. Prior to the twentieth century, English-speaking writers routinely capitalized nouns that were not names. William Byrd II, a highly educated early eighteenth-century American writer, capitalized *Pipe, Eyes, Expectations, Vegetable, Gunpowder, Irony,* and *Tongue.* The *Declaration of Independence,* written by Thomas Jefferson and edited by the Continental Congress, declares that

> all men are created equal, that they are endowed by their Creator with certain unalienable Rights, that among these are Life, Liberty, and the pursuit of Happiness. (Grob and Beck, 1963, p. 187)

The nineteenth-century romantic poet Percy Bysshe Shelley capitalized *Silence, Earth, Poet, Spirit,* and *Death.* Capitalization is merely an editorial convention and such conventions change fairly quickly.

Clearly, we need a more precise definition for the term *proper noun.* Linguists characterize proper nouns in two ways. The first is semantic. Linguists are fond of saying that proper nouns have unique reference. But what does this mean? There are tens of thousands of Maria Garcias in the world and as many John Smiths, so how can such names have unique reference?

Proper nouns have unique reference only in those cases in which both speaker and hearer are familiar with the referent at some level. You wouldn't approach a stranger and immediately begin talking about Henrietta and Ralph without any indication of who these people were. Proper names have unique reference only in a particular setting. *Alice Walker,* for example, has unique reference in the canon of American literature but not in the English-speaking world at large. There are many *Ronald Reagans* in the world but in the context of modern American history this name refers to a single individual.

If a speaker wishes to use a proper name that is unfamiliar to the hearer, s/he will typically introduce it into the discourse by explaining the reference in some way. All of the passages below are from Patricia Cornwall's novel *From Potter's Field* (1995). In each passage the proper noun is double underlined and the information that identifies that proper noun is single underlined. (Underlining added.)

> <u>All of Gault's victims</u> were sitting, heads bowed, hands in their laps. . . . The one exception was <u>a woman prison guard</u> named <u>Helen</u>. (pp. 23–24)
>
> . . . we were greeted by <u>a woman in her fifties with dark hair, a wise face, and tired eyes</u>. . . . She introduced herself as <u>Commander Frances Penn</u> of the New York Transit Police. (p. 25)
>
> Later, I drove Lucy and Janet to work with me and left them at the office with <u>Fielding, my deputy chief</u>. (p. 252)

Before using a proper noun, a speaker must assess the knowledge of the hearer. An American can freely use the proper noun *Bill Clinton* without elaboration but the name *Janos Kadar* would probably require some explaining. (Kadar was the premier of Hungary from 1956–58 and 1961–65.) Upon hearing *Paris,* most of us think of the capital of France, but someone living in Honey Grove, Texas, would be more likely to think of the town just up the road. *Celia Cruz* is a household word among salsa fans in Miami but it would probably draw blank looks on the south side of Chicago, where blues men like *B.B. King* and *Buddy Guy* are cultural icons.

The context in which a proper noun will have unique reference depends on many factors. Occasionally, an individual is so famous within a culture that just the first name is adequate—*Michelangelo, Evita, Judas. Jesus* generally has unique reference in Protestant northern Europe but not in Catholic Hispanic culture. Usually a first name works in an extremely limited context—a family, a club, a small group of friends. When there was only one John in an Anglo-Saxon village, no other designation was necessary. When a second John moved to the village, the first might have become John the brewer and the second John the baker, ultimately John Brewer and John Baker. Scores of English surnames derive from trades—Shoemaker, Smith, Weaver, Webster (a female weaver), Brewster (a female brewer), Wright, Miller, Cook, Cooper, Fowler. Middle names and designations like John Brewer, Jr. or John Brewer III enhanced the social utility of proper names. In the United States, probably the only designation that carries true unique reference these days is one's social security number.

In essence, a proper noun is a special shorthand. Instead of referring to someone as the thirty-seventh president of the United States, I can simply say "Richard Nixon." The phrase "the thirty-seventh president of the United States" also has unique reference, but it is a cumbersome and arcane way to refer to an individual. Similarly, I could refer to *New Orleans, Louisiana,* by providing its longitude and latitude, but while this would identity it uniquely, it would seriously impede communication.

Linguists also categorize proper nouns in terms of their grammatical characteristics. Common nouns may or may not occur with a determiner, depending on the grammatical context. Proper nouns, however, are invariable in this regard. If a proper noun occurs with a determiner (almost always the article *the*), it will always occur with that determiner. If it occurs without a determiner, it will never take a determiner. Thus, we always refer to **the** Hague, **the** Netherlands, **the** Midlands, or **the** Midwest, but never to *the Chicago or *the Nigeria. Similarly, if a proper noun ends in a plural {-s}, it will always do so; there is no contrasting singular form. We say *the Netherlands* but never **the Netherland.* Most proper nouns, especially names of people, are invariably singular in form.

One of the reasons that determiner *the* doesn't co-occur with proper nouns in English is that the definite article is used to express the fact that both speaker and hearer are familiar with the referent in question. The very use of a proper noun assumes that the referent is uniquely identifiable to both the speaker and the hearer. (The fact that some proper nouns invariably <u>include</u> *the* as part of the "name" is a different matter.) Be aware, though, that some languages like Greek do use the definite article with proper nouns, even the names of people.

There is one class of proper nouns in English in which the article *the* is invariably included as part of the name. These are proper noun phrases, the heads of which are common nouns in other contexts—*the Brooklyn <u>Bridge</u>, the Empire State <u>Building</u>, the Snake <u>River</u>, the Love <u>Boat</u>, the Red <u>Sea</u>, the Rolling <u>Stones</u>*. Because the common nouns *bridge, building, river, boat, sea,* and *stone* do co-occur with *the*, it seems natural to include the article, even when these words appear in proper noun phrases. This creates an interesting contradiction in written texts. In these phrases *the* is invariably part of the proper noun, yet editing convention dictates that *the* not be capitalized. (There are common noun heads that occur with *the* in some proper nouns and not in others—*the Bay of Fundy* versus *Biscayne Bay*.)

In some cases *the* is part of the proper noun simply by virtue of a naming convention. Ship names for example often include the article—*the Titanic, the Queen Mary*. In the United States, the acronyms of broadcasting companies do not contain the article—*NBC, CBS, PBS*, while in Great Britain they do—*the BBC*.

Obviously, there are occasions when we do say things like *the Miami of my childhood, all the Susans in the class,* or *the two Georges in the family*. But here *Miami, Susan,* and *George* have lost their proper noun status. They do not have unique reference in these contexts and that is why we find determiners and plural markers occurring with these forms. (While *Miami, Susan,* and *George* are not technically proper nouns here, they are of course still capitalized in written texts.)

Non-Count Nouns

While the ability to pluralize is one of the distinguishing characteristics of nouns as a class, not all nouns have contrasting singular and plural forms. Phrases like *two rices, *six sands,* and *three measles* are ungrammatical. Nouns that cannot be directly preceded by cardinal numbers are called **non-count nouns.** (Many grammar books use the term **mass noun** but this term is a bit misleading because some of the nouns in this category don't refer to "masses.")

Many non-count nouns are **concrete,** i.e., they refer to things that have a physical reality. In order to count a concrete, non-count noun, a speaker must choose a **partitive,** which will usually be a container or a measurement of some kind—*four pounds of rice; six buckets of sand; three yards of silk; a carton of milk*. There are actually a limited number of partitives; some are very general and can be used with a wide variety of non-count nouns, while others can be used with only a few. Most partitives of weight and measurement are quite flexible. We can have *two pounds of* anything that can be weighed—salt, flour, oats, oregano, mercury, etc. We can have *four gallons of* anything that is liquid or suitably viscous—water, ketchup, gas, oil, milk, molasses. Some partitives are much more limited. Only a few things are counted in *bars* (soap, gold, chocolate), *lumps* (sugar, coal), or *sticks* (gum, butter, dynamite). Only paper is counted in *reams* and only bread is counted in *loaves*.

Because concrete, non-count nouns cannot be counted without partitives, they don't co-occur with numerals or the article *a*, which entails the meaning *one*—**a gold, *two dynamites*. A speaker can use a non-count noun with a numeral or the article *a* only when a partitive is conventionally understood. When you ask a waiter for "two coffees," he understands that you mean two cups of coffee, not two pounds or two urns. If you ask a bartender for a beer, she will assume that you want a single serving (a can, a bottle, or a mug); she won't bring you a keg. The partitive can also be omitted if the speaker is referring to types. If I tell you that my deli sells fourteen **cheeses,** you know that I mean fourteen *types of* cheese; if your cousin says that her local pub has twenty imported **beers** on tap, you know she means brands of beer.

Although **abstract non-count nouns** do not refer to concrete entities, they sometimes occur with partitives, too. These partitives are usually rather specialized—*a score of* music, *two works of* art, *three games of* chess.

CATEGORIZING NON-COUNT NOUNS

It is not always possible to explain why a given noun is non-count rather than count. Sometimes a noun that is non-count in one language will be literally translated by a noun that is countable in another language. The key does not lie in the distinction between abstract and concrete nouns. There are a number of abstract non-count nouns, e.g., *music, sincerity, greed,* but there are also some abstract count nouns, e.g., *plans, ideas, wishes,* and *convictions.* Furthermore, many concrete entities are expressed by non-count nouns—*pliers, trousers, sand, linens, milk, furniture.*

But the assignment of nouns to the non-count category is not altogether arbitrary. Anna Wierzbicka (1988b) has noted that in English some non-count nouns can be divided into certain fairly coherent semantic categories. She notes that many non-count nouns are "arbitrarily divisible." If you physically divide water into any number of parts, each of those parts is the same and each is still water. On the other hand, if you divide a chair into parts, the parts are different in form and soon the entity is no longer a chair. If you divide the chair often enough, even the parts will become unrecognizable. Many non-count nouns are arbitrarily divisible, including liquids, gasses, and substances composed of very small particles like salt and sand. These are the kinds of non-count nouns that might reasonably be called "mass nouns."

Foodstuffs represent an interesting subset of the "arbitrarily divisible" category. There are many cases in which food on the hoof or on the vine is a count noun while the same food on the plate is expressed by an identical non-count noun. I have *five pumpkins* and *two watermelons* in my garden but I am eating *some pumpkin* and *some watermelon.* Mary owns *three lambs* but she had *lamb* for dinner. Pumpkins, watermelons, and lambs are discreet, identifiable entities in nature. However, when they are cooked, they lose their discrete boundaries. Furthermore, most of us would never eat a whole pumpkin or a whole watermelon at one sitting, but we regularly consume entire peas, olives, and strawberries, all of which are count nouns, even when they appear on a plate. You may eat *four radishes* which are small and discrete, but you consume *some horse-radish,* because the root from which it is made loses its boundaries when it is ground up.

Wierzbicka has noted a second major non-count category that includes words like *furniture, crockery, linens, silverware, jewelry.* Each of these nouns represents a category of disparate items. Furniture includes chairs, beds, dressers, tables, lamps; silverware includes knives, forks, and spoons; and jewelry includes bracelets, necklaces, rings, etc. While knives, spoons, and forks have different configurations, they are all implements used for eating. Rings, necklaces, and bracelets look very different, but they are all used to decorate the body. Plates and bowls have very different shapes, but both are designed to hold food. In each of the above examples, the non-count noun represents a category of physically different items, all of which have roughly the same function. It is interesting to note that while the inclusive category is non-count, the subcategories are count nouns

- **jewelry**—*one ring, six bracelets, two necklaces*

- **silverware**—*one fork, two spoons, six knives*

- **linens**—*two sheets, one table cloth, four towels*

- **crockery**—*twelve bowls, three plates, five cups*

With the exception of *linens,* all of the non-count nouns we have looked at so far have been invariably singular in form and have occurred with singular verbs. There are, however, a number of non-count nouns that appear to be invariably plural in that they always end in {-s}. In some cases the nature of the object explains its plural form, but in others the marking of a non-count as plural instead of singular seems very arbitrary.

Linguists have long noted the existence of **dual object plurals,** an especially interesting category of non-count nouns. Dual object plurals always refer to items that contain two identical halves, which are mirror images of each other; the two halves must be connected. Virtually all pant-type items fall in this category—*pants, shorts, jeans, Levis, trousers, slacks, knickers, jams, baggies, panties, pedal pushers,* etc. Sweat pants are often called *sweats.* Most eyewear falls in this category—*glasses, spectacles, shades, goggles, binoculars,* etc. Certain categories of tools also constitute dual object plurals—*pliers, scissors, tweezers, pincers, forceps, bellows, tongs,* etc. *Scales* used to be a dual object plural because historically scales were two pans hanging from a central post. Of course scales have changed a great deal in the last century and now *scale* is for most speakers a count noun with both a singular and plural form. Dual object plurals are always counted using the partitive *pair of* and always co-occur with a plural verb—*Two pairs of pants are lying on the bed.* (There is a misconception, spread by some reference books, that non-count nouns are always singular in form.)

The names of games are typically non-count nouns—*golf, tennis, chess, baseball, hockey, poker.* Very old games are often non-count nouns that appear to be plural in form—*billiards, checkers, darts, cards, dominoes, craps, marbles.* The implements used to play these games are sometimes the same word in count noun form. This is not altogether surprising, since the games are abstract sets of rules, while the implements used to play these games are of necessity concrete objects. Thus three darts are required for playing darts and fifty-two cards are usually needed to play cards. Games are typically counted with the partitive *game of* although some sports exploit special partitives, especially when the game itself is divided into parts—*two rounds of golf, a hand of cards, two sets of tennis.*

Some diseases are also plural, non-count nouns—*measles, shingles, mumps.* A *mump* was originally a grimace and a *measle* was a blood blister in the original Dutch. While the {-s} in acronyms like *AIDS* and *SIDS* stands for "syndrome," the fact that so many diseases end in {-s} makes this a natural construction. In order to count such diseases, we typically use the partitive *case of.*

However, unlike the dual object plurals, both the game non-count nouns and the disease non-count nouns often take a singular verb even when they carry the {-s} suffix—*Checkers **is** my favorite board game; Measles **makes** you really sick.* For some speakers, however, the plural marker is compelling and you will hear people say "Darts are a lot of fun" or "Mumps are dangerous in an adult."

A few non-count nouns have countable **homophones.** (Homophones are words that are pronounced in the same way but have distinctly different meanings.) *Iron,* the non-count noun referring to ore, is different from *iron* the count noun referring to an implement used to press clothes. *Paper,* the sheet (non-count), is different from *paper* the essay (countable). As Wierzbicka (1998b, p. 509) points out, *chocolate* is a count noun only when it refers to small, bite-sized bits of candy.

Not all non-count nouns fall neatly into the semantic categories discussed above. *The blues, the news,* and *the tropics* are all hard to categorize.

As you will see in the following chart, non-count nouns never occur with the indefinite article *a.* They occur with demonstrative determiners, genitive determiners, and the definite article *the* and they often occur without any determiners whatsoever.

Summary of non-count nouns

Non-count nouns with singular verbs	Non-count nouns ending in {-s} with singular verbs	Non-count nouns ending in {-s} with plural verbs
The **milk** is sour.	**Checkers** bores my dad.	Your **glasses** have orange lenses.
Beer makes me sick.	**Billiards** requires skill.	The **binoculars** are over here.
Gasoline is cheap.		

Summary of non-count nouns (cont.)

Oil rises to the top.	**Darts** is my favorite game.	His **pants** are plaid.
The sand was hot.		
Salt gets hard.	**Mumps** makes your glands swell.	My **jeans** are on the bed.
Paper costs a lot.	**Rickets** is caused by a lack of vitamin D.	The **pliers** are on the bench.
Iron is a strong metal.		
Chocolate is fattening.	**Shingles** is hard to cure.	The **tweezers** look broken.
This dirt is heavy.	[Some speakers use plural verbs with some or all of these nouns.]	These **linens** are dirty.
Their **jewelry** is ugly.		The **dregs** taste disgusting.
Badminton is strenuous.		

Collective Nouns

Collective nouns are often confused with non-count nouns, but they have very different characteristics. Collective nouns are countable. They are unique among count nouns, however, because they refer to a collective entity with individual members—*army, team, faculty, jury, band, clergy, class, gang.* Because collective nouns refer to a collection of individual entities, they sometimes occur with a singular verb and sometimes with a plural verb, depending on the intention of the speaker. When a speaker wishes to focus on the group itself, the collective noun is usually used with a singular verb—*My team is playing well this week; The band is playing off-key.* However, if a speaker wants to focus on the individual members of the collectivity, s/he might choose a plural verb—*The faculty are angry about their raises; The jury are talking among themselves.*

The following examples are cited by Roger Schwarzchild in his book *Pluralities* (1996). You can see that in each case the collective noun has been interpreted as plural and this fact affects the grammar elsewhere in the sentence. (Italics added in the last example only.)

> *The choir* knelt and covered *their* faces. (p. 172)

> The *committee* congratulated *themselves.* (p. 172)

> Every debate *team* . . . gets disqualified because *they* attack each other instead of attacking their opponents. (p. 173)

British speakers are especially likely to use plural verbs with collective nouns and they do so in contexts that sometimes sound strange to Americans— *The World Bank are considering the problem; The BBC are covering that event.*

Pronouns

Pronouns represent the simplest NPs. Unlike nouns, pronouns are almost never preceded by determiners or adjectives, although after listening to you describe an upcoming trip to Alaska, a friend may say enviously, "Lucky you." Pronouns take many different shapes and have a variety of functions in English. They are most often used as a kind of shorthand to refer to items that have already been introduced into the discourse or conversation. Pronouns can also be used to refer to unknown entities or to underscore the fact that no relevant entity exists. The uses of pronouns in discourse are actually quite complex.

PERSONAL PRONOUNS

Personal pronouns are the most common pronouns in English. Informal discourse is always full of them. The pronouns that we use to refer to ourselves are called **first person**—*I, we*. We use **second person** pronouns to refer to those with whom we are speaking—*you*. **Third person** pronouns refer to others and, unlike other pronouns in English, they reflect gender (or lack thereof) in the singular—*he/she/it, they*. In Old English the grammatical function of a noun or a pronoun dictated its form; a noun or pronoun functioning as an object would carry a different ending or have a different form than one functioning as a subject. Nouns gradually lost these distinctions and the modern personal and interrogative pronouns are the only words left in English in which a distinction between a subject form and an object form has survived.

	Forms of personal pronouns					
	First Person		**Second Person**		**Third Person**	
	Singular	**Plural**	**Singular**	**Plural**	**Singular**	**Plural**
Subject	I	we	you	you	she/he/it	they
Object	me	us	you	you	her/him/it	them
Genitive	my/mine	our(s)	your(s)	your(s)	her(s)/his/its	their(s)

The forms *my, our, your, her,* and *their* are determiners as well as personal pronouns.

Third person personal pronouns have **anaphoric reference.** Once a person (or entity) has been introduced into a discourse with a full NP, a speaker can use a third person pronoun to refer to that person, often for a long period of time. This passage is from the thriller *Hard Aground* by James Hall (1993). In it the character Alvarez imagines what his employer, a Florida State Senator, is doing at the moment. The full NPs are double underlined and the anaphoric pronouns are in boldface. (Underlining and boldface added.)

> <u>The senator</u> finishes **her** chicken cordon bleu, **she** goes up to the podium, looks out at this bunch of lawyers and bankers . . . and then starts in giving them **her** full load of free-enterprise horseshit for fifteen minutes. . . . That was **her** job as near as Alvarez could tell. Twice a month another of these fat cat clubs would invite **her** to lecture after the cordon bleu lunch, just so **she** could tell 'em it was all right what they were doing. . . . Near the end of **her** speech **she'd** tell a joke or two, something downhome **she'd** heard. . . . And then right at the end **she'd** tell them just like **she** always did that it was up to them. . . . **She'd** wave her hand at whatever applause **she** got. . . . And then **she'd** shake a few hands, pat a few good old boys on the back, and **she'd** work **her** way to the back of the room . . . and **she'd** wind up outside on the sidewalk. . . . That was when the guy Alvarez had paid twenty bucks to . . . would come up to **her** wearing Alvarez's white captain's hat. . . . And he'd tell <u>the senator</u> what Alvarez had paid him twenty to say. (pp. 311–12)

Hall begins with a full NP *the senator* and then uses 18 personal pronouns in a row before the full NP is finally restated again. Often when a full NP is used after a series of personal pronouns, it is because the speaker wishes to signal that this part of the story or conversation is over. Using the full NP again is one way of indicating closure (Fox, 1987, p. 40). This is the case in this passage; Alvarez has finished his story about the senator.

We see the same phenomenon in conversation involving two or more participants. Either party can use a personal pronoun once an entity has been introduced into the discourse. The following exchange took place between a woman and her young son, who is somewhat obsessed by airplanes. The mother has just explained that a steward is not the same as Stewart, a family friend (Cloran, 1995). (Underlining and boldface added.)

Mother: That's right. <u>Stewart</u> is Joanne's Dad.

Stephen: Is **he** a printer?

Mother: Yes, **he** is a printer.

Stephen: Is **he** a captain?

Mother: No, **he** doesn't go in an aeroplane.

Stephen: Well why?

Mother: Because **he's** a printer. **He** works in a place where they print magazines and things.

Stephen: Does **he** work in a plane where they print things?

Mother: **He** works in a place, not a plane. (p. 369)

Once Stewart has been introduced into the discourse, he becomes the subject and topic of every subsequent sentence. Every instance of *he* has anaphoric reference.

If a conversation or narrative contains two female or two male characters, the situation becomes more complicated. Here is a passage from *Goosefoot* by Patrick McGinley (1982). (Underlining and boldface added.)

> <u>Monica</u> was thrilled at the prospect of helping to cook for a man of private means who was himself a capable cook. . . . **She** questioned <u>Patricia</u> about how long **she** had know him and told **her** that **she** was so secretive about him that their relationship must be very serious. (p. 71)

The referent of the first instance of *she* can only be Monica. But once Patricia is introduced, we are faced with two potential female referents. In this case the narrator expects us to choose the most recent noun as the referent; the last three pronouns refer to Patricia.

However, a referent can be someone/thing other than the most recent noun if the context makes the connection clear. In the following passage from Michael Dibdin's *Dead Lagoon* (1996), both Saoner and Zen are men, but it is quite clear from the context that the pronouns refer to Saoner, not to Zen.

> <u>Tommaso Saoner</u> scurried out of the other entrance and ran straight into <u>Zen</u>. At first **he** made to turn back, then changed **his** mind and strode past without a word or a flicker of expression. (p. 276)

Personal pronoun *it* can refer back to an inanimate or even a non-human animate entity—*I bought a new computer yesterday; **it** cost $1000; That new puppy is a pain; **it** just peed on the kitchen floor. It* can also be used to refer back to a complex situation or a series of events. Here is another passage from *Dead Lagoon*.

> The regime you serve is morally and financially bankrupt. **It**'s exactly the same as working for the KGB after the collapse of the Soviet Union. (p. 260)

Here *it* refers to everything that is entailed in working for a morally and financially bankrupt regime.

Personal pronouns don't have specific reference if their antecedents don't have specific reference. In *Sonya wants to marry a tall man; he must be handsome,* neither *a tall man* nor *he* has specific reference. However, in *Sonya wants to marry a banker; he lives in Boston,* both the pronoun and its antecedent refer to a specific individual.

While the definite article and the demonstrative determiner both have anaphoric reference, the most frequently used "anaphors" in subject position are pronouns. Using data from oral English, Talmy Givón (1995, p. 51) has calculated that the text frequency of anaphoric subject pronouns is 74.5%, while that of definite NPs is only 25.6%. Even though we have a number of strategies for making anaphoric reference, we most often choose personal pronouns.

The third person personal pronoun must agree with the noun it refers to in gender and number, e.g., *Robert/he, the architects/they, Esther/she,* etc. This creates problems when the noun does not have specific reference or the individual's gender is unknown to the speaker—*Susan wants a new dentist and she?/he? must be willing to use laughing gas; A student has taken my grade book and she?/he? must be apprehended.* A few die-hard traditionalists insist that *he* should be used as a "gender neutral" pronoun in such contexts, but this is patently absurd. Speakers often cope with this dilemma by employing *they* as a singular pronoun—*A student has taken my grade book; they must be apprehended.* Edited English usually demands a more elaborate solution. Some publications (and teachers) accept the hyphenated pronoun used in this book—*s/he, him/her;* others insist that the writer recast the sentence to avoid the dilemma altogether; and a few still demand *he* in such circumstances.

The first and second person pronouns are deictic rather than anaphoric. Whoever is speaking uses *I;* the person to whom the speaker is speaking is always addressed as *you.* The referents of *I* and *you* change when the speaker and hearer change. *We* is deictic as well, although any member of a group can use the word *we* to refer to the same collection of individuals. While fiction and other kinds of written narratives frequently exploit third person pronouns, people engaged in actual conversations tend to use a lot of first and second person pronouns. After examining a corpus of spoken conversation, one researcher calculated that *I* is the most frequently used word in personal discourse and *you* is the sixth most frequently used (Dahl, 1979, quoted in Miller, 1996, p. 126). Another scholar, who examined eight conversations taken from a large corpus of spoken English, found that in 51% of her data the topic was one of the speakers (*I, you*) or a group including one of the speakers or both (*we, you*) (Fries, 1995, p. 331). We obviously spend a lot of time talking with others about ourselves.

During Shakespeare's time, English lost the distinction between singular and plural forms in the second person. In Old and Middle English various forms of *thou/thee/thine* were used for singular reference, while various forms of *ye/you/your* were used in the plural. As happened in other European courts, the monarch's use of the royal *we* led speakers to address him or her in the second person plural, *ye* rather than *thou.* Gradually the use of the second person plural instead of the singular became a sign of respect. The object form *you* supplanted the subject form *ye,* and eventually the singular form disappeared completely in all dialects except that used by Quakers, some of whom still use *thee.* (The refusal of the early Quakers to use the second person plural form was a political act for which they were persecuted.)

As a result of all of these social pressures, there is an unfortunate gap in our second person pronoun system, i.e., there is no distinction in form between singular and plural. But speakers have come up with many creative ways to fashion a distinct second person plural form. In the Southern United States *you all,* usually pronounced "y'all," is ubiquitous; in New York and Chicago one hears *yous* and in western Pennsylvania *you uns* is widespread. *You guys* is a very common strategy for speakers in all regions of the United States (although it, too, raises gender issues). My husband and I were once addressed by a server in Kentucky as "Y'all guys." Among some speakers of British English, *you lot* is a common second person plural. An English mother might say to her rowdy children, "You lot, get over here!"

The importance of personal pronouns in discourse cannot be overstated. The vast majority of subjects in English are pronouns, not nouns. This is because topics usually appear in subject position, and pronouns are always topical, i.e., they always express given information.

REFLEXIVE PRONOUNS

In English if two NPs refer to the same entity (i.e., are **co-referential**) and are used in the same simple sentence, in the second instance the NP must be a **reflexive** pronoun and it must reflect that same gender and number as the first NP. The first co-referential NP is usually the subject.

Henry hates **himself.**

The kids scared **themselves.**

Barb talks to **herself.**

I cut **myself.**

We fooled **ourselves.**

The reflexive allows us to distinguish among possible referents with the same number and gender. Clearly the direct object in *Henry hates him* refers to a different male than the direct object in *Henry hates himself.* In most dialects of English, the reflexive never occurs in subject position.

There are syntactic constraints on reflexive pronouns. Only personal pronouns take the reflexive {-self} form and, as a rule, reflexive objects (which may be direct objects, indirect objects, or objects of prepositions) are animate when the first NP is the subject. This is not surprising because it is usually animate beings that act or reflect upon themselves. The subject is usually an agent or an experiencer in a sentence containing a reflexive pronoun.

Guillermo argued with himself.

Marsha doesn't trust herself.

My mother gave herself a present.

Tom believes in himself.

June considers herself a success.

Sometimes a nonvolitional causer occurs as the subject in such a sentence.

Penelope accidentally hurt herself.

Daniel scared himself.

The baby burned herself.

Although the first co-referential NP in a reflexive construction is usually a subject, it need not be—*Jeremiah offered Esther a picture of herself; We talked to Trudy about herself.* Inanimate reflexives are uncommon but they do exist—*She turned my argument in upon itself.* Inanimate reflexives are particularly likely when we endow inanimate subjects with animate qualities—*The water heater blew itself up; My car destroyed itself; That book sells itself.* The following sentence appeared in a motorcycle owners magazine: "[Bearings] virtually never tighten themselves" (Glaves, 1997, p. 16).

Some normally transitive verbs occur intransitively when the direct object is a covert reflexive pronoun. *Tom shaved* means that Tom shaved himself, while *Tom shaved him* means Tom shaved someone else. We see the same phenomenon with certain other grooming verbs—*Wendy bathed; The kids dressed; Raymond washed.*

There are a few verbs which take only reflexive objects.

The children behaved themselves.

The witness perjured herself.

My brother has bettered himself.

Arlene prides herself on her advanced degrees.

Behave can occur with a covert, unexpressed object, but this, too, always refers back to the subject. While we can say, "The children behaved" (meaning the children behaved well), we can never say "The children behaved their cousins." An individual can never *perjure, pride,* or *better* someone else, although it is possible to *best* another individual or group—*The Chicago Bulls bested the New York Knicks.*

Reflexives don't normally occur with copulas and, when they do, the copula does not express mere existence. When a speaker utters a sentence like *Hamlet is not himself today,* s/he is really indicating that Hamlet is <u>behaving</u> strangely, not that he actually exists as something other than himself.

Reflexives can also be used to mean "alone" or "on one's own." In these constructions the reflexive is often preceded by the preposition *by.*

I'll fix it myself.

The building stood by itself in a field.

The baby tied his shoes by himself.

The difference between a straight reflexive pronoun and one which means "alone" is underscored by this wonderfully ambiguous classified ad.

> "Are you tired of cleaning yourself? Let me do it."

Sometimes reflexives are used redundantly to emphasize the preceding noun or pronoun.

I myself have never smoked.

I handed her the gold itself.

I've never actually talked to the President himself.

Constructions like these work best in larger stretches of discourse—*Tom smokes like a chimney, but I myself have never smoked; She was expecting only a certificate but I handed her the gold itself.*

Possessive Reflexives

If you hear a sentence like *Mary destroyed her toys* out of context, it is impossible to determine whether genitive *her* refers to Mary or to another female. But the modifier *own* can be used be used in conjunction with a genitive determiner to produce a genitive reflexive.

Mary destroyed her own toys.

Benjamin wants his own bed.

Laurie threw out her own tax records.

There are a few cases in which a genitive determiner expressing inalienable possession will always be interpreted as referring back to the subject. These typically involve movements made with a part of the body (Levin, 1993, p. 108).

David craned his neck.

The bodybuilder flexed her muscles.

The teacher pursed her lips.

The dog wagged his tail.

The guest smacked her lips.

*David craned Anastasia's neck and **Fido wagged Fluffy's tail* are impossible sentences.

RECIPROCAL PRONOUNS

Like most reflexive pronouns, reciprocal pronoun phrases typically have the same referent as the subject; the difference is that the subject to which a reciprocal pronoun refers must include more than one entity. Thus, the subject NP must be plural or there must be two or more coordinated NPs. The action in such constructions is reciprocal; each individual subject has the same relationship to the other subjects in the construction.

*My children fight with **each other.***

*Jack and Jill hate **one another.***

*We babysit for **each other's** children.*

*They gave **one another** gifts.*

Like reflexives, reciprocal pronouns are almost always animate.

DEMONSTRATIVE PRONOUNS

When the demonstratives (*this, that, these, those*) are used alone without a noun head, they are considered demonstrative pronouns. They behave very much like demonstrative determiners (i.e., they express spatial and sometimes temporal deixis), except that the noun to which they refer is not part of the NP—***This** is moldy; I don't want **that.*** Demonstrative pronouns are often accompanied by gestures, e.g., a child might point while saying "This is my room." The context will usually make the referent of the demonstrative clear.

A demonstrative pronoun can also be anaphoric, in which case it often refers back to an entire proposition—*I listen to opera all the time. **This** drives my family nuts.* Anaphoric demonstratives can also be used to refer back to an event or even a series of events, as you can see in this passage from Tony Hillerman's novel *Sacred Clowns* (1993). (Boldface added.)

> "[He parked] in front, walked in, went to the open mike, said he wanted to broadcast an announcement. Was told to wait until the end of the record. Waited. Was given signal. Then he made his statement, walked out. Drove away. Right?"
>
> "Right," Yazzie said. "**That**'s what happened." (p. 186)

You will find that in general anaphoric *this* is used for a current situation, whereas anaphoric *that* refers to a past event. So even when demonstrative pronouns are used anaphorically, they retain some of their deictic properties.

The events referred to by demonstrative pronouns need not be expressed linguistically. If a student belches loudly in class, the teacher might respond with "**That** was really rude." A professor who catches a student cheating on an exam might threaten, "I'll expel you for **this.**" In these examples anaphora is much stronger than deixis.

QUANTIFYING PRONOUNS

The forms that were included in the predeterminer and postdeterminer categories can also stand alone as pronouns—***All*** *were crying;* ***Both*** *were stubborn;* ***Four*** *remained.* The plural indefinite article *some* can also stand alone as a pronoun—*I will give you some.* In each of these cases the discourse context should make the referent clear.

Everyone, everything, nothing, and *nobody* are also quantifying pronouns—***Everyone*** *likes her; He ate* ***everything***; ***Nobody*** *attended the meeting. Someone* and *something* can also be included in this category although their primary semantic characteristic is indefiniteness, as you will see below. There are adverb quantifiers as well, e.g., *everywhere, anytime,* etc.; these will be discussed in Chapter 4.

INDEFINITE PRONOUNS

We often need to speak about persons, things, or events whose identity or character is unknown to us. The indefinite pronouns allow us to do just that. But once again, the term **indefinite** is misleading. It means that the referent is not specified, but it does not mean that the referent is nonspecific. Indefinite *someone* and *something* can have either specific or nonspecific reference, depending on the context. Upon being asked out, a young woman might respond with "I'm dating someone." Here the speaker obviously knows the identity of the person she is dating but doesn't wish to divulge it. After breaking down on a country road, you might say to your companions, "Surely, someone will come along and help us." In this case *someone* has nonspecific reference. In the following examples the nature of the reference is indicated.

Someone *will call the police, I'm sure.*	[nonspecific]
You'll find ***somebody*** *to take to the prom.*	[nonspecific]
Something *exploded in the garage.*	[specific]
Someone *is walking on the deck.*	[specific]

Anyone and *anything* never have specific reference—*The baby will eat* ***anything***; *He'll talk to* ***anyone***. Because they don't have referents, these indefinites are most often used in negatives and questions.

Did ***anyone*** *hear you?*

My children won't read ***anything.***

Has ***anybody*** *told you about the new rules?*

Gertrude won't loan her plane to ***anyone.***

If you enter your apartment and you hear footsteps in the upstairs hall, you might yell, "Is someone here?" Your expectation is that the answer will be positive. If your friend's house appears dark and empty, you might yell "Is anybody here?" with the expectation that no one will answer.

Nobody and *nothing* are negative indefinites; no referents exist for these pronouns.

Nobody *came.*

Nothing *bothers her.*

I know **nothing** *about the stolen files.*

I saw **no one** *in the library.*

Since *nobody* and *nothing* already contain a negative form as part of the pronoun, neither form occurs with the negative particle in formal edited English, although sentences like *I didn't see nothing* are quite common in conversational discourse.

It should be obvious that all the indefinite pronouns were once nouns or numerals preceded by a quantifier—*some + body, no + thing, every + one*. *Nobody* was written as two separate words until the eighteenth century and it is only a constraint on our pronunciation of double vowels that prevents us from writing **noone* for *no one* today. Since it behaves exactly like *nobody*, we'll treat *no one* as a pronoun also.

Someone, something, no one, and *nothing* can also be classified as quantifying pronouns; this is not incompatible with being indefinite. As you will see in Chapter 5, there are adverb indefinites as well as pronoun indefinites—*sometime, somewhere, somehow, anywhere.*

Indefinite Pronouns and Gender

Indefinite pronouns are neutral in terms of gender and this creates problems when an indefinite pronoun is the antecedent of a personal pronoun. Consider the sentence *If* **anyone** *calls tell* **him?/her?** *that I'm out.* Since the speaker can't possibly know the identity of *anyone*, it is impossible to assign gender. What form then should be chosen for the subsequent personal pronoun? As you have already seen, most English speakers use *they/them/their* as gender neutral pronouns, even in contexts in which the antecedent appears to be singular.

If **anyone** *calls, tell* **them** *I'm out.*

Everyone *must pack* **their** *own lunch.*

I saw **someone** *in the shadows and* **they** *were watching me.*

Anyone *who thinks* **they** *can fix this is a fool.*

Traditional grammars argue that *anyone, someone,* and *everyone* are <u>singular</u> pronouns because they end in "one." It is true that these pronouns take singular verbs. But in most of the examples above, the number implied by the indefinite is actually indeterminate. In *If anyone calls . . .* , the number could be any-where from zero to any reasonable finite number; in *Everyone must pack their own lunch,* there is a presumption that there is more than one potential lunchpacker; only in *I saw someone in the shadows* does the indefinite pronoun clearly refer to a single individual. For this reason, speakers seem especially willing to use *they* when the antecedent is *anyone* or *everyone.* Certain quantifying determiners pose exactly the same problem and speakers often employ exactly the same solution— ***Every*** *student must pack* ***their*** *own lunch.* ***Each*** *child will bring* ***their*** *birth certificate.* (Although the noun head is singular in both these cases, *every* presupposes more than one student and *each* more than one child.) Edited English usually requires the solutions discussed in the personal pronoun section.

INTERROGATIVE PRONOUNS

When a speaker wishes to learn the identity of someone or something, s/he typically uses an interrogative pronoun to solicit that information. Interroga-tive pronouns always begin with the letters *wh* in written texts, thus they are often called ***wh*** **words**. The interrogative pronoun, regardless of its grammat-ical function, is almost always the first word in the sentence. The one excep-tion is in those cases where the interrogative is the object of a preposition, in which case some speakers place the preposition before the interrogative pro-noun.

Who *left the door open?*	[*Who* is a subject]
What *is Matilda eating?*	[*What* is a direct object]
Who *did you loan your car to?*	[*Who* is an indirect object]
To **whom** *did you loan your car?*	[*To whom* is an indirect object]
What *did Maggie call Cedric?*	[*What* is an object complement]
What *is his name?*	[*What* is a subject complement]

If you have problems identifying the grammatical function of an interrog-ative pronoun, simply recast the question as a statement with questioning in-tonation—*Matilda is eating what? Maggie called Cedric what*? Normal word order should make the grammatical function of the *wh* word clear.

There are adverb interrogatives as well—*where, when, why,* and *how.* We will discuss interrogative constructions in detail in Chapter 3. *Wh* forms also func-tion as relative pronouns and these forms will be discussed in Chapter 5.

Noun Phrases in Discourse

We've already discussed the fact that noun phrases allow us to "deploy" peo-ple and things in conversation. But of course conversation is a two-way street and the kind of NP we choose in discourse will depend on how much we think our hearer knows. If we assume that the referent is not accessible to our hearer, we may use an NP containing the article *a* to introduce the referent into discourse or we might use a proper name with an accompanying explanation.

I bought **a bicycle** *last week.*

Last night I met **Derek Walcott, a famous poet.**

If the referent is identifiable to the hearer because it has already been introduced into the conversation or if it is one of those things that is uniquely identifiable even though it may be new to the conversation, the article *the* or a proper noun can be used.

The bike *is a lemon.*

Mr. Walcott *invited me to his next reading.*

I can see **the moon.**

If the referent is not only identifiable to the hearer but has been talked about enough to become familiar, we might choose a demonstrative determiner.

I really hate **that** *bike.*

That *man is a fabulous writer.*

If the referent of the NP is the current center of attention, we most often choose a personal pronoun.

It *won't go over two miles an hour.*

He *has published both poems and plays.*

The following chart is based very loosely on Grundel, Hedberg, and Zacharski (1993).

Referent introduced to hearer	Referent is now identifiable to hearer	Referent is identifiable and familiar to hearer	Referent is current center of attention
I met **a homeless man** yesterday.	**The poor guy** was looking for food.	**This guy** didn't even have a coat on.	**He** looked extremely cold.
Sue married **a boxer named Buzz.**	**Buzz** has a terrible temper.	**This man** is truly mean.	I don't like to be near **him.**

Summing Up

NPs are the actors and the influenced in human discourse. Without NPs there would be no agents, no patients, no experiencers, no recipients. It is no accident that the first words that babies acquire are nouns. Our world is full of things with physical reality and nouns allow us to refer to those things. But while NPs often refer to entities, they can also refer to abstractions and even propositions. The grammatical roles they play—subject, direct object, indirect object, subject complement, and object complement—place NPs into a complex relationship with the verb phrase. This relationship will be explored in the next chapter.

3

The Verb Phrase

The verb phrase is the heart of the sentence. As I have already noted, every English sentence must contain at least one verb. In some languages (e.g., Hungarian and Swahili), subject and object pronouns are routinely incorporated into the verb form itself, so sentences can occur without any overt NPs whatsoever, but the verb is never optional. Verbs carry a great deal of information; they describe actions, events, and states and place these in a time frame; they tell us whether actions or events have been completed or are ongoing; they tell us whether a state is current or resultative; they allow us to command, to request, to speculate, to wish, and to predict. And, as you will see, this is only a fraction of things that verbs can do.

The English verb phrase (abbreviated VP) is a complicated affair. So far in this text we have dealt primarily with sentences containing simple one-word verb phrases. Sentences like these, however, are not very common in discourse. Multiword VPs like the following are more typical.

*You **shouldn't be eating** that junk.*

*Are *you* **going to be able to help** me later?*

*She **might have been insulted** by that remark.*

Be aware that the term **verb phrase** can have two distinct meanings in linguistics. In generative grammars, it refers to the entire predicate, excluding auxiliaries. Here, however, I am using the term to refer to the "main" verb and its auxiliaries, excluding the rest of the predicate.

I talked about verbs at some length in Chapter 1, but didn't attempt to define the term. When I discussed nouns, I was able to describe them in terms of inflectional endings, grammatical functions, and (very loosely) meaning. In many ways the verb is harder to characterize. Like the noun, it can be identified to some extent in terms of inflectional suffixes. These inflections will be examined at some length in the sections on tense, aspect, voice, and modality. And like nouns, verbs can be characterized to some degree in terms of meaning.

Just as nouns refer to the actors and things in our world, verbs allow us to express states, events, and actions involving these actors and things. This encompasses a very broad range of meanings, but all verbs share one characteristic—they encode information about time. Nouns are relatively time stable. We don't think of time as an important factor in understanding what is meant by *chair, rock,* or *dog.* But verbs carry a great deal of implicit information about time. Some verbs describe actions that are by their very nature constrained in terms of time—*Erin jumped over the wall; Marvin broke the window; The guests arrived at 9:00 P.M.* It's difficult, if not impossible, to prolong the acts of jumping over a wall, breaking a window, and arriving. It takes a split second *to blink, to slap,* or *to sneeze.* On the other hand, many verbs are relatively unconstrained in terms of time. One can *swim, talk,* or *sleep* indefinitely. It always takes much longer to build a house than to raze one.

Some verbs indicate that an action has begun or has ended—*He* **began** *to scream; The baby* **stopped** *crying; It* **started** *to rain.* Others underscore the fact that a situation persists over time—*Bill Gates* **is** *very rich; A statue of Amelia Earhart* **stands** *in the town square; Ammonia* **smells** *bad.* Still others express the fact that a state has changed over time—*The tree* **grew** *tall; The weather* **turned** *cold.*

Regardless of the intrinsic meaning of a verb, a speaker can always manipulate the time frame it expresses by the use of tense and aspect.

Tense

Tense is an often misused technical term. When linguists speak of tense, they are referring to a particular set of inflectional affixes that communicate information about the time frame in which something exists or occurs. Tense is deictic. Present time stands at the center of all tense systems; events that took place before present time are marked in one way; events that are ongoing at the present or somehow include the present are marked in another, and events that have not yet taken place may be marked with yet a different form. Some languages, like English, mark only two tenses—present and past; others have a future tense marker as well. There are even languages like Inuit (Eskimo) that have more than one past tense, each marking a different degree of remoteness (Bybee, 1994, pp. 98–99).

In English, tense is usually but not always communicated by the use of suffixes. The {-s} suffix in *walks* is a present tense inflection, while the {-ed} suffix in *walked* and the vowel change in *rang* are both considered past tense markers. But Old English had a far more elaborate present and past tense system than Modern English. Old English tense markers also reflected the **number** of the subject, i.e., singular or plural. Below are the present tense forms for the Old English word "to judge," the source of Modern English *deem. Deman* is the infinitive form. The Old English letter þ (often called thorn because it looks like one) stands for the *th* sound in *thin.*

Person	Singular	Plural
First person	deme (I) judge	demaþ (we) judge
Second person	demest (you, sing.) judge	demaþ (you, plural) judge
Third person	demeþ (s/he, it) judges	demaþ (they) judge

Some of these singular endings persisted into the seventeenth century, at which time the third person singular *-eþ* was replaced by {-s} and all the other endings disappeared. Much modern English liturgical language is based on the King James version of the Christian Bible, a translation published in 1611 under the auspices of King James of England. Although the Jewish *Scriptures* are the source of the Old Testament of the Christian faith, the first English translation of this body of literature by Jewish scholars didn't appear until the nineteenth century. The standard American version of the Jewish *Scriptures* was published in 1915 and, despite its relative modernity, it features most of the late sixteenth century forms found in the King James version. Old English verb suffixes can be found in many well-known religious passages like "whither thou goest I will go" (Ruth 1:16) and "He maketh me to lie down in green pastures" (Psalms 23:2). A 1935 English translation of the *Koran* by Marmaduke Pickthall (1992), an English convert to Islam, also exploits language that is over three centuries old, e.g., "Allah knoweth: ye know not" (p. 55). Our familiarity with archaic English forms stems from the linguistic conservatism of liturgical language.

By the eighteenth century, all the present tense endings had been lost except the third person singular {-s}, as in *The baby **cries** at night*. In Modern English the other present tense forms are all identical to the infinitive—*I **cry**, you **cry**, we **cry**, they **cry**,* and *to **cry***. The only reason linguists continue to call these uninflected forms the present <u>tense</u> is because there is still that one surviving suffix in the conjugation. In some dialects, even the third person singular {-s} suffix has disappeared. The loss of {-s} is especially evident in the case of the verb *do* when it combines with the negative. Speakers who would never delete the {-s} on another third person present tense verb sometimes delete the {-s} in *doesn't*—*He don't live here anymore*.

The past tense in Old English was also highly inflected. Although the markers that distinguished first, second, and third person have disappeared in Modern English, all persons still carry a distinct past tense marker, except in those rare cases in which the verb has no distinct past tense form whatsoever. The vast majority of verbs mark the past tense with an {-ed} suffix. There are a few verbs the infinitives of which end in the sounds [n] or [nd] that exploit *-t* as a past tense marker in both spelling and pronunciation—*bend/bent, send/sent,* and for some speakers *lend/lent* and *burn/burnt* (A few of these are quite archaic, like *rend/rent* meaning "to tear apart"). There are other verbs, however, that end in [nd] and take the typical {-ed} past tense marker—*fended, mended, tended.* Some verbs exploit a vowel change to communicate past tense—*sing/sang, ride/rode, swim/swam, throw/threw, fall/fell, swear/swore,* etc. There are a few verbs in which the past tense contains both a vowel change and a suffix. This suffix, which is usually pronounced and spelled *-t* and occasionally *-d,* is simply a variation of the {-ed} ending—*think/thought, buy/bought, seek/sought, teach/taught, sell/sold,* and for some speakers *dreamt.* The past tense forms of *go* and *be* are **suppletive.** This means that the past tense forms are historically unrelated to the present tense forms and they look completely different. In just a few cases, the past tense is identical to all present tense forms except the third person singular, e.g.—*cut, put, quit, shut, cost, split.* Small children who have mastered the dominant {-ed} pattern often over-generalize, producing sentences like **I cutted my finger* and **I putted my toys away.*

When new verbs enter the language, they are almost always given an {-ed} past tense ending—*boogied, faxed, dissed.*

	Various forms taken by past tense verbs
{ed} ending	walked, jumped, waited, cried, washed, loved
{t} ending	bent, lent, sent
vowel change	sang, sank, ran, swam, fell, threw, slid, found
vowel change + {t} ending	sought, bought, taught, wept, kept, slept, crept
no change	cut, put, split, cost, shut, quit
suppletive form	went, was/were

If you are not clear about the past tense form of a given verb, simply fill in the blank of this frame: *I _____ yesterday.* Any verb form that naturally fills that spot will be a past tense form.

<u>The first verb in the verb phrase will always carry tense;</u> no other verb can do so. This may seem very counter-intuitive at times, but, as you will see later, this is simply a matter of form, not meaning. In each of the sentences below, the verb in boldface carries tense.

*Janice **loves** Fruit Loops.*

*Janice **does** not like Fruit Loops.*

*Janice **threw** her Fruit Loops on the floor.*

*Janice **was** eating her Fruit Loops.*

*Janice **had** eaten her Fruit Loops.*

*Janice **may** eat those Fruit Loops.*

*Janice **should** not be eating Fruit Loops.*

Non-native speakers sometimes overlook this fact about English grammar and produce sentences like *He didn't wanted any juice* in which both *did* and *wanted* carry the past tense marker.

TENSE AND MEANING

It is relatively easy to identify the tense of a verb in English. But what do these forms communicate; what do they mean? Over the centuries, the time frames associated with tense markers have broadened and sometimes the terms *past* and *present* are somewhat misleading. As you will soon see, past tense markers are occasionally used in non-past contexts and present tense markers can be used to manipulate the time frame in a variety of ways.

Past Tense

As you would expect, simple past tense (sometimes called the **preterit**) does indeed communicate past time and this is its primary function. It is used in conjunction with events that are over and done with—*I played volleyball yesterday; Stephen ate his breakfast early; Marsha walked the dog at noon.*

But past time goes on indefinitely. You might find it odd if I were to announce without preamble, "I broke a guy's arm." Your natural reaction would be to ask "When did you do that?" And in fact when we use a past tense verb, we usually limit the time frame in some way. If I say "General Colin Powell visited our university last year," the phrase *last year* tells you when in past time the event occurred. In other words, it constrains the time frame. (We will discuss adverbs of time in some detail in Chapter 4.) In the absence of an adverb that expresses time, the broader discourse context usually constrains the time frame. If a group of students in history are discussing the American Civil War and one says, "Atlanta burned for days," everyone understands (at least roughly) the time frame in which this event occurred.

In the following passage from E. Annie Proulx's novel *Shipping News* (1993), there is more than one past time frame. The first is explicitly established by the date 1909 and some of the sentences reflect that time frame, but it is clear from the narrative that three of the sentences refer to past times later than 1909; these later time frames are marked by italics. (Italics added.)

"This is in 1909. They gave him a little tin trunk with some clothes. . . . *He told us about that trip many times.* There were three hundred and fourteen children, boys and girls on that ship, all of them signed on to help farmers. *He said many of them were only three or four years old.* They had no idea what was happening to them. . . . *[H]e kept in touch with some of the survivors* he'd made friends with on the Aramania." (p. 167)

This passage moves back and forth between 1909 and later past time frames, but the context indicates the switches quite clearly with "He told us," "He said," and "He kept in touch with some of the survivors. . . ."

Occasionally, a speaker will use the past tense form of a verb, not to communicate past time, but to appear more polite or obsequious. A student who is seeking an extension on a term paper might say, "I wanted to ask you for a favor." This sentence is virtually synonymous with "I want to ask you for a favor," but the past tense verb signals greater politeness. Later we will see the same phenomenon operating with modal auxiliaries.

Present Tense

Present tense is far harder to characterize semantically than past tense. In fact "present" is a misleading term in English and some linguists prefer the term "non-past" for this form. The simple present tense (i.e., a present tense verb without any auxiliaries) is rarely used in conjunction with an event that is ongoing in present time. A fluent English speaker would never announce, "I go to bed now." However, non-native speakers in whose languages the present tense can be used to communicate an ongoing activity, often use the English present tense in just this way.

If the English present tense is not normally used to communicate ongoing activities in the present, what are its functions? One of its primary uses is to express **habitual activities,** activities that began at some point in the past, continue into the present, and will presumably continue into the future.

My cousin **attends** *the University of Hawaii.*

Tracy **works** *at the zoo.*

My brothers **go** *to school by bus.*

The present tense is also used to express **universal truths** and **permanent states.**

Hot air **rises.**

Two and two **equals** *four.*

Lourdes **is** *tall.*

The Statue of Liberty **stands** *in the harbor.*

When a speaker wishes to refer to a **scheduled, future event**, the simple present tense can be used along with a word or a phrase that expresses time.

The train **arrives** <u>*at noon.*</u>

The concert **starts** <u>*after the reception.*</u>

*We **leave** <u>on Tuesday</u>.*

*The Halloween party **is** <u>Wednesday</u>.*

The simple present cannot, however, be used for an <u>unscheduled</u> event. **It rains tomorrow* is ungrammatical.

To heighten the drama of a tale, storytellers often use the simple present tense to relate past events. This is called the **historical** or **narrative present.**

Jack **climbs** up the beanstalk and **creeps** into the giant's castle. He **hides** behind a huge chair. The giant **stomps** into the room.

In her autobiographical account of her work with a death row inmate in *Dead Man Walking* (1994), Sister Helen Prejean casts her entire narrative in the present tense. (Boldface added.)

When Chava Colon from the Prison Coalition **asks** me one January day in 1982 to become a pen pal to a death-row inmate, I **say,** Sure. The invitation **seems** to fit with my work in St. Thomas, a New Orleans housing project. . . . Death **is** rampant here—from guns, disease, addiction. Medical care scarcely **exists.** (p. 3)

Prejean's use of the present tense to narrate past events heightens the immediacy of her encounters with the inmate and the prison system.

Performatives are highly constrained constructions in which speech is action. In uttering a particular sentence, the speaker actually carries out some sort of act. This term was first coined and described by English philosopher J. L. Austin (1962). If a marriage license has been signed and a judge utters the words "I now **pronounce** you husband and wife," the couple is legally married. On the other hand, if I say, "I will now pronounce this word in French," I have not performed any kind of act just by uttering this sentence. Performatives are one context in which the simple present tense is actually used to communicate present time. There are a limited number of performatives in English and they all have the same shape—a first person subject, followed by a <u>present tense</u> verb. Many have legal, procedural, or religious ramifications, and they all have social implications.

*I **move** that this meeting be adjourned.*

*I **sentence** you to life in prison.*

*I **christen** you Hortense.*

*I **bet** you five dollars that the Bulls will win.*

*I **warn** you not to touch me.*

*I **beg** you to leave.*

*We **forbid** you to attend the Phish concert.*

*We **apologize**.*

There is another very specialized context in which the simple present can be used to describe an event which is ongoing in the present. Sportscasters and individuals who are demonstrating some sort of process often use the **commentary present** to lend immediacy to their words. A track announcer calling a horse race always begins with "They're at the gate. (Pause) They're off." A radio sportscaster might say, "Marino carries the ball to the twenty-yard line." Television chefs use the simple present tense constantly, as in "I put the mushrooms in the stock and stir slowly." The following magazine ad exploits the commentary present to generate excitement (*Motorcyclist*, April, 1997). (Boldface added.)

> The green flag **drops.** Fifty finely tuned Formula USA racing machines **accelerate** to life. . . . The crowd **erupts** into whoops of approval and within seconds all 50 FUSA bikes **are** thundering around the circuit. One rider **emerges** at the front the pack. (p. 96)

While only two of the semantic categories discussed above use the simple present to communicate ongoing present activity, all but one of them involve present time in some way. In the case of the habitual and permanent states, the activity or state is one that began in the past, includes the present, and presumably will be continued in the future. While *Joan arrives tomorrow* refers to a future event, this event was planned in the past (before the sentence was uttered); thus, the plan encompasses past and present time. Both the commentary present and the performative refer to events that literally occur in present time. So, except for the historical present, all of the present tense constructions discussed above actually incorporate present time in some way (Comrie, 1985, p. 38).

Summary of the uses of the present tense	
Habitual action	I visit my aunt each week.
State	The Empire State Building is tall.
Universal truth	Hot air rises.
Planned future event	Jenny leaves for college tomorrow.
Commentary	Mighty Casey strikes out.
Performative	I call this meeting to order.
Historical	I walk up to this guy and I say. . . .

What About Future Time?

Many languages, including Chinese and Burmese, have no tense system at all. This does not mean that speakers of these languages cannot talk about past, present, and future events. It simply means that the time frame is communicated, not by different forms of the same verb (e.g., a root word and its affixes), but by additional words in the sentence.

The strategies that English speakers employ to communicate future time is a good example of this phenomenon. Unlike Spanish or Greek, English has never had a future <u>tense</u>. There is no suffix that the English speaker can attach to a verb to make it future. To communicate future time, English speakers must employ one or more of a variety of periphrastic constructions, i.e., they must employ extra words. Most English speakers think of *will* as the primary tool for communicating future time, but it is only one of many. As you will see in the sentences below, the future time frame is often expressed wholly or in part by future time expressions like *tomorrow* and *later*. The phrase *be going to* is frequently used to express future events or states. Those elements that communicate future time appear in boldface.

*It **will** rain **tomorrow**.*

*The baby **is going to** fall.*

*The train arrives **at 9:00 tonight**.*

*They are coming **later**.*

*Yves **is to** arrive **at noon**.*

Auxiliary verbs often express future time implicitly and I will take up this issue again when I discuss modality.

FINITE AND NON-FINITE VERBS

Verb phrases that carry tense are called **finite.** The main verb phrase of the sentence is always finite and, as you will see in Chapter 5, some subordinate clauses also contain finite verbs.

In the following sentences the verb phrases in boldface are finite. Remember that it is the first verb that actually carries the tense.

*Lewis and Clark **explored** the West.*

*George **is chopping** down the cherry tree.*

*I **have forgotten** your name.*

*Heathcliff **knows** that Cathy **is seeing** another guy.*

Verb phrases that do not carry tense are called **non-finite.** Infinitives, present participles, and past participles are all non-finite constructions and they can occur without tensed verbs in subordinate clauses. (In fact, the word *in-finitive* literally means "not finite.") We will discuss this in detail in Chapter 5, but here are a few examples of non-finite verb phrases (in boldface).

*I don't want Inga **to borrow** my book.*

***Running** headlong down the hill, the little boy tripped over a log.*

*I dislike Manny **having quit** his job.*

***Broken** in a fight, the window offered little protection from the wind.*

Aspect

Aspect is difficult to define simply. The term derives from a Latin word which means "gaze" or "view." While aspect refers to time in various ways, it goes beyond communicating information about the linear time frame (past, present, future). Modern grammarians disagree about what kinds of constructions should be called aspect, and over the centuries many different forms have been considered aspectual, including those that express continuous actions, repeated (iterative) actions, habitual actions, beginning (ingressive) actions, and finishing (egressive) actions. Aspect has been defined in many different ways. Bernard Comrie, who has written a seminal book on the subject, defines it as "different ways of viewing the internal temporal constituency of a situation" (1976, p. 3). Like most definitions of aspect, this is somewhat opaque. To complicate matters further, aspect systems are far more varied in form than tense systems. Most linguists use the term *tense* to label inflectional forms only. Thus, the suffix {-ed} in *walked* is a tense marker but the auxiliary *will* in *will walk* is not. But these same linguists are willing to label as aspect markers both inflectional and periphrastic forms; thus, across languages there is a tremendous variation in those forms that are considered aspectual.

There are also some serious terminological problems in the study of aspect. Different languages have different labeling systems, sometimes using the same term for very different constructions. If you are familiar with other European languages, you have probably encountered the terms **perfect** or **perfective** and **imperfect.** The term imperfect is not used in English syntax at all, but in many European languages it refers to a verbal affix that communicates ongoing, continuous action and habitual action. Romance languages have an imperfect form, but it is used only with past time events. In English we communicate ongoing action by the so-called progressive—*Mary is swimming,* but since this construction does not also communicate habitual action, the label imperfect is not used.

While the term *perfect* is used in English grammar, be aware that it means something different here than it does in the grammars of most other European languages. In general, the terms *perfect* and *perfective* refer to an action that is seen as an unanalyzed whole, an action that is over and done with, complete.

Not surprisingly, it is usually used for events that occurred in the past. English does not have a separate construction to express this meaning, but many simple past tense utterances fulfill this criteria—*Judith fixed the clock; The kids built a fort.* Don't be intimidated by this foray into the terminological swamp. The point is that the term *perfect,* which will be explained at some length below, means something different in English grammar than it does in other contexts.

English has two aspects. Grammarians have traditionally called these the **progressive** and the **perfect.** Like the terms *present tense* and *past tense,* the terms *progressive* and *perfect* refer to specific forms of the verb. If a verb does not have the required form, it does not have aspect. As you will see, aspect in English is marked by a combination of inflectional suffixes and auxiliary verbs (i.e., periphrastic constructions).

PROGRESSIVE ASPECT

The progressive in English is always constructed in the same way. It requires the appropriate form of the verb *be,* followed by a present participle.[1] The present participle in English is always the {-ing} form of the verb. (*Present participle* is simply the traditional name for this verb form; it is quite distinct from *present tense.*) All verbs except modal auxiliaries and some semiauxiliaries have a present participle form. The progressive is a hybrid construction, part periphrastic (the auxiliary *be*) and part inflected (the {-ing}).

My daughter │is│ study │ing│ German.

In the following sentences, the component parts of the progressive are in boldface.

*Pete **is** drink**ing** cola.*

*Ling **was** study**ing** last night.*

*The twins **are** scream**ing** for their bottles.*

*We **were** skat**ing** in the park.*

*I **am** attend**ing** Reed College now.*

This, not the simple present tense, is what speakers typically use when they want to refer to an event that is occurring in present time.

Meaning of the Progressive

The progressive is usually used to communicate an ongoing and incomplete event. If you walk into your apartment and your roommates say, "We are studying," you will assume that you have interrupted them. When the progressive is used with the present tense form of the auxiliary *be,* the hearer assumes that the activity is in progress. Speakers would normally contract the auxiliaries that appear in the following examples, e.g., **I'm** *cleaning out my dresser*, but for the time being I will use the full auxiliary to ensure that the component parts of each structure are perfectly clear.

I am cleaning out my dresser.	[I'm not done yet.]
She is building a garage.	[It's not completed yet.]
They are fixing dinner.	[Preparations are still underway.]
Kevin is coughing.	[He is still in the midst of coughing.]

The sentences above reflect *present tense* and *progressive aspect*. Technically there is no tense called "present progressive." When grammarians use phrases like *present progressive*, they are exploiting a terminological shorthand; it is understood that two different grammatical systems are reflected in the label.

In English there is a marked contrast between the semantics of the simple present tense and the present progressive. As you saw above, the simple present very rarely communicates an action or event that is ongoing in present time. This is not true in all languages, however. While Spanish has a progressive construction that is similar to the one in English, the simple present tense in Spanish can also be used to describe an action or event that is ongoing in the present. Many languages use the simple present to express an ongoing event and, as a result, non-native speakers of English often produce sentences like *I study* and *I eat dinner now*.

When the auxiliary *be* of the progressive is in the past tense form, the hearer assumes that a past event was ongoing and incomplete at the time in question or when the event was interrupted or terminated.

I was reading last night at nine o'clock.

We were hiding the money [when Fred came into the room].

She was driving down I-95 [when her tire came loose].

Dynamic and Stative Verbs

Not all verbs take the progressive. In general the progressive suggests activity and verbs that co-occur with it are called **dynamic.** Verbs that express **states** don't readily co-occur with the progressive. This is largely because states are by their very nature ongoing and don't require additional grammatical information to indicate that fact. Psych-verbs (mental state verbs), however, do vary somewhat in their co-occurrence with the progressive. *I am knowing algebra* and *She is believing in God* are ungrammatical sentences for most speakers. When we use the verb *think* to express an opinion or belief, we typically avoid the progressive. *??I am thinking that capital punishment is wrong* is peculiar. On the other hand, when we use *think* to describe an activity in which we are currently engaged, it can readily co-occur with the progressive—*I am think-*

ing about dessert. The verb *understand* takes the progressive only when a recent change of state is suggested—*I am understanding statistics better these days.* Verbs expressing wants and desires vary in their ability to co-occur with the progressive. **I am desiring spaghetti* is ungrammatical but *I am craving spaghetti* is acceptable.

Verbs communicating ownership or possession are also stative and don't take the progressive. **I am having a pickup truck* and **Angie is owning a sailboat* are ungrammatical for all English speakers. Sometimes the semantic difference between a stative and dynamic verb is great. Clearly, *I have a baby* and *I am having a baby* reflect two entirely different circumstances.

The verb *have* can also be used to communicate the state of one's health. When a medical condition is long-term, it is treated linguistically as a state and *have* does not co-occur with the progressive; **I am having Parkinson's disease* and **He is having cancer* are ungrammatical. However, a temporary condition is sometimes communicated by using the progressive. *I am having an asthma attack* is fine, while **I have an asthma attack* is not. On the other hand, *I have the hiccoughs* and *I have a headache* are perfectly acceptable. There is no simple "rule" for determining which short-term medical conditions co-occur with progressive *have* and which don't.

As you saw in Chapter 1, the verb *have* is sometimes semantically empty, while the direct object specifies the nature of the activity. Dynamic *have* occurs in sentences like *We are having dinner, They are having an argument,* and *Theresa is having a bath.* These sentences can be paraphrased by turning the direct object NP into a verb—*We are dining, They are arguing, Theresa is bathing.*

Sensory verbs with experiencer subjects seldom take the progressive. **I am hearing them argue* is a very odd sentence. *I am smelling smoke* is marginally acceptable but *I smell smoke* is fine. When experiencer subjects of sensory verbs do co-occur with the progressive, there is sometimes the presumption that some sort of pathological sensory perception exists—*I am seeing stars; I am hearing things. Feel* is the one exception to this generalization. *I am feeling some pain* suggests no sensory pathology.

Copulas that express relatively permanent states don't co-occur with the progressive. You are unlikely to hear **Azra is seeming sad* and **You are appearing angry.* Sensory copulas can co-occur with the progressive if the speaker is talking about a temporary or recently achieved state—*Gene is looking healthy these days; My stereo is sounding bad.* Copula *be,* however, can be used in two different ways. When it describes a relatively permanent state, it does not co-occur with the progressive. It would be in ungrammatical to say **Michael Jordan is being tall* or **Louisa's eyes are being brown.* However, *be* can also be used to describe temporary states and in doing so can readily co-occur with the progressive—*The children are being noisy; Millie is being obnoxious.* When *be* is used in this way, it suggests current behavior. If a speaker wanted to indicate that Millie was a chronically obnoxious person, s/he would eliminate the progressive—*Millie is obnoxious.*

Copulas that suggest changes of state can readily co-occur with the progressive. *Samantha is getting tall, Tom is becoming crabby,* and *The weather is turning cold* are all perfectly acceptable sentences.

The difference between the simple present tense and the present progressive often signals the difference between a temporary condition and a permanent one. If I tell you that *Linda lives in Tucson,* I am suggesting that she is settled there, but if I say that *Linda is living in Tucson,* I am indicating that her residence may not be permanent. *He attends AA meetings* indicates a truly habitual activity, while *He is attending AA meetings* suggests that the activity may be short term.

Punctual Verbs

English contains a set of verbs called **punctual.** These verbs all refer to a single event that is by its very nature over quickly. *Blink, cough, knock, flash, hit, pinch, slap,* and *stab* are events that end in a split second. But when these verbs occur in the progressive, they communicate repeated activity. *The light flashed* could mean that the light went on and off once, but *The light was flashing* can only mean that it went on and off repeatedly. *Lyle is pinching his little sister* indicates that he has pinched her more than once.

Since the progressive is typically used to talk about ongoing activities, its use with punctual verbs makes sense. Given the very nature of punctual verbs, the only way they can be made to express an activity of any duration is with the progressive.

PERFECT ASPECT

Like the progressive, the perfect is a combination of a separate auxiliary verb and an inflectional morpheme, usually a suffix. The perfect always takes the same shape—the appropriate form of the auxiliary *have* followed by the past participle form of the following verb. (*Past participle* is the conventional term for this form; it is only indirectly related to past tense.)

The most common past participle suffix in English is {-ed}, but {-en} and vowel changes also mark this form. Occasionally a verb will have no past participle form; such verbs have no separate past tense form either, e.g., *cut, put.* In most cases the past participle looks just like the past tense. This is true for all those verbs that form the past participle with {-ed}, those that express past tense with a vowel change plus a {-t} ending—*sought, kept,* and those few cases in which the same vowel appears in both the past tense and the past participle (but not in the present tense)—*read, fed, led.*

	Various forms taken by past participles
{ed} ending	walked, turned, nestled, mingled, carried, washed
{en} ending	written, fallen, given, ridden, gone, thrown, been

Various forms taken by past participles (cont.)	
vowel change	rung, sung, drunk, stung, swum, sunk, fed
no change	cost, quit, cut, shut, put
vowel change + {t} ending	sought, bought, taught, slept, kept, wept, crept

In the following sentences the component parts of the perfect are in boldface.

*We **have** **finished** our lunch.*

*You **have** **offended** my uncle.*

*The dog **has** **eaten** my homework.*

*He **has** **written** two novels.*

*They **have** **gone** home.*

*She **has** **swum** in that creek.*

*I **have** **sung** that song often.*

*I **have** **taught** here for 25 years.*

*Marie **has** **put** the tools in the drawer.*

*I **had** **written** three chapters when my computer broke.*

*Sylvia **had** **washed** the car.*

If you are unclear about the past participle form of a particular verb, simply use it in the following frame. The verb form that naturally follows *have* will be the past participle.

I have _____.

Meaning of the Perfect

The term *perfect* derives from an old meaning of the adjective *perfect*, "something that is thoroughly made or fully accomplished, finished." In most languages the perfect form of the verb communicates exactly that, an event that is completed, but as you have already seen, this is not the case in English.

The semantics of the English perfect is quite complex but many of its uses are closely related. In very general terms, the present perfect (i.e., sentences in which the auxiliary *have* is in the present tense) expresses a relationship between two time points, one in the past and one that includes the present.

Often the present perfect is used when an event or series of events began in the past but continues up to and possibly through the present moment. *Josh has washed four loads of clothes* suggests that Josh is not yet finished with the task; in contrast, *Josh washed four loads of clothes* indicates that the job is over. *Alicia has read three chapters of Moby Dick* suggests that Alicia will keep reading, but *Alicia read three chapters of Moby Dick* hints that she is done reading and doesn't intend to finish the novel. *Roland has lived here five years* indicates that Roland still lives here, while *Roland lived here five years* means that he is no longer at this address. A sentence like *William Shakespeare has written 37 plays* is inappropriate, since Shakespeare won't be writing any more plays.

Sometimes the present perfect is used to discuss an event that is technically over but which has generated a result that is still relevant. This is called the **perfect of current relevance**—*I have cut my finger [and I'm bleeding all over the floor]; Josh has washed four loads of clothes [and he's tired]; I have studied hard [and expect to get an A on the exam].* The various uses of the perfect discussed here are not necessarily mutually exclusive and you will find that the notion of current relevance infuses many of them.

The present perfect can also be used to indicate that the subject of the sentence has had an experience at least once in the past leading up to the present moment. *I have been to Russia* does not specify <u>when</u> the speaker was there; the sentence simply indicates the event took place any time in the past right up to the present moment. We often used this **experiential perfect** in questions and negative utterances—*Have you ever been to Egypt? Has your daughter had the measles? I've never eaten sweetbreads.*

The present perfect is sometimes used to discuss events that have occurred in the **recent past**—*Summer vacation has ended; Mike has arrived; Eva has left the room.* While these events have already taken place, the perfect underscores the fact these events occurred recently, e.g., summer vacation ended only days ago. Because this use of the perfect encompasses only the recent past, sentences like *World War II has ended* and *The Watergate scandal has shocked the nation* are unacceptable in most contemporary contexts.

The past perfect (constructions in which the verb *have* is in the past tense) behaves very much like the present perfect, except that the entire event and any result take place in past time. In the sentence *I have read three pages of the report*, the reading begins in the past and continues up to the present moment; in *I had read three pages of the report [when Jerry walked in]*, the reading starts in the past and continues up until another moment in the past. In other words, the present perfect reflects a past event that somehow bumps up against the present, while the past perfect communicates a past event which bumps up against another, more recent past event.

Novels and short stories are often written in the past tense. In this context, events that precede those being described in the story line are usually related in past perfect. The following passage occurs in Tony Hillerman's *Sacred Clowns* (1993). (Boldface added.)

> Four figures **had** emerg**ed** on a roof across the plaza. . . . The sacred clowns of Pueblo people. Chee **had** first s**een** similar clowns perform at a Hopi ceremonial at Moenkopi when he was a child. . . . Two of them now stood at the parapet of the building. (p. 15)

Here past perfect communicates past time within the past.

When the perfect and progressive constructions are combined, the *have* of the perfect always precedes the *be* of the progressive.

Simone | has | be | en | eat | ing | your chocolates.

Note that the component parts of the perfect are not contiguous nor are the component parts of the progressive. In the following examples the component parts of the perfect construction are in capital letters and the component parts of the progressive construction are double underlined.

Those children HAVE beEN throwing rocks at dogs.

Dave HAS beEN sleeping all day.

We HAVE beEN studying organic chemistry.

Note, too, that in each of these sentences the word *been* participates in both the perfect and progressive constructions; it carries the {-en} of the perfect and the *be* of the progressive. In each sentence the first auxiliary carries the tense for the entire verb phrase. *Been, throwing, sleeping,* and *studying* are not marked for tense. In all of the sentences above the {-ing} of the progressive attaches to the main verb; that will no longer be the case when a passive construction is added, as you will see shortly.

When the perfect and progressive are combined, the meaning is basically a combination of their respective meanings as discussed above. In *Dave has been sleeping all day,* the speaker indicates that Dave began sleeping in the past and that this is an incomplete, ongoing activity that includes the present. Tense and aspect work together semantically, but they are completely separate grammatical systems.

Summary of the uses of the present perfect

State or activity begins in past, continues into present	I have painted three walls [and I have one more to go].
Past event with current relevance	I have spilled some juice [now it's staining the floor].
Experience at any point in the past	Have you ever driven a sports car?
Event of the recent past	Susan has arrived.

Tense and Aspect in Discourse

In natural language, sentences don't occur in isolated bursts but rather follow one another in (more or less) coherent discourse. Tense and aspect work together in some interesting ways to forge connections between predicates and between separate sentences. Often a series of past tense "action" verbs are processed as representing activities that occur in the order in which they are mentioned, i.e., the actions are temporally sequenced. This is especially obvious when two predicates are joined (coordinated) with *and*.

She tripped and plunged down the stairs.

He sipped some coffee and put his cup on the table.

Trish opened the car door and got in.

The above examples seem a little fraudulent, however, because the second predicate follows logically from the first; in each case the reverse order would be odd given the nature of the physical world, e.g., *?He put his cup on the table and sipped some coffee.* But even in cases where there is no predictable order of actions, we find the same phenomenon.

Mort ate dinner and took a nap.

Sue smiled and took the boy's hand.

He shrugged and walked over to the bar.

Although the two events captured in each of these sentences could easily occur in the opposite order, we assume that the order of the telling is the order in which the events occurred. *Jane stopped the car and got out* conjures up a very different image from *Jane got out and stopped the car.* There can be significant time gaps between events that are ordered in this way—*He got married and had six children.*

Not all coordinated past tense action verb phrases express this kind of temporal sequencing, however. Actions like taking a boy's hand, walking over to the bar, and getting out of the car take place over very short periods of time. But when the actions in both predicates continue over a longer period, they may be interpreted as intermingled—*We ate pizza and drank soda all evening; The kids tapped their feet and whispered during the service; I coughed and sneezed all night.* In these cases the predicates aren't temporally ordered.

Action verbs in separate but contiguous sentences can also be interpreted as representing a temporal sequence of events. This passage is from Sara Paretsky's short story collection *Windy City Blues* (1995). Only the main verb(s) in each sentence will be considered. (Boldface added.)

They **frog-marched** me down the hall to the closet before untying my hands. I **knelt** to work on the lock. As it clicked free Vico **grabbed** the door and **yanked** it open. I **fell** forward into the wires. Grabbing a large armful, I **pulled** with all my strength. (p. 73)

There is a clear-cut temporal sequence here; the order of the main verbs represents the order in which the actions occur.

However, when verbs express states or habitual actions, there is no real temporal ordering. Consider the following passage, also from *Windy City Blues*.

Cinda Goodrich and I **were** jogging acquaintances. A professional photographer, she **kept** the same erratic hours as a private investigator; we often **met** along Belmont Harbor in the late mornings. (p. 296)

Here a stative verb *were* is followed by two habitual verbs. The circumstances that are described in this passage persist over time and their ordering is unspecified.

The progressive has an interesting effect on the way we interpret events temporally. As you saw above, progressive events are ongoing, incomplete. When a progressive verb follows a past tense verb, we usually interpret the action of the first verb as being included within the time frame of the second (Dowty, 1986, pp. 53–54). In *I sat down next to Sammie; he was crying*, the hearer is likely to assume that Sammie was crying before I sat down next to him. We see the same pattern when the second verb is stative—*I looked over at Beth. She was bored.* In each of the following sets of sentences, the second predicate overlaps the first in terms of time frame.

I heard a loud thump. Someone was climbing the trellis outside my window.

Esther looked outside. It was raining.

Moira called me up last night. She was mad.

The boys entered the locker room. It was very humid in there.

You might imagine the time frame for the last example as looking something like this:

(Time Frame)

-->

[I t   w a s   v e r y   h u m i d   i n   t h e r e]
[The boys entered the locker room.]

By combining the simple past tense with progressive and stative predicates, English speakers can talk about situations or events inside other situations or events.

Passive Voice

Voice is a very different phenomenon from aspect. Where tense and aspect work together to place an event or state within a time frame, voice provides a strategy for focusing on different participants in an event.

English contains two so-called voices—the **active** and the **passive**. Active sentences are unmarked; in other words, if a sentence is not specifically marked passive, it is technically active. All of the examples in this chapter thus far have been active sentences.

Like the perfect and the progressive, passive sentences have a distinctive structure. Most passive sentences contain the auxiliary *be* followed by a verb in past participle form. (As you will see later, some passives contain the auxiliary *get*.)

$$Jack \;\boxed{was}\; push \;\boxed{ed}\; by \; Jill.$$

Some passives include a prepositional phrase containing the preposition *by*— *Guido was fired **by the Board of Directors***, but this is not required. In the following sentences, the component parts of the passive are in boldface.

*The dog **was** saved by its owner.*

*The trees **were** damag**ed** by high winds.*

*He **is** offended by crude language.*

*Amy **was** promot**ed** last week.*

*The village **was** destroy**ed.***

Most speakers of English have no difficultly turning an active sentence into a corresponding passive form. *The cat chased the rat* becomes *The rat was chased by the cat*; *Goldilocks ate the porridge* becomes *The porridge was eaten by Goldilocks*. In these sentences the direct object of the active sentence becomes the subject of the passive sentence, while the old subject appears at (or near) the end of the sentence preceded by the preposition *by*. This suggests that only transitive verbs participate in passive constructions and this is usually, but not always, the case. Sentences like *This bed was slept in by George Washington* do exist in English but they aren't common.

TRANSITIVE VERBS THAT DON'T (READILY) PASSIVIZE

While almost all passive sentences contain transitive verbs, not all transitive verbs can participate in passive constructions. As was indicated in Chapter 1, some sentences are more transitive than others, depending in part on the relative agentiveness of the subject and the degree to which the direct object is affected by the action of the verb. The degree of transitivity a sentence exhibits affects its ability to passivize.

Transitive verbs with agent and causer subjects passivize easily, largely because they have affected direct objects.

Gerald broke the VCR. / The VCR was broken by Gerald.

Those roots destroyed my plumbing. / My plumbing was destroyed by those roots.

The dogs frightened the children. / The children were frightened by the dogs.

Sensory verbs with experiencer subjects can passivize, but such passives sometimes sound a bit strained.

The employees heard the explosion. / The explosion was heard by the employees.

The guests smelled smoke. / ?Smoke was smelled by the guests.

Three students saw the accident. / The accident was seen by three students.

Psych-verbs with experiencer subjects resist passivization.

*Martha wants this book. / *This book is wanted by Martha.*

Manny hated the movie. / ?The movie was hated by Manny.

Orson enjoys romances. / ??Romances are enjoyed by Orson.

You will find that both sensory and psych-verbs are somewhat more acceptable in the passive if the NP in the *by* prepositional phrase is indefinite, e.g., *The movie was hated **by everybody**; Tiny Tim was loved **by all**; The accident was seen **by everyone***. But in general, sentences with experiencer subjects don't make good passives. This is in large part because their direct objects are relatively unaffected by the action of the verb.

There is a small category of stative verbs called **reciprocal verbs.** Sentences containing these verbs are unusual semantically because the subject and direct object have the same relationship to one another. If *Sophia resembles Alexander* then *Alexander resembles Sophia*; if *House means maison* then *Maison means house.* Neither of these sentences contains an agent nor an affected patient. It is not surprising then that reciprocal verbs do not take the passive—*Sophia is resembled by Alexander.* English contains two verbs *to marry*; one is reciprocal and one is not. In *A Roman Catholic priest married the young couple,* the verb is clearly not reciprocal and this sentence can be turned into a passive—*The young couple was married by a Roman Catholic priest.* In *Othello married Desdemona,* however, the verb is reciprocal and the passive is impossible for most speakers. Reciprocal verbs do not co-occur with the passive because in the passive there is typically an agent (or instrument) and an affected party. That dichotomy simply doesn't exist with reciprocal verbs.

Possession verbs are always stative but some passivize and some do not. *Have* (meaning possess) always rejects the passive and, as a result, constructions expressing inalienable possession never passivize—**A beard is had by Toby; *Two cousins are had by Zia. Possess* is marginally acceptable in the passive— *?That land is possessed by the Jones family. Own*, however, passivizes readily— *This corporation is owned by a billionaire; That cabin is owned by a recluse.*

GET PASSIVE

Increasingly, English speakers are using a passive construction that exploits some form of *get* as its auxiliary. Written examples of the so-called **get passive** date back to the middle of the eighteenth century and it is undoubtedly older than that in the spoken language (Givón and Yang, 1994). The *get* passive is especially common in colloquial speech. It is most often used when the subject of the sentence suffers adversely as a result of the action. One study has shown that in spoken English about 80% of *get* passives reflect an adverse effect upon the subject, as opposed to only 40% of *be* passives. (These data are from an unpublished 1986 study by R. Herold, cited in Givón and Yang.)

*My dog **got** bitten by a snake.*

*They **got** mugged by some teenagers.*

*The unruly students **got** punished.*

*My wife **got** fired.*

The following passages are from *The Bone People*, a novel by New Zealander Keri Hulme (1986). (Boldface added.)

"You'll probably **get sued** by the shop owners, or their insurance people. He's smashed in nearly all the glass fronts along Whitau street." (p. 306)

"He's too young to prosecute, Joe, but it's about time something **got done**." (p. 306)

But she hadn't been hit there. She hadn't **got hurt** at all. (p. 187)

Even the passive *got done* suggests an adverse result; the speaker is recommending that disciplinary action be taken against a young vandal.

Even when a subject does not suffer adversely, the *get* passive usually suggests that the subject has been truly affected by the action. *Bill got promoted last week* and *The hikers got rescued* are acceptable sentences but *??Tina got seen* is very odd unless Tina was doing something surreptitiously. (*Tina was seen* is fine in any context, however.)

In a few cases the *get* passive is preferable to the *be* passive. For most speakers, *Crystal got married last week* is more natural than *Crystal was married last week.*

It is not always easy to tell a passive construction from a copula plus a subject complement. This is because past participle forms often function as adjectives—*the **broken** window, a **stolen** necklace, **unfinished** business, a **tattered** coat, **bleached** hair*, etc. When a construction like *They were married* is considered out of context, it is impossible to determine whether *married* is functioning as a predicate adjective noting a married state or as part of a passive construction that is describing an activity. Usually the discourse context will make things clear, e.g., *They were married, but they acted like boyfriend and girlfriend* versus *They were married in a beautiful garden.*

Because the subject of the passive is usually the direct object of the corresponding active, the passive subject is typically a patient. But there are exceptions to this pattern. When the verb is ditransitive, two objects are available, either of which could theoretically become the subject of a corresponding passive. Thus, *Scott loaned Michelle a bike* yields two passives—*A bike was loaned to Michelle by Scott* and *Michelle was loaned a bike by Scott.* (Note that when the direct object becomes the subject of the passive, the indirect object must occur in a prepositional phrase.) But indirect objects that can be paraphrased as *for* prepositional phrases do not become the subjects of passives. *Jerry baked Elly a cake* and *Jerry baked a cake for Elly* yield a passive that most speakers find unacceptable—**Elly was baked a cake by Jerry.* Similarly, *Mary built the kids a sandbox* yields the infelicitous **The kids were built a sandbox by Mary.*

When the active sentence contains no object, i.e., the verb is intransitive, the object of a preposition can sometimes become the subject of a corresponding passive, e.g., *Someone slept in this bed last night. / This bed was slept in by someone last night.*

PASSIVES WITH NO CORRESPONDING ACTIVE

There seem to be a few passives that have no corresponding active.

Bugsy is reputed to be a gangster.

James is rumored to be a CIA agent.

A sentence like *My uncle is wanted by the police* is also interesting in this regard. While we can say *The police want my uncle*, this active does not carry quite the same meaning as its passive counterpart. In fact *wanted* has taken on a life of its own, even appearing as a descriptive adjective on "wanted" posters.

THE PASSIVE IN DISCOURSE

When you consider two sentences like *The cat chased the rat* and *The rat was chased by the cat*, there seems to be little if any difference in meaning. Both contain the agent *the cat*, the affected party *the rat*, and the action *chased*. Given the no synonymy rule, why does English have two related constructions that appear to communicate the same meaning?

There are a number of different discourse reasons for the existence of the passive. One important function of the passive is maintaining the topic of a discourse. As you have already seen, once an entity has been introduced as a topic, a speaker will try to keep that topic in subject position. Consider the following narrative.

> My daughter Alice works in a bank. Last week she **was** called to the supervisor's office because a customer had complained about her behavior. Alice **was** not allowed to defend herself. She **was** suspended for a week without pay. Of course she **was** shocked by this callous treatment.

Alice is obviously the topic of this little story. Once Alice is introduced in the first sentence, the passive is used to maintain Alice as the subject (and thus topic) of the next four sentences.

Related to the issue of topic is the egocentrism of human beings. Humans like to talk about themselves and other humans. We are likely to make a human the subject of a sentence even when there is no topic to be maintained. *A man was hit by a bus* is a more natural utterance than *A bus hit a man*. The passive allows us to make this human the subject of the sentence even though he is not an agent.

Agentless Passives

While agents are usually subjects, they can appear in prepositional phrases as well. If a passive contains an agent, causer, or instrument, that role will expressed by the NP in a *by* prepositional phrase—*Timmy was saved by his dog.* But, in fact, most English passives contain no such prepositional phrase. These constructions are called **agentless passives,** since the agent/causer/instrument is unspecified—*My car was vandalized.* (From now on I will simply refer to an agent, causer, or instrument in the passive as the agent.) A number of linguists have studied passives in written texts and media broadcasts and have found that between 80% and 85% of English passives are agentless. Since most passives are agentless, we can conclude that speakers typically use the passive to omit the agent.

Often the agent is omitted simply because it is unknown.

> My cousin was mugged yesterday.

> The car door was scratched last night.

> My great-grandfather was wounded in the Civil War.

The agent is also omitted when it is irrelevant to the speaker, indefinite, or obvious from the rest of the discourse. When the doctor's husband says, "She was called to the hospital at midnight," <u>who</u> called is irrelevant, even if caller's identity is known. When Miamians say "Yuca can be bought at any Cuban grocery," the omitted agent is the nonspecific indefinite "by anyone." Often the agent is obvious from the rest of the sentence or discourse—*An elephant fell on her and she **was killed** instantly; He stepped in front of the train and **was crushed***.

The agentless passive has other related functions as well. Sometimes the agent is known but deliberately omitted in order to avoid assigning or taking responsibility—*An important file was misplaced; The clothes were left in the dryer.* The Watergate scandal produced the weak admission that "Mistakes were made."

For scientific and technical writers, who are required by editorial convention to suppress the first and second person pronouns, the agentless passive is an important linguistic tool. The following passages are from a highly technical computer science article (Lui and Layland, 1973). (Boldface added.)

The deadline of a request **is defined** to be the time of the next request. (p. 49)

None of the computation requested . . . **was carried** out before *T*. (p. 57)

Some of these tasks **are executed** in response to events. (p. 47)

When an agent or causer does occur in a passive, it is almost always new information. Such constructions often appear as answers to questions.

What happened to your avocado tree? Oh, it was damaged by the wind.

Because *by* prepositional phrases in passives usually carry new information, we very rarely find pronouns acting as agents in passives. (Remember that pronouns always express given information.) Sentences like *?Cynthia was hurt by me* and *?The city was destroyed by it* are odd precisely because we don't expect given information in these positions.

The passive, especially the agentless passive, is ubiquitous in English. It is an extremely useful syntactic tool. I am, therefore, baffled by teachers and editors who insist that writers should not use the passive and am annoyed by computer grammar-checkers that mark passive constructions as errors. College students most often write nonfiction essays, and Givón (1993b, p. 53) has demonstrated that, among professional writers, this type of essay contains even <u>more</u> passives than fiction writing or newspaper reporting. Nevertheless, the academy sometimes discourages the use of the passive in just this context.

I suspect that this anti-passive bias stems in part from undergraduate student writing in which the full passive (including the *by* prepositional phrase) is used in a stilted fashion. Including a first person agent in an English passive is always awkward, since the agent is almost always new information, but novice writers often generate infelicitous sentences like *?The computations were made by me.* However, if over 80% of our spoken passives are agentless, it is reasonable to assume that a significant number of our written passives will be agentless as well. Proscribing the passive altogether in student or professional writing simply generates bad prose.

Constructions That Are Active in Form and Passive in Meaning

There are some active constructions in English that behave very much like passives. In one type the agent is omitted altogether—*Cotton washes well; Tangerines peel nicely; These shirts iron easily.* Note that in these sentences the subjects are patients, not agents, despite the normally transitive verbs. Clearly, cotton cannot wash anything, nor can shirts iron. Although these sentences do not have the verb morphology required of passives, they resemble passive sentences in some interesting ways. Unlike normal active sentences, some of the sentences above can be turned into passives by retaining the original NP in subject position—*These shirts can be ironed easily.* Unlike the subjects of normal transitive, active sentences, the subjects of these sentences are affected by the action of the verb. These constructions are sometimes called **pseudo-passives.**

English speakers also use a generic *they* as a subject in cases in which the agent is unknown, unimportant, or conceptually complex—*They're paving over Paradise; They buried my grandfather last week; They're repairing the old train station.* In each of these cases no NP specifying *they* has been previously introduced into the discourse; thus, *they* does not have anaphoric reference. Nonanaphoric *they* constructions and agentless passives have similar functions in that they both allow us to talk about events without specifying an agent. Remember, however, that a true passive must be passive in <u>form</u>.

WORD ORDER AND THE PASSIVE

The passive frequently co-occurs with the perfect and somewhat less frequently with the progressive. While the conventional passive construction very rarely occurs with both the perfect and progressive, *get* passives appear more frequently in this context—*We have been getting burglarized every Friday night; I have been getting stopped by the police [whenever I go out].*

The passive always comes last in the VP and, as a result, its past participle always attaches to the last verb.

Stephanie | has | | be | en | chos | en | for the job.

In the following sentences, the component parts of the perfect are capitalized, the component parts of the progressive are double underlined, and the component parts of the passive are in bold.

*Jimmy <u>is</u> **be<u>ing</u>** tormented by his little sister.*

*I HAVE **beEN** promoted.*

*The machines <u>are</u> **being** repaired by a professional.*

Remember that the first verb always carries the tense. If there is a perfect construction, it precedes the progressive and/or passive constructions; if there is a progressive, it precedes the passive. In other words, the order is always **perfect + progressive + passive.**

Primary Auxiliaries and the Lexical Verb

The *have* of the perfect, the *be* of the progressive, and the *be* of the passive are called **primary auxiliaries.** These auxiliaries have no meaning apart from their participation in these constructions.

In a sentence, auxiliary verbs are always followed by a **lexical verb.** There are a very small number of auxiliary verbs in English, but lexical verbs number in the thousands. The *Collins English Dictionary* lists 14,190 different verbs (Miller and Fellbaum, 1992, p. 214) and all but a few of these are lexical.

Primary auxiliaries have no independent semantic content, and, as you will see later, modal auxiliaries express a somewhat limited range of meanings. Lexical verbs, however, communicate an extraordinary number of meanings as a class, and individual verbs tend to be semantically complex as well. A single verb form may have five or six different but related meanings. Consider a verb like *run.*

Margot ran to the store.	*The engine is running.*
The kids ran him ragged.	*The baby's nose is running.*
The canoeist ran the rapids.	*My uncle runs a grocery store.*
The doctor is running late.	*Gore is running for President.*

A group of verbs that is unrelated in terms of form may be very closely related semantically. All of the following verbs refer to walking; they differ only in the style of gait they describe—*stroll, amble, saunter, shuffle, stagger, stride, strut, tiptoe, march, limp, stomp.* Verbs can refer to a tremendous variety of speaking styles—*talk, whisper, chatter, whine, mumble, yell, babble,* as well as many ways of interacting verbally with another person—*converse, argue, gossip, gab, quibble, rap, chat, yak, debate.*

The lexical verb is always the last verb in the verb phrase. If there is only one verb in the verb phrase, it is a lexical verb. You are probably accustomed to calling the lexical verb the "main" verb. This is risky, however, because, as you will see later, every clause in a sentence has a lexical verb, but the sentence itself has only one main verb. In the following sentences, the verbs in boldface are lexical.

*Bert has been **working** for hours.*

*Sandy **has** two bicycles.*

*Michelle has been **hired** by a prestigious firm.*

*Billy has **had** the measles.*

*Donna is being **tormented** by her boss.*

*My uncle is **being** polite.*

*I **am** a social worker.*

*Boris **loves** Shakespeare.*

Remember that auxiliary *be* and auxiliary *have* are completely different from lexical *be* and *have*; thus, two *haves* or two *bes* can occur in the same utterance— *Mick is being obnoxious; Mary Jane has had trouble with her car.*

Many of the sentences cited as examples above are actually somewhat artificial. In informal speech, most primary auxiliaries are contracted. This means that in terms of pronunciation the auxiliary is reduced to its final consonant and is attached to the subject.

Auxiliary	Contracted form
am	I**'m** being eaten by mosquitoes.
is	Dudley**'s** leaving the party now.
are	They**'re** eating all your pretzels.
was	[no contracted form]
were	[no contracted form]
has	She**'s** finished her project.
have	We**'ve** seen that movie
had	They**'d** been there before.

In the following transcription of actual speech, the speaker is describing a short film clip s/he has just seen. Each primary auxiliary is contracted. (Boldface added; all but the final ellipses are in the original.)

He**'s** very deliberately . . . plucking the . . the um . . . the pears off the tree, . . . and . . . you know you hear this . . . a sh:arp little crunch as . . he pulls each one off, and he**'s** doing it . . very slowly, and putting them in . . . [breath] . . . his apron. . . . [H]e**'d** never make it as a fruitpicker. (Tannen, 1984b, p. 35)

Lexical verb *be* can be contracted in exactly the same ways that primary auxiliary *be* can—*She's a lawyer; We're angry.* Americans rarely contract lexical verb *have,* but British speakers often do so—*I've no money today; They've no hope whatsoever.*

Multi-Word Lexical Verbs

Before I launch into a discussion of multi-word lexical verbs, let me briefly explain **prepositions.** Prepositions constitute a class of short function words that combine with NPs to make prepositional phrases like *I put the book **on the table*** and *The baby threw my hat **in the toilet**.* Many prepositions express location or direction—*in, on, at, to, through, over, under, above, around,* etc. Typically a preposition is followed by an NP that functions as its object—*Sam put the cows in **the barn**.* Prepositions typically occur in modifying phrases, i.e., adverb phrases and adjective phrases.

Over time, some prepositions have become semantically attached to preceding verbs, creating new multi-word verbs with new meanings. When the preposition becomes figuratively attached in this way, it is called a **verb particle** and the entire construction is called a **multi-word verb** (or sometimes a **phrasal verb**). Some multi-word verbs have one particle and some have two.

*The police **tracked down** the killer.*

*Nina **gave back** the book.*

*The baby **threw up** her lunch.*

*Art **chewed out** his employees.*

*Brian **gave up on** his son.*

*These plans don't **conform to** our standards.*

*Grace **looks down on** her relatives.*

*The newspaper **hinted at** scandal.*

*Ted **broke in on** their conversation.*

In a sentence like *Donna turned out the light,* the lexical verb is *turned out* and the direct object is *the light.* In *Charlotte called on Emily, called on* is the lexical verb and *Emily* is the direct object.

Some multi-word verbs are very old. *Give up* as in *She gave up her title* appears in print as early as the twelfth century; *put on* (*He put on his clothes*) and *blow out* (*She blew out the candle*) date back to the fourteenth century. *Throw out* developed in the sixteenth century and *give in* meaning "to yield" in the seventeenth. As contemporary as it sounds, *fork over* as in *May forked over the money* dates back to the nineteenth century. The creation of multi-word verbs continues unabated—*Jimmy grossed out his friends; Anne ripped off her employer; Hannah blew off her homework.*

Verb particles derive from prepositions and in some multi-word verbs, the particle retains a great deal of its original prepositional meaning. *Out* is used quite literally in *The dentist took **out** three teeth* and *Susan has put **out** the cat,* and a bit less literally in *Mark has thrown **out** your comic books.* The particle *out* is often added to verbs to denote <u>removal</u>—*yank* versus *yank out, pull* versus *pull out, pry* versus *pry out, tear* versus *tear out.* But *out* has lost its prepositional meaning in *I can't figure **out** this problem* and *I found **out** her secret.* Even when a particle loses its literal prepositional meaning, however, it is often possible to see a metaphorical connection between the original preposition and the current particle. While the preposition *down* literally indicates a direction, *down* is often used in expressions to suggest the result of a social or psychological decline—*down and out, down in the dumps.* In these contexts *down* always has a negative connotation. In *George is always putting down his partner, put down* means to denigrate or insult. In *They turned down my request, turn down* means to reject. Clearly, these constructions are metaphorically linked to others in which *down* has taken on a strongly negative meaning. Many verb particles exploit this kind of metaphor.

Some verb particles have specialized meanings. While the particle *up* in *He picked up the baby* retains the directional meaning of preposition *up, up* means something very different in *She cleaned up the room.* Here particle *up* means "completely or thoroughly." A number of verbs exploit *up* in this way—*sweep up, wash up, burn up, tie up, close up, rip up, fix up, cover up, use up,* etc. Something that is *used up* has been used to the point of exhaustion; something that has *burned* may or not be totally consumed, but something that has *burned up* most assuredly is. As you saw above, many languages exploit the perfect to indicate that an event or action is complete; in English the particle *up* performs much the same function.

MOVABLE PARTICLES

There are two distinct types of multi-word verbs. In the first type the verb particle can move to a position after the direct object. Any preposition-like word that can move in this fashion is a verb particle.

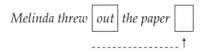

The particles that are most likely to be movable are *out, up, down, over,* and *off,* although others do move on occasion.

*He drove **out** everyone else./ He drove everyone else **out.***

*Azar put **out** the light. / Azar put the light **out.***

*They blew **up** the dam./ They blew the dam **up.***

*They gave **up** the hostage./ They gave the hostage **up.***

*Teresa swept **up** the debris./ Teresa swept the debris **up**.*

*You screwed **up** my wiring. / You screwed my wiring **up**.*

*They burned **down** the house./ They burned the house **down**.*

*Dan put **down** the baby./ Dan put the baby **down**.*

*They tracked **down** the killer./ They tracked the killer **down**.*

*She looked **over** the exams./ She looked the exams **over**.*

*Paul forked **over** the money./Paul forked the money **over**.*

*They ripped **off** their friend./ They ripped their friend **off**.*

*He took **off** his clothes./ He took his clothes **off**.*

*You must break **in** a new car./ You must break a new car **in**.*

Pronouns have an interesting effect on movable particles. When the direct object of a multi-word verb is a pronoun, the particle must appear after the direct object. *Linda threw out the paper* is fine but **Linda threw out it* is ungrammatical for most speakers. In this case, the particle must be moved—*Linda threw it out.* You will recall that we witnessed this same phenomenon in ditransitive constructions with pronoun direct objects. Since pronouns typically express given information and since new information usually appears last in the sentence, pronouns resist occupying final position.

UNMOVABLE PARTICLES

In the second type of multi-word verb, the particle does not move. In these cases, it is not always easy to distinguish a verb plus particle construction from a verb plus prepositional phrase construction. Usually in a verb phrase containing an unmovable particle, the particle has little in common semantically with the preposition from which it derives. In *Angela called on her grandparents, on* has lost its spatial meaning. (Clearly, Angela did not stand on top of her grandparents and call.) Unmovable particles are usually more stressed in speech than movable particles but the difference is very subtle. See if you can perceive a stress difference in *She threw on her clothes* versus *She called on her grandmother.* The most common unmovable particles are *on, of, to, for,* and *at.*

*Michaela insisted **on** imported beer.*

*I don't approve **of** your behavior.*

*Eve commented **on** Adam's good manners.*

*They must conform **to** our standards.*

*I object **to** your inference.*

*Judith applied **for** a post abroad.*

*The reported hinted **at** scandal.*

*The candidate called **for** a referendum.*

*That leather gives **off** an unpleasant odor.* (*Off* may be movable for some speakers.)

Turn into is a multi-word copula—*The prince turned into a frog; My little girl has turned into a teenager. Turn into* can be paraphrased with *become,* although *turn into* usually suggests a more dramatic transformation.

There are some multi-word verbs containing two particles. Multiple particles never move.

*They will not put **up with** her arrogance.*

*I want to catch **up on** my reading.*

*The operator broke **in on** my telephone call.*

*His girlfriend walked **out on** him.*

*My roommate looks **down on** everyone.*

*Children look **up to** professional athletes.*

*We ran **out of** milk.*

*Istvan looks **out for** his brother.*

*The kids must cut **down on** expenses.*

Sometimes the same verb plus particle construction will have different meanings in different contexts. *Rip off* can mean to remove completely—*She ripped off the sleeves,* and it can also mean *steal* or *steal from*—*She ripped off that stereo; She ripped off her brother.* Transitive *give up* means to relinquish something—*He gave up his inheritance,* while intransitive *give up* means to surrender or cease—*The fugitive gave up; I couldn't open the child-proof container so I gave up.* Transitive *take off* means to remove—*The child took off his shirt,* while intransitive *take off* means to leave or become airborne—*The kids took off; The plane took off.*

IDENTIFYING MULTI-WORD VERBS

Because multi-word verbs derive from old prepositional phrase constructions, it is not always easy to distinguish a verb plus particle from a verb plus prepositional phrase. A movable particle is, of course, a definitive diagnostic. If the preposition-like word moves to a position after the following NP, it is a particle.

Paraphrasing is also a useful diagnostic tool. Verb plus particle constructions can often (but not always) be replaced by a single-word lexical verb.

conform to	*meet*	*hint at*	*suggest*
put out	*extinguish*	*give in*	*yield*
call on	*visit*	*give up*	*relinquish*
call up	*telephone*	*break in on*	*interrupt*
throw up	*vomit*	*look down on*	*disdain*
give back	*return*	*look up to*	*admire*
put down	*denigrate*	*put up with*	*tolerate*
take off	*remove/leave*		

(It is interesting to note that most multi-word verbs contain Old English verb heads, e.g., *give, blow, throw, rip,* but their single word counterparts are often words borrowed from French or Latin, e.g., *extinguish, visit, vomit, relinquish.* This is some measure of just how "native" verb particle constructions are.)

If a given verb routinely occurs with a given preposition-like form, it is reasonable to treat that form as a particle. *Apply* frequently co-occurs with *for, approve* frequently co-occurs with *of,* and *object* almost always co-occurs with *to.* If a verb that is normally transitive is followed directly by a preposition-like word (instead of an NP), that word is probably a particle, as in *give up* and *give in, throw up* and *throw out, put away* and *put up with.* In addition, there are some verb heads that participate in a great many different multi-word constructions.

blow	*blow up, blow out, blow down, blow over, blow off*
throw	*throw out, throw up, throw down, throw in* (e.g., *The boxer threw in the towel.*)
look	*look up, look up to, look over, look down on, look in on*
give	*give up, give in, give away, give off, give out*
put	*put out, put up with, put down, put in* (e.g., *The canoeists put in at the bridge.*)
burn	*burn up, burn out, burn down, burn through*
call	*call up, call on, call for, call in* (e.g., *He called in his pledge* or *She called in the chips.*)

While some of these verbs can be followed by prepositions as well as particles, the presence of one of them in a construction suggests that you should employ another test for verb particle status.

In some cases, however, it is not at all clear how a construction should be categorized. Should *talk to* be considered a multi-word verb or a verb plus preposition? *Talk* often co-occurs with *to* but it can also be accompanied by *with, about,* or nothing at all. *Talk to* cannot be readily replaced by a single verb paraphrase and the *to* is not movable. On the other hand, *to* has lost much of its spatial meaning in this construction. When *to* occurs as a full-fledged preposition it usually expresses a physical goal—*Ida is going to Prague; Sandra is going to the store.* In *The CEO talked to her staff,* that sense of goal is significantly diminished. The evolution of preposition to particle represents a continuum and *talk to* seems to fall somewhere near the middle.

The classic verb particle conundrum is this:

> Why does a match *burn out*, a building *burn down*, and paper *burn up*?

Modality

Examples in grammar books do not constitute a representative sample of actual human speech. Textbook examples tend to reflect statements of fact—*The little girl threw the ball over the wall; The cat chased the rat; Ella gave the dog a bone.* But we do so much more than that with language; we speculate, we hedge, we predict, we suggest, we order, we demand, we hope, we want, etc.

The abstract term **modality** is used to refer to these kinds of meanings in language. Modality has nothing to do with form; many different kinds of constructions can be used to express modality, including lexical verbs, modal auxiliaries, semi-auxiliaries, adverbs, the imperative mood, and the subjunctive mood. Modality in English sentences is usually divided into two general types—epistemic and deontic.

EPISTEMIC MODALITY IN GENERAL

The term *epistemic* is related to the word *epistemology* (theories of knowing). Epistemic modality encompasses all the ways in which speakers indicate their degree of commitment to the truth of a given proposition. It allows speakers to indicate that they are certain about something, unsure about it, or deem it impossible. (Some grammarians use the terms "possibility" and "necessity" to describe these meanings.) English has a whole range of strategies for communicating this kind of information.

Sometimes we use nonlinguistic cues to communicate epistemic modality. If you tell someone that your sister is a financial planner, but you use quotation marks in the air as you say "financial planner," your hearer will know that you don't see your sister as the real thing. Sarcasm in the voice has a similar effect. What seems to be a positive statement of fact, "She's very efficient," can become an indictment when said sarcastically.

We often preface assertions with expressions like *I **think/believe/assume/guess/suppose/hear** that Joan is taking the job.* Here the speaker is unwilling to make the unqualified assertion *Joan is taking the job;* instead, s/he is hedging. By prefacing the assertion with an expression like *I hear that...* , the speaker makes someone else the source of the information; by using *I assume, I guess,* or *I suppose,* s/he indicates that this proposition is a deduction and not a known fact. *I think* and *I believe* reveal that the proposition is personal opinion. In each of these sentences, epistemic modality is being expressed by the lexical verb. In expressions like *I am sure/positive/certain that Joan will take the job* and *It is likely/possible/conceivable/doubtful that Joan will take the job,* the predicate adjective expresses epistemic modality.

Sentence modifiers can also express epistemic modality. These constructions will be discussed more fully Chapter 4.

Maybe it will rain tomorrow.

Supposedly, he composed it himself.

Allegedly, she has robbed four banks.

In his book *Mood and Modality,* F. R. Palmer (1986, p. 67) describes modality in the Tuyuca language of Brazil and Columbia. Tuyuca speakers mark their verbs to indicate what kind of evidence exists for the assertion they are making. A verb can be marked to indicate visual evidence (the speaker saw the event being described), aural evidence (the speaker heard the event but didn't see it), indirect physical evidence (the speaker saw physical signs that the event took place), second-hand account (someone told the speaker the event took place), or a reasonable assumption (the speaker assumes the event took place). We can do all of this in English, of course, but our strategies are far wordier.

DEONTIC MODALITY IN GENERAL

Like the term *epistemic,* **deontic** is a semantic label. It derives from the Greek word *deontology* which refers to "the science of duty." And like epistemic modality, deontic modality goes beyond the simple proposition. Deontic modality involves language and potential action; when speakers order, promise, or place an obligation on someone, they usually exploit linguistic forms that express deontic modality. (Deontic modality is sometimes called **root** modality because, historically, the epistemic meanings derive from the deontic.)

Directives represent one important type of deontic modality. A directive is any utterance in which a speaker tries to get someone else to behave in a particular way. Directives take many forms, as the examples below indicate.

I want you to get your feet off the coffee table.

You should help Deanna fix that tire.

These errors must be corrected.

I insist that you leave.

Sit down, shut up, and eat your spinach.

Don't be late.

Please have some more pie.

You might call me when the shipment arrives.

STOP

No smoking.

Any expression of **volition** also encodes deontic modality. *Volition* includes wanting, willingness, intention, and wishing. Sentences that express promises and threats are also volitional.

Adam wants to taste tripe.

I promise to take you to the zoo.

I will wash the dishes later.

My daughter insists on dating that idiot.

I am going to repair the roof next week.

I wish to leave.

I'll punish you if you do that again.

As a rule, in an active sentence deontic meanings attach only to animate, usually human, subjects. Epistemic modality can coexist with any kind of subject.

A common way to express modality of any sort is through the use of modal and semi-auxiliaries.

MODAL AUXILIARIES

Modal auxiliaries represent a very special class of verbs in English. These odd verbs predate even Old English; their peculiarities are the result of linguistic events in the ancient Germanic languages (ca. 500 B.C.). All the other major modern Germanic languages (Dutch, Swedish, Danish, Norwegian, and German) have these same auxiliaries. In contrast to the primary auxiliaries *be* and *have*, modal auxiliaries are semantically rich and inflectionally impoverished. Modal auxiliaries carry no third person present {-s} ending (*Bruce cans go now* is absolutely ungrammatical) and they have no past participle forms, no present participle forms, and no infinitive forms.

Most modals do have distinct past tense forms, however. While you may find this counter-intuitive, the past tense of *can* is *could*, the past tense of *will* is *would*, the past tense of *shall* is *should*, and the past tense of *may* is *might*. Remember that tense is simply a matter of <u>form</u>, not meaning. The {-d} or {-t} ending on these words is simply a manifestation of the typical {-ed} past tense inflection, and all of these forms date back to Old English. *Must* was an Old English past tense form; the corresponding present tense *mot-* was lost during

Middle English times. *Ought* was the past tense form of the Old English verb meaning *to own* from which Modern English *owe* is derived. *Ought to* is the only two-word modal auxiliary.

Present tense form	Past tense form
will	would
can	could
shall	should
may	might
[no form exists]	must
[no form exists]	ought to

Will and *would* are the only modals that are routinely contracted in speech—*I'll come over later; I'd have been here sooner [if my car hadn't broken down].*

Modal Auxiliaries and Epistemic Modality

Among the most common sources of epistemic modality in English are the modal auxiliaries *can, could, should, will, may, might, must,* and *ought to.* Taken as a group, these modal auxiliaries express a whole range of epistemic modality. When Cory's wife says "That might be Cory at the door," she is expressing doubt. When she says "That should be Cory at the door," she communicates greater certainty; maybe Cory always gets home at this time. When she says, "That must be Cory at the door," she is indicating that the evidence is overwhelming; maybe no one else has a key. Epistemic modals express meanings that range from slight possibility to absolute certainty.

It **might** rain tomorrow.

Angelo **may** come to the party.

We **ought to** be in Cleveland by 10 P.M.

The office **should** be open by now.

Kerry **must** have taken the folder home.

The airport **can't** be closed!

That **will** be Zulah at the door.

Epistemic *can* usually occurs only in questions, negatives, or passives; **That can be Zulah* and **It can be midnight* are ungrammatical for most speakers. *Will* expresses very strong epistemic modality, to the point that it <u>predicts</u>. *Would* occasionally occurs in epistemic occurrences. If someone asks you who the best plumber in town is you might reply "Oh, that would be my Uncle Walter." *Shall* is never used epistemically.

Modal Auxiliaries and Deontic Modality

Most of the modal auxiliaries discussed above can also express meanings that are decidedly non-epistemic. There is a marked difference in the meaning of *must* in *That must be Cory* and *You must clean your room*. In the second sentence the speaker is expressing deontic modality.

Modal Auxiliaries Used in Directives. The directive is an important subcategory of deontic modality. As you saw above, the term directive refers to all of the strategies that speakers use to direct the behavior of someone else. Modal auxiliaries are especially important in this regard; they can be used to order, insist, reprimand, lay an obligation, make a suggestion, and give permission. The same modal can appear in different types of directives.

*You **will** put that candy down!*	[an order]
*You **must** pay for your food.*	[strong obligation]
*She **should** help her sister.*	[obligation]
*Your partner **should** see this first.*	[suggestion]
*He **ought to** be ashamed.*	[obligation]
*The employer **shall** provide medical benefits.*	[contractual obligation]
*You **might** call me when the package arrives.*	[suggestion]
*You **might** have let me know about this problem.*	[reprimand]
*You **could** have told me in advance.*	[reprimand]
*The kids **can** have some ice cream.*	[permission]
*You **may** not take drum lessons.*	[permission]
***Can** you pass the potatoes?*	[request]

(While prescriptive grammarians argue that only *may* can be used for permission, *can* has supplanted *may,* even in the speech of highly educated speakers.)

American speakers rarely use *shall* in routine conversation or writing. It is a bit more common in British English. Like *should, shall* originally meant "to be obligated," and this meaning persisted well into Modern English times. This use is ubiquitous in the King James version of the Bible and as a result many contemporary English speakers are familiar with this older meaning of *shall.*

Thou shalt not kill.

Thou shalt not commit adultery.

Thou shalt not steal. (Exodus 20:13–15)

While this deontic use of *shall* has faded in most conversational contexts, it is still widely used in legal and contract language and it indicates that the subject of the sentence has an absolute obligation to act (or not act), e.g., *The defendant shall pay the plaintiff the sum of $37,000.*

While the modals *should, must,* and *ought to* can express both epistemic and deontic modality, they are most often used to express deontic modality. A study of the use of modals in British and Australian speech and writing and American writing revealed that the deontic uses of these auxiliaries far outnumber the epistemic uses (Collins, 1991). A particularly dramatic statistic shows American writers using *should* deontically 73% of the time and epistemically 5% of the time (p. 161). The remaining instances of *should* reflected other uses.

There is an interesting semantic parallel between modals in their epistemic and deontic modes. Those modals that express the strongest sense of obligation in deontic mode are also the modals that express the strongest likelihood in epistemic mode (Bybee, 1994, p. 195).

You must leave by noon. / That must be Mom at the door.

You should leave by noon. / That should be Mom at the door.

You might mail me the results. / That might be Mom at the door.

Modal Auxiliaries Used to Express Volition and Commitment. Speakers also direct their own behavior by expressing willingness and making promises. The modal auxiliary *will* actually derives from an Old English lexical verb *wille,* which literally meant "to want." In some dialects *wille* was pronounced and spelled *wolle,* which is the source of the [o] sound in Modern English *won't.* Originally *will* was used only to express volition; it was not a future marker in any way. But wants are always projected into the future; if you want something, you don't yet have it. For this reason, over many centuries *will* also took on the role of predicting. But even in Modern English *will* is more often used to express volition than simple future time. This is especially obvious in negatives. Compare *It won't rain tomorrow* with *We asked Martha to help us but she won't.* In the first example *won't* (*will not*) simply expresses a prediction, but in the second example it expresses a refusal. In a sentence like *I'll clean up the mess,* the speaker is not really predicting that s/he will clean but is expressing a willingness to do the job.

Stressed *will* can be used to express very strong volition on the part of the subject of the sentence—*My daughter <u>will</u> play in the street even though I punish her.* (In other words, she insists on doing it.) Directive *will* also expresses strong volition but it is the volition of the speaker that is at issue, not that of the subject—*You <u>will</u>* finish your homework!

We routinely use modal auxiliary *will* to make commitments, promises, and threats. A threat is, after all, simply a promise to do something hurtful. Commitments and promises are always projected into the future, but here, too, prediction is not the primary meaning of *will*. *I'll probably be late* is an epistemic prediction, but *I won't be late* is a promise. When a modal expresses willingness, it often reflects a willingness to do something at the moment of speaking—*I'll dry the dishes for you*. A promise typically expresses willingness to do something in the future; your niece might say "I'll do the dishes later; I promise," but she wouldn't say "I'll dry the dishes for you, I promise," as she picks up the dishtowel.

Modal auxiliaries expressing volition

Strong volition	He <u>will</u> play with matches [even though I punish him].
	You <u>will</u> clean your room [or you'll be grounded].
Willingness & unwillingness	I'll carry those groceries for you.
	She won't help me mow the lawn.
	I'll bring you some ice cream after work.
Promises	I'll take you to the zoo tomorrow.
	We'll fix your computer when we get the parts.
Threats	I'll break your arm [if you touch me].
	I'll scream [if you come any closer].

Dare and Need.   Dare and *need* are modal auxiliaries for some speakers and not for others. Even those who can use them as modals, use them only in negative and interrogative constructions.

*She **dare** not utter a sound.*

***Dare** Jack tell his boss the truth?*

***Need** you play that music so loud?*

*Marsha **needn't** be told.*

Note the lack of a third person {-s} inflection in those sentences in which *dare* or *need* has a third person subject. This is strong evidence that these forms are modal auxiliaries. The modals *dare* and *need* are loosely deontic. A construction like *Felice needs to rent her apartment* does not contain a modal auxiliary (note the third person {-s} ending on *need*), although *need* still has deontic force in this context.

Modal Auxiliaries Used to Express Ability

Not all modal auxiliaries are epistemic or deontic. Since ability is not necessarily an expression of behavior, it is usually treated as a separate semantic category. *Can* and *could* are of course the modals that perform this function.

*Andre **can** speak Ukrainian.*

*I **can** run a marathon.*

*Ricki **can't** roller skate.*

*I **could** skate when I was young.*

There are some constraints on *could* in terms of expressing ability, but we will discuss these later.

Can and *could* are sometimes used in questions to make a polite request. If I ask, "Can you pass the potatoes?" I'm not really asking you to assess your potato-passing skills. I am simply using *can* here to express politeness. The use of *can* or *could* in a question strikes hearers as much softer than a bald imperative like "Pass the potatoes."

Modal Auxiliaries Used to Express Habitual Actions

As you saw in the section on aspect, the habitual is expressed by an imperfect form in many languages. English has no such form, so habitual actions must be expressed in other ways. You've already seen the present tense in this role—*Jake attends the University of Michigan.* Occasionally *will* is used to express present time habitual activities—*First he'll fill his pockets with bread crumbs; then he'll go to the park and feed the pigeons.* The modal *would* expresses habitual action but only in past time—*Each Sunday she would visit her family in the city; He would always end his day with a glass of sherry.* Habitual represents a separate semantic category, so when *will* and *would* express habituality, they are neither epistemic nor deontic.

It is important to remember that each modal auxiliary can potentially express a variety of meanings. It is also important to remember that, while there are a number of modals, there are only a few general semantic categories into which these modals fall. As you have seen, most modals can be used to direct or influence the behavior of others in some way and every modal except *shall*, *need*, and *dare* can express some degree of epistemic modality.

Modals and Word Order

Modals always appear first in the VP—*Pedro **might** have been detained; Claudia **should** have finished the project.* Some grammarians maintain that there can be only one modal auxiliary in a VP. While this may be a rule of edited

English, individuals living in the southeastern United States routinely use two or more modals in a VP. The following sentence, which contains three modal auxiliaries in a row plus a semi-auxiliary, was uttered by a speaker from southeastern North Carolina: "If she might should ought to have to go to the hospital, she's worried about what she'll do with her children."[2] The expression *might could* is extremely common in the South, even among highly educated individuals. *I might could help you with that* expresses both epistemic and deontic modality; it is possible that I will have the ability. As you will see later, some speakers use a second modal to negate *ought to—You shouldn't ought to do that*. This usage is fairly common, although highly informal.

Summary of modal auxiliaries

Epistemic modals

It **will** rain tomorrow.

That **must** be Dad's car.

It **can't** be snowing! [It's June.]

She **should** be home by now.

They **ought to** be done by now.

They **may** enjoy the play.

Marcella **might** be on time.

Ability and habitual modals

I **can't** speak Twi.

Each day she **would** work out.

Deontic modals

He **will** play with matches.

I **will** fix that for you.

You **should** help your sister.

You **ought to** wash your car.

You **can/may** attend the party.

You **might** call me tomorrow.

The plaintiff **shall** honor the contract.

Need Jake be here?

She **dare** not tell them.

SEMI-AUXILIARIES

Modal auxiliaries are very ancient forms and constitute a closed class. More recently, English has admitted into the language a class of "semi-auxiliaries"—constructions that behave very much like modals semantically but that do not share the same grammatical form. Semi-auxiliaries are always lexically complex; they are composed of two or three words and usually end in *to*. With one exception, semi-auxiliaries take the third person {-s} in the present tense and have participle and infinitive forms. As a class, semi-auxiliaries express both epistemic and deontic modality. In the following sentences, the semi-auxiliaries are in boldface.

*Wilbur **is going to** be late.*	*I'll **be able to** come.*
*Yesim **is sure to** succeed.*	*That helicopter **is about to** crash.*
*Your old boyfriend **is bound to** be there.*	*You **have got to** leave.*
*Helge **is supposed to** dust the furniture.*	*Dad **seems to** be upset.*
*Reginald **appears to** be crying.*	*Tobias **has to** finish that project.*
*Maxine **is unlikely to** pass.*	*She **is certain to** fall.*
*You **were supposed to** clean your room.*	*Dahlia **is to** arrive at noon.*

Semi-auxiliaries are highly problematic. They behave inconsistently and somewhat idiosyncratically. One reason for this is that they are relative newcomers. Many semi-auxiliaries have been borrowed from other languages either directly or indirectly. *Have to, have got to,* and *had better* all use native lexical items, but while *be going to* contains native English words, the actual construction is modeled on the French *Je vais* ("I go; I am going"). The words *able, certain,* and *sure* were borrowed from the French, and *seem* and *likely* were borrowed from the Norse (Scandinavians). Some of these words entered into semi-auxiliary constructions early on. *Seem to* and *had to* appear in texts by 1300 and *be sure to* by 1400. But *appear to* and *be able to* don't materialize until the sixteenth century. (For a discussion of the history of these constructions, see T. Th. Visser, Vol. 4, 1978.)

Because they are lexically complex and because they are relatively new constructions, semi-auxiliaries are still in a state of flux. Even highly educated native speakers are sometimes stymied when they attempt to exploit a semi-auxiliary in a particular sentence.

Epistemic Semi-Auxiliaries

Be going to is a widely used semi-auxiliary that has both epistemic and deontic meanings. Epistemic *be going* to is used to predict events, very much like epistemic *will—It is going to snow tomorrow; That chair is going to crack.* If an event is imminent, a speaker will choose *be going to* rather than *will—I'm going to be sick; That car is going to crash. Look out! The baby is going to fall* is perfectly natural, while *??Look out! The baby will fall* is very odd. *Be going to* is usually uttered with the contracted form of *be* followed by a form that is often pronounced *gonna—He's gonna be late.* Although traditional grammar books cite *will* as the auxiliary that expresses future, *be going to* actually projects a stronger sense of futurity than *will* does. A construction that expresses a weak sense of future will be accompanied by an adverb that specifies the time frame. The progressive, for example, can express future time only when it is accompanied by an adverb that delineates the time frame—*I am leaving tomorrow*. A researcher who employed this adverb test discovered that *be going to* has a higher "inherent futuric value" than *will*. In other words, *be going to* was less likely than *will* to be accompanied by an adverb of time (Mindt, 1991, pp. 183–86).

English has a whole set of semi-auxiliaries that express varying degrees of certainty.

It is going to rain tomorrow.

Sylvia was bound to hurt herself.

They were certain to be late.

Pat is sure to love the present.

James is (un)likely to buy the house.

The culprit has (got) to be your sister.

Seem to and *appear to* are also semi-auxiliaries that express degrees of certainty or, more accurately, uncertainty. These semi-auxiliaries share the same meanings as their homophones copula *seem* and copula *appear*. But *seem to* and *appear to* are semi-auxiliaries and they can co-occur with any kind of lexical verb, including some copulas.

Harold seems to be unhappy.

This milk seems to be getting sour.

Your brother appears to be sleeping.

Helen appears to hate her job.

Tran Le seems to have recovered.

Deontic Semi-Auxiliaries

Semi-auxiliaries express roughly the same range of deontic meanings that we found among modals. Although semi-auxiliaries and modal auxiliaries look very different and have very different histories, combined they represent a relatively unified semantic system.

Semi-Auxiliaries Used to Express Obligation.   *Have to* and *have got to* are used deontically in directives and other contexts in which obligation is being expressed.

You have to clean the garage today.

You have got to talk louder.

Kyle has to move his car.

Had better is an oddly constructed semi-auxiliary that is used in softer directives—*You **had better** leave now*. The contracted form, as in *You'**d better** leave*, is often further contracted to *You **better** leave*. Some speakers can use the superlative form of *better* as in *You'**d best** finish your lunch*.

Be to can be used in a directive—*You are to clean your room immediately!* It is also used to communicate a scheduled event—*Adrienne is to arrive at noon*. In this second usage it resembles the simple present—*Adrienne arrives at noon*. The difference is that the semi-auxiliary places a hint of obligation on the subject of the scheduled event. Adrienne is not only scheduled to arrive at noon, she has some obligation to do so. This is why inanimate subjects sound odd with *be to* constructions—*?The bus is to arrive at noon*.

Be supposed to is another semi-auxiliary that lays an obligation, although that obligation is not necessarily imposed by the speaker.

Betsy **is supposed to** file these reports.

You **were supposed to** be here by 10 A.M.

We **are supposed to** mail our tax returns by April 15.

Be sure to and *be certain to* are often used to reinforce deontic modality in imperatives—*Be sure to lock the door*. (Imperatives will be explained shortly.)

Semi-Auxiliaries Used to Express Volition, Commitment, and Threats. *Be going to* can be used deontically as well as epistemically. In *I am going to finish the project later,* the speaker is making a promise or a commitment, not a prediction. A woman who is standing on a narrow ledge might yell, "I am going to fall" (epistemic) or "I am going to jump" (volitional deontic). A speaker who yells "I'm going to call the police if you don't leave" is using the semi-auxiliary deontically to make a threat.

Semi-Auxiliary Used to Express Ability

Just as there is a set of modal auxiliaries that express ability, there is a semi-auxiliary that carries this meaning—*Mbola **is able to** read Latin; My daughter **is able to** swim*. Like *can* and *could, be able to* expresses physical ability—*She is able to run a mile in five minutes*, a mental or intellectual ability—*Bob is able to multiply large numbers in his head*, or a simple lack of constraints—*I am able to help you now*. *Be able to* is often used in conjunction with modal auxiliary *will* to indicate a future lack of constraints—*I will **be able to** help you with the laundry later*.

The Habitual Semi-Auxiliary

Used to is the habitual semi-auxiliary. It has only one function in English, to refer to habitual activities or states that existed in past time but have ceased to exist. *Used to* is never used to refer to a single event—**He used to die*. This semi-auxiliary represents the past time equivalent of the present habitual construction—*I ride horses; I used to ride horses*.

Semi-Auxiliaries and Discourse

Despite the fact that semi-auxiliaries are extremely common in English, traditional grammars often ignore them altogether. This is unfortunate. Semi-auxiliaries provide crucial information about modality. A non-native speaker who fails to master the uses of the ubiquitous *be going to* construction will never sound casually fluent. Elmore Leonard is a novelist who is famous for his natural dialogue. His characters make constant use of *be going to* (*gonna*) in his novel *Out of Sight* (1996).

"You're not gonna give up the life you have." (p. 270)

"Listen, these guys, they're gonna be out here any minute looking for me." (p. 293)

"Are you gonna leave your tie on." (p. 266)

"You're gonna kill me anyway." (p. 254)

Semi-Auxiliaries and Word Order

Semi-auxiliaries always appear after modals, if there are any, and before the lexical verb—*Wilson will **be able to** fix it*. They have a complicated relationship with perfect and progressive constructions, as you will see below. While only speakers of certain dialects can employ multiple modals in the same VP, all English speakers use multiple semi-auxiliaries.

She | *is going to* | *have to* | *apologize.*

Children | *have to* | *be able to* | *reach the drinking fountain.*

Semi-Auxiliaries and Aspect

Because semi-auxiliaries have internal structure, some of them can carry aspect. Consider the following sentences.

*Doris has to **have fixed** the car.*	[*have to* + perfect]
*Ned has got to **be working** on his report.*	[*has got to* + progressive]

In these sentences, the aspectual construction <u>follows</u> the semi-auxiliary. In the sentences below, however, the semi-auxiliary actually participates in the aspectual construction.

*Doris **has had to** fix the car.* [*has had to* is the perfect form of *has to*]

*Ned **is having** to work on his report.* [*is having to* is the progressive form of *have to*]

The location of aspect can have a significant impact on meaning. In *Doris has to have fixed the car,* the semi-auxiliary is epistemic, while in *Doris has had to fix the car* the semi-auxiliary is deontic.

Not all semi-auxiliaries exhibit this kind of flexibility in terms of aspect. *Be able to* can participate in a perfect construction—*Scott has been able to speak German for years,* but it cannot precede a perfect construction—**Scott is able to have spoken German for years. Be going to* precedes perfect constructions—*She's going to have completed the project by then,* but it does not, as a rule, participate in the perfect—*??She has been going to finish it for years.*

Summary of semi-auxiliaries

Epistemic semi-auxiliaries	Deontic semi-auxiliaries
It**'s going to** rain tomorrow.	I **am going to** arrest you.
Ginny **is about to** leave.	You **have to** be quiet.
That **has (got) to** be Dad at the door.	You**'ve got to** mow the lawn.
Tom **is bound to** hurt himself.	You **had better** wash your hair.
The baby **is sure to** fall.	You**'d best** leave now.
Kids **are certain to** hate it.	We **were supposed to** help her.
He **is (un)likely to** be late.	**Ability and habitual semi-auxiliaries**
Sherry **seems to** be content.	Janine **is able to** splice rope.
They **appear to** be angry.	Esther **used to** be wealthy.

AUXILIARIES, TIME, AND TENSE

While most modal auxiliaries have a distinct past tense form, this form is not always used to communicate past time. Stressed *would* can be used to communicate strong volition in the past—*I told him not to cross the street alone, but he would do it.* (This usage may sound archaic to many of you.) Similarly, *would* can be used to express past willingness or intention—*I invited her but she wouldn't come.* But there are times when *would* is almost synonymous with *will. Would you help me?* is just slightly more polite or more obsequious than *Will you help me?* and it in no way suggests past time. Exactly the same situation pertains in *Can you help me?* versus *Could you help me?*

Occasionally epistemic *would* is used for expressing future time in the past, especially in highly literary contexts—*She would marry within the year* and in dependent clauses—*She hoped that he would be better soon.* But the past tense forms of *be going to* are more commonly used for predicting in the past. This is especially true in past tense narratives.

The lamp was going to fall, [but I caught it.]

It was going to snow later.

I knew that she was going to be angry.

As you have already seen, *would* is sometimes used to express a habitual action in the past—*Every day she would go to the gym.*

Could communicates past, long-term ability—*I could sing when I was young.* *Could* can also refer to the subject's ability in a single situation or event, but only in a negative sentence—*I couldn't find you last night; She couldn't fix my carburetor yesterday.* Inexplicably, *could* can't be used to refer to a single past act in a positive sentence. **I could find you last night* and **She could fix my carburetor yesterday* are both ungrammatical. The semi-auxiliary *be able to* is perfectly acceptable in such sentences—*She was able to fix my carburetor yesterday.*

Should, which is technically the past tense of *shall*, almost never communicates past time. *You should clean your room* clearly lays a future obligation. Only in an exclamation like *Who should I see but my old boyfriend!* does *should* refer to the past. *Might* is technically the past tense of *may* but, as you have already seen, the deontic meanings of *may* and *might* are different. *Might* never communicates past time; *You might call me when the shipment arrives* is clearly a suggestion projected into the future. While both *ought to* and *must* are past tense forms in Old English, neither of these verbs can communicate past time in modern English.

While many past tense modals are incapable of expressing past time on their own, most of them can do so when they are combined with the perfect.

Using the Perfect to Express Past Modality

The following deontic modals must co-occur with the perfect in order to communicate past time.

You should have cleaned your room.	[an (unfulfilled) past obligation]
I would have fixed that for you.	[willingness in the past]
You might have called me.	[reprimand regarding a past omission]
Marilyn ought to have told you.	[an (unfulfilled) past obligation]
Chandra could have done it.	[past ability not acted upon]

In some cases, however, a semi-auxiliary is required to communicate past time. While *must* means strong obligation when it stands alone, it loses that meaning when combined with the perfect. The deontic modality of *Thomas must clean his room* becomes epistemic when the perfect is added—*Thomas must have cleaned his room [there aren't any pizza boxes under the bed].* To communicate strong obligation in the past, a speaker can use the past tense of *have to*—*Thomas had to clean his room last night,* although this construction implies that the obligation was met, i.e., Thomas did indeed clean his room. The past tense of *be to* can be used to express an <u>unfulfilled</u> obligation. *Thomas was to clean his room last night* suggests either that Thomas failed to do so or that the speaker does not know the outcome.

Most epistemic modals require the perfect to place an event in past time—*She might have lied; He may have stolen the jewels; They couldn't have cheated; It can't have been Jim; My cousin should have arrived by now.* (Note that some of these modals are past tense and others are present tense.)

Most semi-auxiliaries can communicate past time alone but a few require the perfect. Deontic *has to* can simply be put in the past tense—*I had to leave*, while epistemic *has to* can be used with the perfect—*She has to have been there*— or without it—*She had to be there.* (This last example is more likely in casual speech than in formal discourse and it is potentially ambiguous.) Despite the fact that *had* in *had better* is technically a past tense form, *had better* requires the perfect to communicate past time—*He had better have finished that assignment.* (Some speakers may find this sentence marginally acceptable.) Those semi-auxiliaries that begin with *be* require only that *be* carry past tense—*Bill was going to take us to the zoo, but he got sick; Nora was able to finish the painting; Olga was certain to fail.*

Modals and semi-auxiliaries requiring the perfect to communicate past time

	Deontic	Epistemic
can	_____	That **can't have** been my car.
could	_____	That **couldn't have** been Brenna.
would	I **would have** helped but . . .	He **would have** survived if . . .
should	She **shouldn't have** knocked me down.	It **shouldn't have** been that cold in June.
may	_____	It **may** have rained yesterday.
might	You **might have** informed me that you'd be late.	It **might have** snowed last night.
must	_____	She **must have** hidden the keys.
ought to	You **ought to have** told him.	They **ought to have** arrived by now.
had better	You **had better have** finished that.	[*had better* is never epistemic]
has to	_____	Bonnie **has to have** finished by now.

MOOD AND MODALITY

In all of the examples above, modality has been expressed by auxiliaries. This strategy for communicating modality is periphrastic, i.e., extra words are required. Mood markers, however, communicate modality by inflectional endings or special verb forms. The term "mood" simply refers to a particular way of expressing modality. (The words mood and modality are etymologically related.) Unlike Latin or classical Greek, Old English did not have an elaborate system of mood markers. There are even fewer left in Modern English and some of these are very weak.

Imperative Mood

The imperative is a very distinctive kind of **directive.** In Old English the imperative required special forms of the verb. The only surviving remnant of these special imperative forms in English is the verb *be.* Assume for the moment that the subject of an imperative is *you.* In a nonimperative (i.e., indicative) sentence, the appropriate verb form for *you* is *are.* But in an imperative, the verb takes the infinitive *be,* the lone survivor of the Old English imperative form. Other imperative verbs look exactly like their second person indicative forms.

Be *a good boy.* / *You* **are** *always a good boy.*

Eat *your spinach.* / *You always* **eat** *your spinach.*

Fortunately, the imperative has other grammatical features that make it very distinctive. The most notable one is the absence of an overt subject—*Sit down; Be quiet; Give me some milk.* This is the only case in English in which a subject is not required in the main clause of a sentence. We all "know" that the subject of the imperative is an understood *you,* but how do we know it? The following sets of sentences supply the evidence.

Yogi closed the door, didn't he?	*Sharon helped herself.*
She closed the door, didn't she?	*They helped themselves.*
They closed the door, didn't they?	*Harry helped himself.*
<u>*Close the door, won't you?*</u>	<u>*Help yourself.*</u>

Simon held his breath.

We all held our breath.

Susanna held her breath.

<u>*Hold your breath.*</u>

The imperative has no tense distinctions; the verbs always take the same form. The imperative almost never co-occurs with the perfect and only occasionally with the progressive—*Be cleaning your room when I get back.* The passive often occurs in negative imperatives—*Don't be alarmed by Noah's appearance; Don't be upset by her remarks* and occasionally in affirmative imperatives—*Be assured that this procedure is correct; Be forewarned that the road is impassable.* Affirmative passive imperatives are usually quite formal in tone.

Normally the word *not* or its contracted form *n't* can follow any form of *be* in English, including the lexical verb—*Miguel is not angry; Ken isn't leaving.* But in an imperative a semantically empty *do* must be added, and *not* follows *do*—*Do not be angry; Don't be surprised by Ruth's attitude.* In the seventeenth century, John Donne could write "Death, be not proud" but today we would say, "Death, do not be proud." (Death is not a subject in these sentences; the speaker is simply addressing death.) Negative imperatives have odd forms in a number of languages.

The auxiliary *do* is also used in persuasive affirmative imperatives—*Do have some more candy; Do sit down.* Semantically these constructions are offers rather than orders, but they are still considered imperatives.

First Person Imperative. English has a special first person plural imperative that always employs the form *let's* or in very formal, often liturgical contexts, *let us.* This imperative form is semantically weaker than the second person imperative; *let's* constructions typically sound like suggestions rather than orders and they direct the speaker as well as the hearer.

Let's eat Thai food tonight.

Let's go over to Joe's house.

Let us pray.

The first person imperative does not require empty *do* in creating a negative. The *not* simply follows *let's* (or *us* in more formal discourse).

Let's not wake up the baby.

Let's not get crazy.

Let us not fall into bad practices.

You will on occasion hear speakers who insert *do* into the first person negative imperative—*Let's don't invite your cousin.*

Imperatives with Overt Subjects. While the prototypical imperative is subjectless, there are imperative constructions with overt subjects. In *You be quiet,* the verb is clearly not in its normal indicative form *are,* and this utterance is considered an imperative by grammarians. *You sit here* is ambiguous out of context. It might be an imperative or it might express a habitual action; *You (usually) sit here.*

There are also a very limited number of third person imperatives; they require a subject pronoun with indefinite reference.

Somebody close the window.

Nobody move!

Somebody hide the beer.

(If these were indicative sentences, the verb would contain a third person singular {-s} ending.)

The first person imperative can also contain an overt subject as long as the subject includes both the speaker and the hearer(s).

*Let's **everyone** keep calm.*

*Let's **all of us** agree to keep this a secret.*

*Let's **you and I** paint the kitchen this weekend.*

The Imperative in Discourse.   While the imperative occurs in all types of discourse, it is especially common in situations in which a speaker or writer is giving explicit instructions or directions. Not surprisingly, it is ubiquitous in cookbooks. This recipe for making mushroom lasagna is typical (Martin et al., 1991) (Boldface added.)

> **Puree** farmer's cheese, ricotta, egg whites and Parmesan. **Blend** in chives, parsley and pepper by hand. In a large pot of lightly salted boiling water, **cook** lasagna noodles until just tender. . . . **Remove** noodles with a slotted spoon. (p. 95)

Instruction labels usually feature a string of imperatives. The following directions accompany an inhaler for asthmatics. (Boldface added.)

> **Breath out** as fully as you comfortably can. **Hold** the inhaler in the upright position and **put** the mouthpiece in your mouth. **Close** your lips around the mouthpiece, keeping your tongue below it. (Instructions for a Vanceril® inhaler.)

In conversational situations, a speaker who has social power will use more and stronger imperatives than one who does not. Teachers often use the imperative with students—*Turn to page twenty three; Take out a sheet of paper; Pipe down; Get rid of that chewing gum,* but most students are wary of using the imperative with teachers. Children hear imperatives from their parents constantly—*Pick up your toys; Take out the garbage; Stop bothering your brother,* but kids respond in kind at their peril.

To some extent politeness moderates our uses of the imperative, even among equals. If I covet your Godiva chocolates, I am more likely to say "Can

I have some?" than "Give me some." In general, the more <u>indirect</u> the directive, the more polite the utterance. Probably the most polite directives are those that combine a past tense auxiliary with a question—*Could you loan me five dollars*? There are, however, a few polite, formulaic expressions that always take the standard imperative form (Brown and Levinson, 1987, pp. 96–98).

Excuse me.

Forgive me.

Have a nice day.

Have a good time.

Pardon our dust. (A sign that always seems to accompany commercial remodeling projects.)

Subjunctive Mood

Like the term imperative, the term subjunctive refers to a particular verb form. In Old English, special verb forms existed to communicate non-facts, e.g., wants, hopes, and hypothetical situations. The subjunctive is somewhat weak in Modern English, but there are speakers who use it routinely. In many cases, the subjunctive is a form learned in school or through reading, so it is educated speakers who use it most. The modern subjunctive expresses a variety of deontic meanings

Mandative Subjunctive. So far we have examined three different ways of issuing directives—modals, semi-auxiliaries, and the imperative. The subjunctive can also be used as a directive. The term **mandative** derives from the Latin root for *mandate*, "a command or order." The mandative subjunctive is a very distinct kind of directive and it always takes the same form.

*I suggest [that he **leave**].*

*I beg [that he **return** the money].*

*I demanded [that she **give** me her files].*

*We asked [that Marsha **tell** the truth].*

*Beth moved [that the meeting **be** adjourned].*

*I insist [that you **be** quiet].*

*I require [that term papers **be** turned in on time].*

In each of these sentences, the main verb makes some sort of demand, from very mild (*ask/suggest*) to very strong (*demand/insist*). In each case, the direct object of the main verb is a clause (the structure in brackets). Note that when the subject of the clause is third person, its verb does not take third person {-s} ending and *be* is in its infinitive form. These atypical verb forms are the vestiges of the Old English subjunctive system. The same meanings can be communicated by a verb in present tense—*We insist that Marsha **tells** the truth* or by a modal auxiliary—*We insist that Marsha **must** tell the truth*. Technically, however, these are not subjunctive utterances because they lack subjunctive verb forms. All of these sentences are directives, however.

Volitional Subjunctive.   Just as there are volitional modals, there are volitional subjunctive constructions. These, too, exploit unusual verb forms—*I wish I **were** a bird; Joseph wishes he **were** a cowboy*. The use of *were* with first and third singular subjects is also a remnant of the old subjunctive system. *I wish I **was** a bird* expresses exactly the same meaning, but technically *was* is not a subjunctive form. The subjunctive is gradually disappearing in English and even highly educated speakers sometimes use non-subjunctive forms in such utterances.

Formulaic Subjunctive.   English has a small set of phrases and sayings that are so old that they still contain uniquely marked subjunctive verbs. These utterances are learned as whole pieces, often as part of religious liturgy. The expression *God bless you* contains a third person subject and an uninflected verb. This sentences is communicating, not a statement of fact, i.e., *God blesses you*, but rather a wish on the part of the speaker, i.e., *I hope that God blesses you*. Some remnants of the formulaic subjunctive in Judeo-Christian liturgy are:

> *The Lord **make** his face to shine upon thee . . . .*
>
> *Thy kingdom **come**, thy will **be** done . . . .*

There are formulaic subjunctives that are less tied to liturgy, but most still have a religious cast.

> *God **save** the Queen.*
>
> *Heaven **forbid.***
>
> *God **be** with you.*
>
> *God **help** him.*
>
> ***Be** that as it may.*
>
> *Long **live** the King.*

Summary of modality markers

Construction	Epistemic modality	Deontic modality
Lexical verb	I **think** that Mary is coming.	I **wish** to leave now.

Summary of modality markers (cont.)

Modal auxiliary	Sue **might** be there.	He **should** fix that furnace.
Semi-auxiliary	The baby **is going to** fall!	You **have to** leave now.
Imperative mood	_____	**Eat** your liver.
		Somebody **open** that door.
Subjunctive mood	_____	I demand that she **leave**.
		God **bless** you.

The Verb Phrase and Scope of Negation

As English speakers, our primary tool for negation is the negative particle *not*. *Not* always follows the first auxiliary in the verb phrase. In most cases *not* is contracted *n't* and attached to that auxiliary—*Edwina can't attend the party; She isn't working now.* So ubiquitous are contracted negatives, that speakers usually sound stilted or even non-native when they use the full negative particle *not*. The one notable exception to this pattern is *am not*; here *am* is contracted to the subject and *not* remains uncontracted—*I'm not leaving. Will* changes pronunciation when *not* is contracted to it; *will not* becomes *won't. Shan't* and *mayn't* are old contracted forms that are rarely heard today.

The first auxiliary in an English sentence has a special role not available to other verbs in the verb phrase. The first auxiliary is manipulated in negatives, questions, and tag questions and for this reason it is called an **operator**[3] (Quirk et al., 1972).

Not always follows the operator in a negative construction. The following sentences illustrate the role of operator in positioning *not* and *n't*.

*Bernard **was**n't lying.*

*Merle **has** not arrived yet.*

*David **can**'t swim.*

*You **should**n't drink so much.*

*Ariel **does**n't eat green peppers.*

***Don't** leave.*

For most American speakers, *be* is the only lexical verb that can become an operator—*Jasmine isn't an administrator; Irving wasn't upset.* A few Americans and most British speakers can make lexical *have* an operator—*Ian hasn't any money; They hadn't a scrap of evidence.*

If there is no lexical *be* or no auxiliary to act as the operator in a negative construction, semantically empty *do* occupies this position, as in *Carol doesn't eat meat* or *Ozzie didn't finish his dinner.* (This is the same *do* you saw in negative imperatives—*Don't be silly.*) The insertion of this extra word is called ***do* periphrasis.** (*Periphrasis* is simply the noun form of *periphrastic.*) Because *do* is semantically empty, it is considered a primary auxiliary along with *be* and *have*.

When a verb phrase contains negation, only certain parts of the sentence are negated by the negative particle *not* or its contracted form *n't*. These portions of the sentence are said to be within the **scope of negation.** Usually only those elements in the sentence after *not* are negated. The difference in meaning between *Donna is definitely not going* and *Donna is not definitely going* is a difference in the scope of negation. In the first sentence *definitely* occurs before *not* and is outside the scope of negation, i.e., *It is definite that Donna is not going.* In the second sentence *definitely* occurs after *not* and is within the scope of negation, i.e., *It is not definite that Donna is going.* One of the reasons that the negative particle always <u>follows</u> the subject in a statement is that the subject is typically a topic and it would be strange for a speaker to negate the topic of the discourse (Lambrecht, 1994, p. 153).

SCOPE OF NEGATION AND AUXILIARIES

In perfect, progressive, and passive sentences, as well as those containing periphrastic *do*, the primary auxiliary carries no meaning on its own, so whether or not the auxiliary is semantically negated is moot; it means nothing to negate a word that has no semantic content in the first place. But when the VP contains a modal, the situation becomes more complicated. Despite the fact that modals always <u>precede</u> *not* or its contracted form *n't*, some are included within the scope of negation, i.e., the meaning of the modal is negated.

Jenny can/may not attend the concert.	[Jenny is not permitted to attend.]
That can't be Julie at the door.	[It is not possible that it's Julie.]
Sam won't come to our party.	[Sam is not willing to come.]
I can't help you.	[I am not able to help you.]

In the following sentences, however, the modal is not within the scope of negation. Only the meaning of the lexical verb is negated.

Tom may/might not pass the exam.	[It is possible that Tom does not pass the exam.]
I won't tell your mother.	[I promise to not tell.]
Jan should/must not cheat on her taxes.	[She is obligated to not cheat.]

Contracted *n't* can be used when *must* has a deontic reading but not when it has an epistemic reading. *Jan mustn't cheat on her taxes* is fine but **Jan mustn't have paid the phone bill* is ungrammatical.

Since the negative particle typically follows the first auxiliary in the verb phrase, the multi-word auxiliaries pose some interesting problems. Most speakers are unsure of where to put *not* in negating modal *ought to*. Does it go after *ought to — You ought to not do that* or before the *to — You ought not to do that*. (Some speakers omit *to* in this last construction.) The dilemma can be solved by adding another auxiliary, which then becomes the operator—*?You shouldn't ought to do that*, but many speakers find this construction questionable and simply avoid using *ought to* with a negative.

If the first word of the semi-auxiliary is some form of *be*, *not* follows it routinely—*Laurie is not going fix it; I'm not sure that Hakeem is right. Be going to* usually falls within the scope of negation in both epistemic and deontic readings.

It's not going to rain tomorrow.	[It is not possible that it will rain.]
I am not going to wash the dishes for you.	[I am not willing to wash the dishes.]

When *be going to* expresses a promise, however, it is not included in the scope of negation.

I'm not going to hurt you.	[I promise to not hurt you.]

Semi-auxiliaries that contain *have* reflect certain inconsistencies. Negative *had better* has some interesting characteristics. If the *not* is contracted, it attaches to *had — You hadn't better eat that.* (Of course, *n't* is routinely contracted to *had* in other constructions as well.) If *not* is uncontracted, it follows *better—You had better not eat that.* In both cases the scope of negation does not include the semi-auxiliary; both sentences mean "you are obligated to not do that."

As we've already seen, *have to* requires *do* periphrasis for negation—*You don't have to sing.* Here the semi-auxiliary is included in the scope of negation— "You are not obligated to sing."

Different speakers exploit different strategies in negative constructions with *used to*. Some exploit *do* periphrasis—*He didn't used to be mean;* and others use *used to* as an operator—*He used to not be mean.*

The Verb Phrase and Questions

Questions almost always involve a variation on normal word order, i.e., they are highly marked. Very rarely do we ask questions by simply using rising question intonation at the end of a sentence—*Mike is fixing dinner?* In fact, this kind of question sometimes suggests incredulity rather than information seeking: "Mike is fixing dinner? Wow, he never cooks." Questions that exploit only intonation are called **echo questions** because they often repeat information provided by a previous speaker.

YES/NO QUESTIONS

Questions soliciting a yes or no answer typically require that the operator precede the subject—*Is Danielle running that marathon? Can Istvan speak Hungarian?* Periphrastic *do* becomes the operator if there is no other auxiliary in the VP—*Does Lena drink ouzo? Did Patrick give you the file?* Any statement can be turned into a yes/no question by this operation.

*Lincoln **has** finished his project. / **Has** Lincoln finished his project?*

*Nancy **is** reading the paper. / **Is** Nancy reading the paper?*

*The kids **have** been eating popcorn. / **Have** the kids been eating popcorn?*

*Jackie **should** have gone. / **Should** Jackie have gone?*

*Malka **can** help. / **Can** Malka help?*

*Felipe crashed. / **Did** Felipe crash?*

Here, too, lexical *be* always acts as its own operator—*Is Amos an electrician? Are those kids your grandchildren?* Some American and most British speakers can make lexical *have* an operator, especially in sentences containing the indefinite quantifier *any—Have you any money? Has Ian any prospects?*

As you have already seen, *n't* is usually contracted to the previous auxiliary. When that auxiliary moves in a question, *n't* moves with it— *Hassan isn't playing volleyball; Isn't Hassan playing volleyball?* However, uncontracted *not* does not move—*Is Hassan not playing volleyball?*—and is usually stressed. In a sentence like this, the speaker is questioning a strongly held assumption; s/he had believed that Hassan was playing volleyball and now something has happened to challenge that belief.

INFORMATION SEEKING QUESTIONS (WH QUESTIONS)

Information seeking questions, also called *wh* questions, always contain an information seeking word—*who, what, where, when, why, whose, which,* or *how,* and this form is usually first in the sentence. These are typically called *wh* words, even though *how* is not spelled with *wh.* The word order in a *wh* question is always the same.

Who is sleeping in my bed?

What are you eating?

Where are the children playing?

When will you return?

Why did he lie?

Whose book did you borrow?

Which piece of meat do you want?

How is the project going?

In each case the operator precedes the subject and the *wh* word precedes the operator. Note that in the first example the *wh* word is the subject, so it automatically precedes the operator.

It is always possible to paraphrase a *wh* question using noninterrogative word order—*What is Harry doing?* becomes *Harry is doing what?* These two constructions are rarely used in the same discourse context; a speaker who uses such a *wh* echo question is typically asking for a reiteration or clarification of something that has already been said. However, you will find that an echo question paraphrase is a useful strategy in determining the grammatical function of the *wh* word.

The *wh* words in questions have a variety of grammatical functions. The pronoun forms *who* and *what* are NPs and can occupy any NP position. In each of the following examples the grammatical function of the *wh* pronoun is indicated in brackets.

Who *ate all the potato chips?*	[subject]
What *did she say?*	[direct object]
What *have they named the baby?*	[object complement]
What *is that thing?*	[predicate nominative]
Who *did you hand the money to?*	[indirect object]
To **whom** *did you hand the money?*	[indirect object]

The interrogative words *when, where, why,* and *how* all function as adverbs in *wh* questions. I will discuss these in Chapter 4.

There is a small inventory of interrogative *wh* words that function as determiners within NPs.

I want **this** *book.* / **Which** *book do you want?* [often means which of a known or specified set]

I learned **a** *lesson.* / **What** *lesson have you learned?* [which of an unspecified set]

They are driving **her** *car.* / **Whose** *car should we drive?* [genitive]

TAG QUESTIONS

The operator is also exploited in the creation of **tag questions.** Tag questions follow statements and they seek affirmation of the proposition contained in the statement.

*That politician **is** lying, **isn't** she?*

*Janie **has** been a problem, **hasn't** she?*

*Ted **won't** cheat, **will** he?*

*Gene **can't** do the tango, **can** he?*

*Those kids **are** sweet, **aren't** they?*

*Ricki took your toys, **didn't** she?*

*Frieda **didn't** get that job, **did** she?*

The creation of a tag question in English is a very elaborate operation. To construct a tag question for the sentence *Lara is moving to Sweden*, the speaker has to be able to identify the pronominal form of the subject and the first auxiliary in the VP; these appear in reverse order in the tag question. Then the speaker must determine whether the sentence is affirmative or negative and construct a tag that is the opposite—*Lara is moving to Sweden, isn't she?; Lara isn't moving to Sweden, is she?* A positive tag is used when a speaker seeks to confirm a negative proposition, i.e., s/he believes that Lara is not moving and wants confirmation. A negative tag is used when a speaker wants to confirm a positive proposition, e.g., Lara is moving to Sweden.

English speaking children learn how to construct tag questions fairly late in their linguistic development; when they are young, they resort to a much simpler alternative—*You're taking me to the zoo tomorrow, right?* In fact, in many languages tag questions are created by the addition of a single word, as in Spanish—*Lourdes va a Argentina, verdad?* [Lourdes is going to Argentina, true?].

There is also a positive tag in English, i.e., one in which both the sentence and the tag are in the affirmative—*Lara is moving to Sweden, is she.* Positive tags are not real questions. They tend to reiterate something that has been said before and they often have a sarcastic, threatening, or otherwise negative tone—*You borrowed my car, did you; He's dating my sister, is he.*

Like most questions in English, tag questions are highly marked constructions.

MULTI-WORD AUXILIARIES AS OPERATORS IN QUESTIONS AND TAGS

All modal auxiliaries except *ought to* function comfortably as operators. Because *ought to* is a two-word modal, it creates problems. Some speakers are comfortable with *Ought you to be doing that?* and others are not. *Ought to* almost never appears in tag questions. As you saw earlier, *ought to* poses problems in negative constructions as well.

Most semi-auxiliaries contain their own operators. When *be* is the first word in a semi-auxiliary (and the semi-auxiliary is the first auxiliary in the VP), the *be* becomes the operator and separates from the rest of the semi-auxiliary in a question.

Is *Susan <u>likely to</u> finish this project?*

Are *you <u>going to</u> attend?*

Was *Jamie <u>able to</u> register last semester?*

Am *I <u>supposed to</u> take out the garbage?*

The *be* also becomes the operator in a tag question.

*Scott <u>is going to</u> attend, **is**n't he?*

*We'<u>re sure to</u> be chosen, **are**n't we?*

The *have* in *have got to* can function as an operator in a question—*Have you got to play that music so loud?* Some speakers can use *have* as an operator in a tag question—*I have got to clean my room, haven't I?* but most use *do—I have got to clean my room, don't I?* The *had* in *had better* functions as an operator in yes/no questions only when the construction is negative—*Hadn't you better clean your room?* There is no way to construct a positive question with *had better. Had* can also be found as the operator in negative tags—*You had better clean your room, hadn't you?* But positive tags with *had* sound strange—*?You hadn't better eat that, had you?*

Do periphrasis is always required with *have to—**Do** you have to leave now? **Don't** you have to finish your homework? You have to finish your homework, **don't** you?*

Used to poses a problem. The only way to construct a question or tag with this semi-auxiliary is to exploit *do* periphrasis—*Did you used to attend Purdue? You used to attend Purdue, didn't you?*

There is considerable variation in how speakers handle the problem of choosing an operator in the case of a multi-word auxiliary. This is a symptom of a grammatical system in a state of flux.

HISTORICAL DEVELOPMENT OF THE OPERATOR

The widespread use of auxiliaries as operators is a fairly late development in English grammar. Old and Middle English speakers and writers typically made the lexical verb the operator (although auxiliaries sometimes did occupy this position). The following questions are posed by an Anglo-Saxon schoolmaster to his students (Moore and Knott, 1955). This work was probably written in the tenth century. (The Old English letter æ is pronounced like the vowel in *bad* (standard American pronunciation) and the Old English letter þ is pronounced like the *th* in *thin*.)

Hwæt sægst þū, yrþling (p. 263)	[What say thou, farmer?]
Canst þū ænig þing (p. 263).	[Know thou anything?]
Hwær cyþst þū þīn fixas (p. 265).	[Where sell thou thy fishes?]

Shakespeare (1564–1616) is a transitional figure who sometimes uses the lexical verb as the operator and sometimes employs *do* periphrasis. Compare the following lines:

"Do you not hope your children shall be kings?" *Macbeth,* Act I, Sc. iii, line 18

"What say'st thou, my dear nurse?" *Romeo and Juliet,* Act II, Sc. iv, line 207

By the eighteenth century, the operator is normally an auxiliary in all discourse contexts except poetry.

Exclamations

Not all sentences in which the subject and operator are inverted are questions.

Am I furious!

Is Zack ever hungry!

Did Marilyn ever chew me out at work today.

Wow. Has Nigel gained weight!

In each of these sentences the marked word order signals an exclamation.

Wh words can also be used to mark exclamatory utterances. In the following sentences the *wh* word modifies the following NP, but there is no subject/operator inversion.

What a marvelous person he is.

What an idiot that director is!

What an amazing performance that was.

What a good time I had last night.

One interesting feature of these constructions is the fact that the initial structure cannot be moved into the predicate unless *what* is omitted—*He is what a marvelous person; *That director is what an idiot.*

Existential *There* Constructions

There is another commonly used English construction that violates standard word order. When English speakers want to point something out or introduce something new into the discourse, they often exploit a special construction called **existential *there*.** (This is sometimes termed **expletive *there*.**)

There's an elephant in my office.

There are fourteen people sitting in your bathtub.

There is a real problem brewing in the accounting department.

There's some mold on my bread.

There are some threads on your sweater.

There arose an incredible outcry.

There exists no antidote to this poison.

This is a very odd construction. For one thing, *there* does not have its usual location meaning. In fact, all but two of these sentences contain another clear-cut expression of location (in each case a prepositional phrase). As you will see in Chapter 4, words and phrases that describe location are usually adverbs. But in the sentences above, *there* is not an adverb; it is in fact the subject of these sentences. This may seem counterintuitive but a couple of simple syntactic tests will demonstrate it.

Most declarative English sentences can take a tag question in which the pronominal form of the subject is repeated in the tag. Note what happens when an existential *there* sentence receives a tag.

*There are fourteen people in your bathtub, aren't **there**?*

*There's some mold on my bread, isn't **there**?*

*There is a problem in the accounting department, isn't **there**?*

The very fact that *there* appears as the subject of the tag question is strong evidence that it is also the subject of the sentence.

Another test exploits the operator. As you saw above, a statement can be turned into a yes/no question by moving the first auxiliary or the lexical verb *be* to a position in front of the subject. Look at what happens when existential *there* sentences are turned into questions.

There are some frogs swimming in Carolyn's pool. / Are there some frogs swimming in Carolyn's pool?

There is a stain on your shirt. / Is there a stain on your shirt?

Existential *there* sentences contain odd VPs. In *There <u>are</u> some strangers <u>walking</u> up the path,* the auxiliary verb is separated from the lexical verb by an NP even though this is not an interrogative sentence. Existential *there* constructions have a number of other unusual features as well. Since *there* is not a conventional noun or pronoun, it has no number, i.e., it has no separate singular and plural forms. English subjects agree with their verbs in number— *Mary **goes** to the beach every weekend; Her kids **go** to the mountains.* But in existential *there* constructions, the verb often agrees in number with the noun phrase that <u>follows</u> it—*There is a child in the room; There are children in the room.*

In fact many existential *there* sentences can be paraphrased (more or less) with this noun phrase in subject position, e.g., *There are some guests in the garden. / Some guests are in the garden.* Some syntacticians argue that existential *there* sentences have two subjects—*there*, which acts as subject in most grammatical operations, and the noun phrase following the verb, which controls subject/verb agreement.

However, in casual conversation, even highly educated speakers of English often use a singular verb with a plural noun phrase in existential *there* constructions. This is especially common when the verb is contracted onto *there*. *There are fourteen people sitting in your bathtub* easily becomes *There's fourteen people sitting in your bathtub.* Similarly, it is not uncommon to hear a sentence like *There's been four earthquakes in Santa Rosa this year.* The {-s} here is short for *has*, the singular form of the auxiliary.

The VPs in existential *there* sentences usually contain the copula *be*, which typically means "to exist" or "to be located" in this context. Intransitive verbs of existence and appearance can also appear in these constructions but such sentences tend to sound formal or archaic.

There's a crack in the window.	[A crack exists in the window.]
There are ants all over my sandwich.	[Ants are located all my sandwich.]
There's no room for your stuff.	[No room exists for your stuff.]
There developed a problem in the ignition.	[A problem developed.]
There appeared a bright light in the sky.	[A bright light appeared.]
There exist many solutions to this problem.	[Many solutions exist.]
There arose a great cry from the crowd.	[A great cry arose.]

In existential *there* sentences, the noun phrase following the verb is almost always indefinite, In other words the noun will never be preceded by *the* and will never be a proper noun. *There is a man on the porch* is fine but **There is the man on the porch* is ungrammatical unless *there* is reanalyzed as a redundant adverb of location, i.e, *There is the man, on the porch.*

Many languages have such "pointing out" constructions and they are often syntactically unusual. Existential *there* constructions are ubiquitous in English. The following passage is from Walter Mosley's novel *Gone Fishin'* (1997). (Boldface added.)

> The road wasn't paved or landscaped. On either side **there** were dense shrubs and bushes. . . . **There** are stretches of land that have hardly anything growing, but even then it's no simple story. Texas is made up of every kind of soil;

there's red clay and gray sod and fertile brown. . . . But **there**'s no such thing
as a desert town near the gulf. (pp. 22–23)

Narrative Discourse and the Verb Phrase

As you have already seen, a speaker's choice of tense, aspect, and voice will
depend a great deal on real world circumstances—is the event over and done
with, is it ongoing, does it have current relevance, is the agent known, etc. The
nature of a discourse will also influence the form of its VPs.

In an action sequence of the sort found in crime novels, the actual events
are often encoded in transitive and intransitive verbs with highly agentive subjects. This is called **foregrounding** because such constructions serve to push
the action to the forefront. The following passages are from James Lee Burke's
novel *Burning Angel* (1995). (Boldface added.)

> He **dropped** his ring of keys in his pocket and **called out** to a man sweeping
> the wood floors in front. . . . Then he **spat** his chewing gum neatly into a trash
> bag and **clanged** through a metal door into the back alley. (p. 65)

> I **took** two paper bags from the kitchen pantry, **put** a clean shirt in one of them,
> **stopped** by the bait shop, then **drove** up the dirt road through the tunnel of
> oak trees and over the drawbridge. (p. 84)

Background information and descriptions typically employ stative verbs,
copulas, and agentless passives.

> [Moleen Bertrand] **was** over six feet and could not **be called** a soft man, but
> at the same time there **was** no muscular tone or definition to his body. . . . He
> **had been born** to an exclusionary world of wealth and private schools. . . . He
> **was** Phi Beta Kappa at Springhill and a major in the air force toward the end
> of the Viet Nam War. He **made** the *Law Review* at Tulane and **became** a senior
> partner at his firm in less than five years. He **was** also a champion skeet shooter.
> (p. 20)

> An aluminum boat with an outboard engine **was tied** with a chain to a cypress
> knee on the bank, and beyond it a shack **was set** back in the willows on pil-
> ings. The screens **were webbed** with rust, dead insects, and dirt, and the tin
> roof had long ago **taken on** the colors of a woods in winter. The base of the
> pilings **glistened** with a sheen like petroleum waste from the pools of stagnant
> water they sat in. (p. 393)

Different kinds of discourse will tend to use foregrounding and back-
grounding differently. Most adult fiction is a mix of the two techniques. Stories for small children, however, are very heavy on foregrounding. Little kids
respond well to action and children's literature is full of highly transitive verbs

and agentive subjects, as in the following passages from Richard Scarry's *Huckle Cat's Busiest Day Ever!* (1992).

> Huckle and Lowly **run** to the bathroom. They **wash** their faces. They **brush** their teeth. Huckle **combs** his hair. Then they **make** their beds. They **dress,** and **run** to breakfast. (p. 2)

> Mother Cat **drives** the Cat family car through the streets of Busytown. Huckle and Lowly **see** many sights. Trucks **are making** deliveries of things. Shops **are opening** their doors. Garbage workers **pick up** the garbage. Postman Pig **delivers** letters. Sergeant Murphy **directs** traffic. (pp. 5–6)

In this passage even the inanimate noun *shops* is treated as an agent. The only stative verb used here by Scarry is *see*.

Sportswriters also exploit foregrounding heavily. The following passage is from the *Denver Post* sports section (May 6, 1997). (Boldface added.)

> Hundley **crushed** two home runs, **went** 4 for 4 and **knocked in** five runs, and Bobby Jones **scattered** six singles as New York **whipped** the Rockies 6–1. (p. 1–D)

These are highly transitive verbs and the subjects are all very agentive. Even the normally intransitive *went* takes a direct object here.

Histories and biographies, on the other hand, often include long sections of background information, like this passage from *Undaunted Courage: Meriwether Lewis, Thomas Jefferson, and the Opening of the American West* (Ambrose, 1996). Note that most of the finite verbs are either copulas or stative verbs. (Boldface added.)

> When Thomas Jefferson **took** the Oath of Office as the third president of the United States on March 4, 1801, the nation **contained** 5,308,483 persons. Nearly one out of five **was** a Negro slave. Although the boundaries **stretched** from the Atlantic to the Mississippi River, from the Great Lakes nearly to the Gulf of Mexico . . . only a relatively small area **was** occupied. Two-thirds of the people **lived** within fifty miles of tidewater. Only four roads **crossed** the Appalachian Mountains. (p. 51)

Even normally dynamic verbs like *crossed* and *stretched* are stative here.

Since epistemic modality usually expresses the doubts and certainties of the speaker/writer, it is most often used in conversation and first person narrative. The following passages from Prejean's autobiographical book *Dead Man Walking* (1994) illustrate both contexts. The narrative is written in the first person but it includes accounts of conversations with others, as in the first two examples below. (Boldface added.)

When I go up to him, he says in a whisper, "I **think** it was Mrs. Harvey's patriotic speech about America there at the end that did me in. I **think** I was winnin' before that little part of her speech." I am amazed at his naïveté. He **thought** he had a chance. (p. 168)

Marsellus is angry. "No way. . . . He knew the real score. He **may** have said that to you to save face, but he was the one who worked out the deal with the woman." (p. 172)

It **must** have been a terrible ordeal to know all the wheeling and dealing going on. (p. 173)

In contexts like these, epistemic modality is entirely appropriate. But a scholarly article or an instruction manual that was filled with epistemic constructions would not inspire confidence.

We've already seen that cookbooks and directions for product use are heavy on imperative constructions. Textbooks and manuals exploit the imperative and a variety of other deontic devices as well. The following passages are from the *Inside Windows 95* manual (Boyce et al., 1995). (Boldface added.)

To remove a device, **choose** the System object in the Control Panel, then **click** on the Device Manager tab. (p. 124)

. . . you **should** avoid copying objects to the Startup folder to make them start automatically. (p. 178)

You might **have to** download fonts to the printer . . . before you can print the document. (p. 234)

In this situation, you **need to** rename your Config.sys. (p. 99)

While most of the constructions discussed in this chapter can theoretically crop up anywhere, you will find that often the nature of the discourse will affect, however loosely, the kinds of verb constructions that a speaker/writer chooses.

Summing Up

As you can see, the English verb phrase is complex both grammatically and semantically. The verb phrase is in essence the command center of the sentence. Verbs dictate the semantic roles of subjects, direct objects, indirect objects, etc. They dictate whether or not a sentence will even contain a direct object, an indirect object, a subject complement, or an object complement. Most expressions of modality are contained in the verb phrase. The verb phrase is important in establishing the time frame of an utterance and the status of event (complete, in process, currently relevant, etc.).

Some of the most knotty problems in English syntax revolve around the verb phrase. There are still many disagreements about the nature of semi-auxiliaries; their treatment in this book reflects only one approach. Some verbs are followed by clauses that are difficult to categorize. (I will touch upon this in Chapter 5.) The terminology traditionally used to describe elements in the VP is often problematic.

Nevertheless, you should now have a clearer understanding, not only of the VP itself, but of how it relates to the various NPs in the sentence. Once you have acquired some mastery of the structure and semantics of the noun phrase and the verb phrase, even the most complex English sentences yield to analysis.

4

Modification

If English sentences contained only determiners, nouns, and verbs, they would be colorless indeed. Many parts of speech can be modified in some way. In traditional grammar, modification relationships are usually subsumed under the categories **adjective** and **adverb**. Adjectives are typically described as words or phrases that modify nouns, while adverbs are often defined as structures that modify adjectives, verbs, and other adverbs. But there are modification relationships that cannot be comfortably included in these two categories. Furthermore, modification is a complex and problematic phenomenon and not all modification relationships are the same.

Modification of the Noun and the Noun Phrase

Grammatical categories like subject and direct object are internally complex. Not only does the typical noun phrase contain a noun and some sort of determiner, but it often contains adjective constructions as well. The adjective usually appears between the determiner and the noun. Unlike the categories determiner, predeterminer, and postdeterminer, the category adjective is an **open class**. There are thousands of adjectives in English and speakers invent new ones—*a **scuzzy** guy, a **spacy** teenager* and readily assign new meanings to old ones—*a **hairy** problem, a **gay** friend, a **gnarly** surfboard*.

Adjectives are not altogether easy to characterize, however. Words from many grammatical classes can modify nouns. There is of course the prototypical adjective, a word that can take the comparative form (*sweeter, smarter, bigger*) and the superlative form (*sweetest, smartest, biggest*). These {-er} and {-est} suffixes are inflectional endings; the adjectives that can take these suffixes usually date back to Old English, although even neologisms (new words) like *scuzzy* sometimes carry them—*He's the scuzziest guy I've ever seen*. Multi-syllabic adjectives borrowed from French during the Middle English period typically require periphrastic comparative and superlative forms—***more** intelligent, **more** beautiful, **most** difficult*. Borrowed adjectives of a single syllable are sometimes inflected, however—*larger, finest, nicer, closest*.

There are a few adjectives in English in which the root form is different from the comparative and superlative forms, e.g., *good/better/best; bad/worse/worst; little/less/least*. All of these suppletive forms are very old.

Many of the words that modify nouns are not prototypical adjectives. Verb participles readily take on this function. When a noun is modified by a present participle, there is a sense that the state being described is ongoing; *a galloping horse* is in the process of galloping and *a screaming child* is in the process of screaming. Present participle adjectives are relatively common.

The **laughing** clown delighted the baby.

The **coughing** patient contaminated the whole office.

He walked into the **raging** river.

The fire fighters doused the **smoldering** ashes.

The **ringing** bells awaken us every Sunday.

Some {-ing} adjectives are very idiosyncratic. The following present participle forms rarely occur with nouns other than the ones indicated here (Fillmore and Kay, 1995, p. 4-4).

Jane's cousins are **blithering idiots**.

They were **consenting adults**.

He was excused due to **mitigating circumstances**.

Adjectives formed from past participles are ubiquitous in English.

I threw out the **wilted** gardenia.

The athlete soaked her **swollen** foot.

That **wrecked** car must be moved.

The **wounded** soldier was airlifted to the hospital.

Cynthia raked up the **fallen** leaves.

When a noun is modified by a past participle, there is a sense that the state being described is resultant. *Broken* glass has already been broken, while *breaking glass* (as in *the sound of breaking glass*) is in the process of being broken; *a stolen necklace* has already been filched and *a scratched cornea* has already been damaged. When I'm driving on mountain roads, I find the sign that warns of "Falling rocks" far more ominous than the one that says "Fallen rocks," even though I know that fallen rocks are a direct result of falling rocks. You can see the meanings of the progressive and perfect reflected in these participial adjective forms.

There are a number past participles that can function as adjectives only when they contain the prefix {un-}—*the unread manuscript; an unsold car; an un-*

sung hero. Without the prefix, none of these participles can modify nouns (**a* *read manuscript*, **a sold car*, **a sung hero*), unless the participle itself is modified in some way—*a **seldom** read manuscript; an **easily** sold product*. (Constructions like these will be taken up in detail later.)

Even words that are usually noun heads can modify other nouns—*a **paper** airplane, the **senior** trip, **apple** cider, the **county** jail, a **stone** wall*. While these words are functioning as adjectives, they rarely take inflected or periphrastic comparative and superlative forms; **a more apple cider* and **the paperest airplane* are impossible. These are called **denominal adjectives**. (The term *denominal* indicates that a word has lost its nominal status; it can be used to refer to any noun form that takes on a non-nominal grammatical function.)

Adjectives can sometimes be identified by their **derivational suffixes**, i.e., the endings that derive adjectives from other parts of speech.

Noun to adjective	**Verb to adjective**
hunger → *hung**ry***	*to select* → *select**ive***
metal → *metal**lic***	*to inflate* → *inflat**able***
beauty → *beaut**iful***	*to harm* → *harm**less***
fool → *fool**ish***	*to tip* → *tip**py***
nation → *nation**al***	*to watch* → *watch**ful***
danger → *danger**ous***	
scholar → *scholar**ly***	
irony → *iron**ic***	
ice → *ic**y***	

Most derived adjectives can take comparative and superlative forms—*hungriest, more scholarly, most dangerous*.

All the modifiers discussed so far can be considered adjectives because they express some attribute or quality held by the following noun, but the underlying semantic relationships vary a great deal. Consider the following adjective plus noun constructions and their paraphrases:

a tall woman	[a woman who is tall]
a crying baby	[a baby who is crying]
a brick building	[a building made of brick]
a country road	[a road in the country]
a cracked mirror	[a mirror that is cracked]
the class picnic	[the picnic for the class]

a Thanksgiving feast	[a feast held on Thanksgiving]
a spring day	[a day in spring]
Shaker furniture	[furniture made by or in the style of the Shakers]
a personal computer	[a computer designed for individual use]
a personal attack	[an attack on an individual]
advance payment	[payment made in advance of services]

English is very rich in adjectives. For any general attribute you might name, there are likely to be a great number of adjectives that can express some aspect of that attribute. Usually the real world context will dictate the choice of adjective. Think about the extensive inventory of adjectives that express "wetness"—*wet, moist, damp, sopping, swampy, soaked, humid, dank, water-logged, rainy, foggy, sweaty*. Obviously many of these adjectives are quite constrained in terms of context; *humid, rainy,* and *foggy* are typically limited to weather, *dank* is used to describe a damp environment and it usually entails "unpleasant," while *sweaty* is used to refer to moisture excreted by some mammals. The variety is impressive, nevertheless.

It's hard to imagine English discourse without adjectives. The passage that follows describes a Lap man in traditional dress (Beach, 1993). Despite its brevity, this passage contains 12 adjectives. (Boldface added.)

> He wore a **faded blue Saami** costume decorated with strips of red and yellow and a **matching** hat with a **huge** topknot of **red** yarn. This was the **traditional** dress of the Karesuando district, I later learned. Even with his **odd** hat he was not very **tall**. His posture was **stooped**, and he walked with an **elastic** gait. He was an **old** man. (p. 10)

Even the driest academic texts exploit adjectives constantly. Here is a paragraph from an advanced computer graphics text (Glassner, 1995). (Boldface added.)

> The **conceptual** side of computer graphics often deals with *continuous-time* (CT) or *analytic* signals. These have a **symbolic** representation that enables us to evaluate them for any **parameter** value. . . . An **analytic** signal need not be *smooth* (i.e., **differentiable** everywhere), or *continuous* (i.e., **unbroken**). (p. 128)

This highly technical passage contains 10 adjectives in just a few lines.

In English, adjectives most often occupy one of three positions. They occur prenominally (i.e., before the noun), after the copula (i.e., as predicate adjectives), or after a complex transitive verb and a direct object (i.e., as object complements). However, sometimes an adjective will follow a noun or a pronoun in the absence of a complex transitive verb. These are **postnominal adjectives**.

*This is a **risky** business.*	**Prenominal adjective**
*This business seems **risky**.*	**Predicate adjective**
*She considers this business **risky**.*	**Object complement adjective**
*Something **risky** is being planned.*	**Postnominal adjective**

Most adjectives can readily occupy both prenominal and predicate adjective position, although there are exceptions as you will see below. The adjectives that can occupy object complement position are severely limited by the semantics of complex transitive verbs, and postnominal adjectives are also highly constrained.

PRENOMINAL ADJECTIVES

A prenominal adjective can modify virtually any noun, regardless of its position in the sentence. In a sentence like *This is a risky business, risky* is not a predicate adjective, even though it appears in the predicate. *Risky* precedes and modifies the noun *business* and the entire NP, *a risky business*, is a predicate nominative. Similarly, an adjective which <u>precedes</u> a direct object noun (as in *I hate a risky business*) is not an object complement. This term is reserved for adjectives that <u>follow</u> the noun head of the direct object; furthermore, object complements usually occur with complex transitive verbs.

Prenominal adjectives are sometimes called ***attributive***. This terminology is somewhat misleading, however, because adjectives in other positions also attribute some quality to the noun head they modify.

While most adjectives can occur in both prenominal and predicate adjective position, a few are limited to one position or the other. The adjectives that are limited to prenominal position fall into four general categories:

1) most denominal adjectives
2) a few adjectives derived from nominal forms by means of derivational suffixes
3) present participles functioning as adjectives
4) non-inherent adjectives
5) relationship adjectives

As you saw above, some noun forms can function as prenominal adjectives—*the freshman class, the city park, county jail, the garden gate.* Many of these sound ungrammatical or at best odd in predicate adjective position—**the class was freshman, *the park was city, ??the jail was county; *the gate was garden. Criminal court* means something very different from *The court was criminal.* I suspect the reason for this discrepancy lies in the grammatical differences between predicate adjectives and predicate nominatives. When something that looks like a noun follows a copula, we process it as a predicate nominative, not a predicate adjective. While a predicate adjective describes the subject NP, a predicate nominative must have the same referent as the subject NP, a significantly different function. A sentence like *Billy is a criminal* can be characterized as *Billy = a criminal*, but *the park = city* is not a reasonable paraphrase of *the city park.*

There are some nouns that have, over the centuries, taken on real adjective status. In a sentence like *The building is stone, stone* is a descriptor, not a co-referential NP. Nouns that name the materials out of which things are made often take on this descriptive function and they can appear in both prenominal and predicate adjective position.

This is a brick wall. / The wall is brick.

This is a cardboard table. / The table is cardboard.

This is a paper hat. / The hat is paper.

That is a tin can. / That can is tin.

Even adjectives that have been derived from nouns via derivational morphology occasionally resist predicate adjective position. We speak of *atomic scientists* but no one would say **Those scientists are atomic;* Jack the Ripper was described as *a serial killer* but no journalist would have written that "The killer was serial." The phrase *presidential assistant* means something quite different from *the assistant was presidential.* On the other hand, many other adjectives derived from nouns are perfectly comfortable in predicate adjective position— *The baby is hungry; This book is scholarly; That sport is dangerous.*

Complex expressions can sometimes be used as prenominal adjectives, especially in informal conversation.

*Roger is an **early-to-bed** guy.*

*Linda was a **take-charge** executive.*

*My daughter is in her **I-can't-stand-adults** phase.*

*It was a **take-no-prisoners** situation.*

As you saw above, adjectives derived from past participles readily occupy predicate adjective position—*The mirror is cracked; That chair is broken.* Since past participle adjectives encode states, they can also follow copulas other than *be*— *That chair looks broken; This lens seems cracked; That C.D. sounds scratched.* However, adjectives derived from present participles behave quite differently, due to the semantic differences between past and present participles. As you have already seen, the condition described by a past participle is a resultant state; *a cracked mirror* has already been cracked. A present participle, however, describes an ongoing condition; *a babbling baby* is still in the process of babbling. As a result, any present participle that directly follows *be* will simply be interpreted as a component part of the progressive—*The baby is babbling.* Present participles never follow other copulas either—**That baby seems babbling; *That boy sounds screaming; *It appears snowing.*

Noninherent adjectives constitute a special class that can only be used prenominally. In most cases an adjective names some quality held by the noun being modified. Noninherent adjectives, however, do not actually describe the following noun, but rather another, related noun. In a sentence like *Terence is a big fool,* the speaker is not describing the stature of Terence, but rather the extent of his *foolishness.* An expression like *my old friend* refers to the length of the friendship, not to the age of the friend; even a child can have an old friend. *Attila is a poor loser* means that Attila is poor at losing, not that he is short of funds and a *wooden actor* is one whose acting is wooden, not a marionette. When a noninherent adjective is moved to predicate adjective position, its meaning changes and it loses its noninherent status. The meaning of *old* in *my old roommate* is quite different from that of *old* in *My roommate is old.*

Former, previous, and *late* are also prenominal adjectives that don't appear in predicate adjective position.

> *Martha's former boss is now in jail.* / **Martha's boss is former.*
>
> *Jackson's late uncle left him millions.* / **Jackson's uncle is late* (i.e., deceased).
>
> *The previous tenant left a mess.* / **The tenant was previous.*

Each of these adjectives refers to a relationship that no longer exists; Martha's boss is no longer her boss, the tenant no longer lives there, and Jackson's uncle is dead.

You will find that two or more adjectives that derive from different parts of speech sometimes resist being coordinated with *and.* While a scientist may be *tall and handsome,* he cannot be **tall and atomic.* A horse might be *strong and beautiful* but we would never speak of the **beautiful and galloping horse.* Furthermore, not all adjectives derived from nouns can be coordinated. Rugby might be described as *a bloody and dangerous sport* but not a **bloody and national sport.* Relationship adjectives and noninherent adjectives seldom coordinate with other types. **Martha's former and rich boss is coming to dinner,* and **My old and brilliant roommate is visiting next week* are ungrammatical, although *An old and dear friend is visiting* is fine. Past participle adjectives are quite flexible and can be coordinated with many other adjective types—*The witty and talented Bette Midler is being honored tonight; He is a quiet and reserved man; It was an exciting and animated performance.* This is a measure of how thoroughly some past participles have taken on adjective status.

PREDICATE ADJECTIVES

As you saw in Chapter 1, predicate adjectives always follow copulas and constitute one type of subject complement.

Those exam questions were **tricky.**

Calvin seems **honest.**

Ellen looks **pale.**

There is a set of adjectives all of which begin with *a-* (*asleep, afraid, ablaze, afloat, alive, ashamed,* etc.) that readily occur in predicate adjective position but do not occur prenominally. Phrases like **the afraid child, *the asleep baby,* and **the afloat raft* are ungrammatical. *Afraid* and *ashamed* both derive from the past participle forms of now archaic verbs, while *asleep, ablaze, afloat,* and *alive* derive from very old prepositional phrase constructions—*on sleep, on blaze, on float,* and *on life.* It is certainly not surprising that adjectives derived from prepositional phrases cannot occur prenominally, since prepositional phrases themselves never occur in prenominal position—**the on fire house, *the in the box cookies. Well,* meaning "healthy," does not, as a rule, occur prenominally, although "well baby clinics" exist in some communities.

There are other constraints on predicate adjectives. Some can co-occur with both stative and dynamic verbs and others cannot. As you saw in Chapter 3, adjectives that describe relatively permanent states do not follow the progressive. **Nate is being tall* is unacceptable under most circumstances, but *Nate is being noisy* is fine. Normally an English speaker would not say **Danica is being musical* or **James is being thin,* since being thin and being musical are long-term qualities. Adjectives which describe relatively permanent states are called **stative.** Thus, a sentence like *Jessica is smart* contains both a stative copula and a stative predicate adjective.

Of course some adjectives can be used to describe both permanent and short-term states. As we have already seen in Chapter 3, a short-term state can be communicated by the use of the progressive—*Your sister is being obnoxious; Those boys are being mean.*

Unlike prenominal adjectives, predicate adjectives are rarely stacked. *That old, tan couch is mine* is fine but **That couch is tan, old* is unacceptable unless there is a significant pause between *tan* and *old.*

POSTNOMINAL ADJECTIVES AND ADJECTIVE PHRASES

On rare occasions a lexical adjective <u>follows</u> a noun in the NP.

Some of the people **present** *voted against the amendment.*

The person **responsible** *was never found.*

All of the individuals **concerned** *were there.*

Adjectives in this position are called **postnominal.** While adjectives seldom follow full nouns, they often follow indefinite pronouns, despite the fact that adjectives rarely <u>precede</u> pronouns of any sort.

*Nobody **new** has joined the sorority.*

*Something **strange** has occurred.*

*Someone **tall** snatched the oranges from the tree.*

*Nothing **bad** happened at the meeting.*

*Somebody **important** is attending the reunion.*

Prepositional phrases frequently function as postnominal modifiers, usually following full NPs.

*The little girl **in the blue dress** is my niece.*

*Do you know the kid **with the freckles**?*

*The house **across the street** burned down last night.*

In each of these sentences the prepositional phrase helps the hearer identify the referent of the NP. A sentence like *The little girl is my niece* is not especially informative if the room is filled with little girls, and a speaker who hears *The house burned down last night* will have no idea <u>which</u> house. In the section on determiners, I discussed the fact that *the* typically has anaphoric reference; it is used with entities that have already been introduced into the discourse. However, in the sentences above, *the* has cataphoric reference. The prepositional phrase tells the hearer which entity is being referred to; *in the blue dress, with the freckles,* and *across the street* restrict the possible referents to one (presumably). As you will see in Chapter 5, restrictive relative clauses have much the same function.

OBJECT COMPLEMENT ADJECTIVES

Those adjectives that make bad subject complements tend to make bad object complements as well. Denominal adjectives rarely appear in this position—*I consider that park city; *They deemed the class freshman; *They made the gate garden.* Past participles are fine as object complements—*The insurance company considered the building damaged,* but present participles are not—*The jockey considered the horse galloping.* In *I considered the fool big, big* loses its noninherent status and *I considered my boss former* is totally unacceptable.

On the other hand, adjectives that make good subject complements (but don't occur prenominally) also make good object complements.

*The pyromaniac set the building **ablaze**.*

*The Captain set the life raft **afloat**.*

*A package of Fig Newtons kept the victim **alive**.*

*The new medicine made the child **well**.*

A prenominal adjective is in no way sensitive to the verb in the sentence. Many predicate adjectives are relatively indifferent to their copulas—*Morgan is/became/seems/ appears angry*, but a sensory copula must be followed by a predicate adjective that reflects the sense in question. A compact disc can sound *scratched* but not *red*; a surface can feel *rough* but not *noisy*. While *become* can take almost any subject complement, *turn* usually suggests a relatively rapid change of state—*The milk turned sour, The weather turned cold*. *My grandparents turned old*, and *My family has turned poor* are ungrammatical, but, surprisingly, *Bob has turned grey* is fine.

Object complement adjectives are highly sensitive to their verbs. Complex transitive *paint* requires that the object complement adjective indicate some sort of color—*We painted the dining room purple*. A verb like *prove* requires that the adjective name a quality that can in fact be proven—*The attorney proved his client innocent*. Similarly, *deem* must be followed by a quality that requires judgement; *We deemed the candidate suitable* is fine but *We deemed the candidate tall* is unacceptable.

Whether an adjective occupies prenominal or object complement position can have a profound effect on the meaning of a sentence.

(a) *I considered the* **interminable** *debate*.
(b) *I considered the debate* **interminable**.

In example (a), *considered* means "to think about" or "mull over"; it's a dynamic verb in this context. But in (b), the object complement forces us to reinterpret *considered* as a stative verb meaning loosely "to judge."

INTENSIFYING AND DOWNTONING ADJECTIVES

In phrases like *an* **utter** *fool, a* **complete** *disaster, a* **total** *failure, an* **absolute** *idiot*, and *a* **real** *mess*, the prenominal adjectives do not carry much meaning of their own; instead they intensify the meaning of the noun. When someone says, "My brother-in-law is a real idiot," the speaker is using *real* to underscore the extent of the idiocy, not to express the opposite of "imaginary." Such adjectives are called **intensifying adjectives** and they are often interchangeable—*My best friend is an utter/total/complete/absolute/real failure*. Sometimes *horrible* and *terrible* can be used in this way as well—*It was a terrible mess; It was a horrible fiasco*. While most intensifying adjectives can be used in both positive and negative contexts, *horrible* and *terrible* are usually reserved for unpleasant situations. *The party was a horrible success* would be anomalous for most speakers, and ?*The party was a terrible success* would be problematic for many.

Intensifiers vary in their ability to act as subject complements. *Total* and *absolute* retain their intensifying meaning in predicate adjective position —*The destruction was absolute; The chaos was total*. *Complete* is somewhat marginal in this regard—?*The destruction was complete*. *Utter* cannot occur in predicate adjective position at all, and *real* loses its intensifier status when it occupies this position—*The destruction was real*.

English also contains constructions that downplay rather than intensify meaning. These constructions precede the entire noun phrase rather than the noun head, so they are not technically adjectives. Since there is no traditional grammatical label for these constructions, they are known simply by their semantic label, **downtoner.**

*My boss is **sort of** a jerk.*

*She is **kind of** a prima donna.*

*Your cousin is **rather** a fool.*

*Boris is a **bit of** a snob.*

*Zoila is **kind of** an accountant.*

The function of downtoners is to soften the negative connotations of an uncomplimentary noun or to undermine the literal meaning of a neutral noun. It is certainly better to have a boss that is *sort of* a jerk than a boss that is a *real* jerk. On the other hand, you may not want to trust your taxes to someone who is *kind of* an accountant.

LIMITERS

In the following sentences the items in boldface are **limiters**. They limit the hearer's attention to the noun phrase that follows and exclude other possibilities. Like downtoners, limiters modify the entire NP. Unlike the other modifying structures in this section, limiters can modify proper nouns.

*He ate **only** the grapes.*	[He didn't eat the apples, oranges, or bananas.]
*I invited **just** the women.*	[Not the men]
***Only** Evelyn knew the answer.*	[No one else knew the answer]
***Just** the oak trees survived.*	[Nothing else survived.]
***Only** the bedroom was ransacked.*	[No other room was ransacked.]

As you will see later, intensifiers, downtoners, and limiters can also modify adjectives, adverbs, and verbs.

GRADABILITY

As you have already seen, some adjectives can be inflected with comparative and superlative suffixes and others require the periphrastic forms *more* and *most*. While {-er} and *more* and {-est} and *most* communicate the notions "greater" and "greatest," respectively, *less* and *least* accomplish the same thing on a descending scale—*Otto is less friendly than Frieda; Max is the least friendly.*

Comparative and superlative forms of all types require a context for comparison. They are always anaphoric or cataphoric. In the following sentences the context for the comparison is in boldface.

*Eric is smarter **than Leslie.***

*The youngest child **in the family** asks the questions at Passover.*

***There are ten kids in the class** and Sarah is the tallest.*

***Of all the people I have ever known**, Anne is the most frugal.*

*Charlotte is more competent **than her sister.***

*Anastasia seems less confident **than Sergei.***

*I am the least talented member **of my team.***

If you marched into a room an announced without preamble, "I am older," those present would undoubtedly want to know "older than <u>who</u>?" The comparative context, however, need not be expressed in the sentence itself; it might emerge from the previous discourse or be obvious from the situation. When workers strike for *higher wages*, the employer knows that they want wages higher than the ones they currently earn.

Be aware that {-est} and *most* are not <u>always</u> superlative forms. Sometimes speakers use these forms as intensifiers without implying a comparison.

*I am dating the **most wonderful** woman.*

*Rachel is the **nicest** person.*

*He is a **most** happy baby.*

*This is the **worst** course.*

In each of these sentences *most* or {-est} is semantically closer to the intensifier *very* than the superlative.

Adjectives that can take comparative and superlative forms of either type are said to be **gradable**. Gradability means that the quality expressed by the adjective can be seen as a continuum. Gradable adjectives can always be modified by intensifiers and downtoners—*a very nice gift; a rather nice gift*.

Not all adjectives are gradable, however. Adjectives that derive from other parts of speech seldom express scalar qualities. Sentences like **This class is more freshman than that one* or **That was a very school picnic* are completely unacceptable. Even adjectives carrying adjective producing derivational morphology are sometimes problematic—*??This bowl is more wooden than that one; ??My suit is very woolen*. Some past participle adjectives are gradable—*This chair is more damaged than that one; That's a very damaged chair*, but present participle adjectives never are —**This brook is more babbling than that one; *This is a very babbling brook*.

Gradable adjectives have some interesting characteristics. Because they refer to qualities that are inherently scalar, some gradable adjectives have opposites—

hot/cold, tall/short, big/small, dark/light, smart/stupid, old/young, rich/poor. Of course in order to be opposites, two words have to have a great deal in common; both *hot* and *cold* refer to temperature; they merely represent the poles of the same semantic continuum. Be aware that not all adjective opposites are scalar. Some, like *alive* and *dead*, represent absolutes. *Dead = not alive* and *alive = not dead*. While we use expressions like "half-dead," someone who is half-dead is in fact alive. These **absolute opposites** are not normally gradable but sometimes speakers use intensifiers to engage in hyperbole—*The gangster was very dead.*

A few commonly used scalar opposites exhibit **markedness**. In the context of pairs of adjectives, markedness reflects the fact that one member of the pair represents the "norm" in the grammar. *Short* and *tall* are opposites that refer to height, but *tall* is the more generally used and therefore "unmarked" form. No matter how short an individual is, the appropriate question is "How tall are you?" *Short* and *long* usually behave in the same way (although the constraints on *short* are somewhat less stringent). If you go to a hardware store to buy piece of lumber, the clerk will probably ask "How long do you want it?" Although *young* is the opposite of *old*, we ask even three-year-olds, "How old are you?" *Tall, long,* and *old* are the commonly used **unmarked** adjectives. *Short* and *young* are considered **marked**, even though they don't carry any special morphology, because they are used in more limited circumstances.

Unmarked adjectives can be modified by measurement terms—*The child was **eight years** old; The room was **ten feet** long*, but marked adjectives cannot—**Tom was **two years** young; *The room was **ten feet** short.* (The last sentence is possible in a different context, one in which the room is ten feet short of some goal.) When someone says "I am seventy years young," we smile in part because *young* is a highly marked form here.

ADJECTIVES AND COMPOUND NOUNS

Sometimes an adjective becomes so closely associated with a noun that the construction becomes a **compound noun**. A compound noun carries different stress from an adjective plus noun construction. In an adjective plus noun construction, the second element (i.e., the noun) carries primary stress, while in a compound the first element carries the primary stress. A house that has been painted green is a *green hóuse* but a place for growing plants is a *gréenhouse*. A bird which simply happens to be blue is a *blue bírd*, while there is an avian species called a *blúebird*. Gardening may be *dirty wórk*, but your boss may expect you to do her *dírty work*. A tall chair is a *high cháir*, but if that chair is for a baby, it is a *híghchair*. Spelling is irrelevant; compound nouns may be written as separate words long after they have become compounds in speech. There are, in fact, many compounds that are still spelled as two words—*hót tub, yéllow jacket* (a bee), *blúe book* (an examination booklet), *hígh school, pótato salad,* etc.

Compound nouns can be formed from a number of different elements. The most common types are adjective plus noun constructions of the sort discussed above and noun plus noun constructions, e.g., *cupboard, freight train, wristwatch, fanny pack, windbreaker, snowshoes, roller blades.* But verb plus preposition/particle structures can also function as nouns—*a sit-in, a cookout, the lift off, a rip off, a put on, a turnover* (in pastry or basketball). Present participles sometimes function as the second element of a compound noun—*channel crossing, bungee jumping, ice fishing*. Compounds can be found in other grammatical categories as well. Among adjectives we find *pigheaded, foolproof, bloodthirsty,* and *out-to-lunch* and among verbs *typeset, stir fry, spot weld, sidestep,* and *broadcast*.

In a written text, a phrase like *French history teacher* is ambiguous. If *history teacher* is a compound noun, then *French* modifies the entire compound, e.g., [French [history teacher]]. If, however, this individual is a teacher of French history, the internal structure is different, e.g., [French history [teacher]]. In speech, pauses and stress usually make the meaning clear.

Since compounds often depend heavily on metaphor, their meanings are sometimes opaque. A non-native speaker would have difficulty interpreting *a **hotbed** of discontent* or *a **highbrow** publication*. A *sóft spot* for animals has a distant semantic relationship to *a soft spót* on the ground. Over time, the underlying structure of even relatively straightforward compounds can become muddy. Most English speakers have lost sight of the fact that a *cupboard* was literally a board on which cups were placed. Sometimes the nature of the referent changes; these days a lighthouse is often just a tower made of steel beams. Very few English speakers know that *daisy* derives from an Old English compound *dægeseage* [day's eye], *garlic* from *gar lēac* (spear leek), *warlock* from *wærloga* (oath breaker), and *lord* from *hlāfweard* (loaf ward, i.e., the protector of the bread).

We have already seen that adjective plus noun constructions embody many different semantic relationships. The same is true for the elements of a compound. *Alligator shoes* are made from alligator skins, *horse shoes* are made for horses, and *running shoes* are made to facilitate running but are worn only by people. A *lumberyard* sells lumber, a *lumber mill* cuts timber into lumber, and a *lumberjack* cuts down trees that will be made into lumber (or paper). A *bench-warmer* warms the bench by sitting on it, while a *babysitter* sits with, not on, the baby. A song called "Why Don't a Tow Truck Haul Toes?" (Penn, 1997) exploits the variable semantics of compound constructions. (Unfortunately, this pun loses force when written.)

Occasionally a compound is formed by an NP and a word that was originally a postnominal adjective, i.e., an adjective that <u>follows</u> the noun. Such compounds tend to refer to quasi-legal or governmental entities—*president elect, the body politic, an attorney general, the heir apparent.* Just as in conventional compounds, the stress here falls on the original modifying element, which in this case is the second word in the compound—*president eléct, body pólitic.*

Adjective + noun	Compound noun
a bad print	a footprint
a hard rock	a hard hat [for construction]
a brick walk	brickwork

Adjective + noun (cont.)	Compound noun (cont.)
a soft ball [like a Nerf ball]	a softball
a short child	shortbread
good food	soul food
a big yard	a barnyard
a light room	a lighthouse
high gear	high school
a large box	a cigar box
a proper gentleman	the city proper
a public event	a notary public

Usually a compound noun is semantically distinct from a comparable adjective plus noun counterpart, e.g., *a blúebook* is a completely different entity from *a blue bóok* and a *gréenhouse* has little in common with a *green hóuse*. In each of these examples the stress signals the difference. Unfortunately, there are occasions when a construction feels like a compound but does not carry compound stress. Most English speakers use compound stress in *ápple sauce* but not in *apple cíder, apple píe,* or *apple strúdel. Pótato salad* and *pótato chips* usually carry compound stress but often *potato sóup* and *potato páncakes* do not. To some extent the familiarity of the item in the culture is a factor; most Americans eat potato chips but far fewer eat potato pancakes. But this doesn't explain *apple píe,* which is a cultural icon and yet doesn't carry compound stress. For some reason cakes are more likely to carry compound stress than pies— *cárrot cake, ángel food cake, lémon cake* but *rhubarb píe, lemon meringue píe, pecan píe.* My intuition tells me that in terms of semantic structure *carrot cake* and *apple pie* are identical, since both constructions refer to pastries made from a specified fruit or vegetable. To argue on the basis of stress alone that *carrot cake* is a compound and *apple pie* is not seems unsatisfactory.

ADJECTIVE ORDER IN THE NOUN PHRASE

While an NP can have only one determiner, it can contain many adjectives. Utterances like *my old, brown couch* or *a tall, brick building* are extremely common. In these phrases, each adjective modifies the noun independently; the couch is both brown and old and the building is both tall and brick. When there is more than one adjective in an NP, English speakers usually put these adjectives in a particular order. Most speakers would not say *the brown, old couch,* nor would they say *a brick, tall building. A beautiful Russian vase* is a perfectly acceptable phrase, but *??a Russian beautiful vase* is odd, if not ungrammatical. You will find that adjectives communicating such attributes as color, size, nationality, and the material from which the noun is made often occupy relatively predictable positions in the noun phrase. While there is no sure algorithm for adjective order, English speakers tend to exploit the following pattern:

$$\text{size + age + color +} \left\{ \begin{array}{c} \textbf{material characteristics} \\ \textbf{national origin} \end{array} \right\} \text{+ noun}$$

a tall, young woman

an old, brown, leather briefcase

a red, wool coat

an immense, stone barn

a plump, dark-haired child

big, brown eyes

a tall, muscular, Swedish athlete

a tiny, five-year-old boy

You will undoubtedly find exceptions to the pattern described above.

INTERNAL STRUCTURE OF THE ADJECTIVE PHRASE

Sometimes the adjectives in an NP have their own internal structure. In a phrase like *a large white building*, *large* and *white* each modify *building* but a phrase like *a light blue dress* is potentially ambiguous. The interpretation depends on whether *light* is construed as modifying *blue* or *dress*.

a | light | blue | dress   a | light | blue | dress

In actual speech, stress and pauses will probably disambiguate the phrase. We tend to pause a bit more between adjectives of equal status. (This pause can be signaled by a comma in edited English.) The following exchange, allegedly between two state representatives, was passed around the Internet. It underscores the potential for ambiguity in structures with multiple modifiers.

Speaker A: "The Knights of Peter Claire is a large Catholic organization."

Speaker B: "I'm a large Catholic and I don't belong to it."

When gradable adjectives are modified, they can express a quality in terms of degree. A painting can be *more* or *less beautiful* than another painting, an athlete can be *too tall* or not *tall enough,* and music can be *sort of loud* or *really loud.* We use various kinds of **degree modifiers** to express these differences including *intensifiers* and *downtoners.*

Intensifiers

Intensifiers are ubiquitous in English. We have already seen that *very* plays this role; forms like *absolutely, really, totally,* and *extremely* have exactly the same function—*a **very** loud noise; an **extremely** irritating child; a **totally** awesome experience; a **really** nice woman; a **terribly** bad accident.* So can be used as an intensifier, but only with predicate adjectives and object complements—*You are **so** smart; Gwen is **so** lucky; Tom finds Lena **so** annoying.* In New England *wicked* is often employed as an intensifier—*It's **wicked** cold out today* and in England *bloody* serves this same function—*That was **bloody** rude. Stark* can be used as an intensifier, but usually only with the adjective *naked—The swimmers were **stark** naked. Super* has been an informal intensifier for decades—*This is a **super** good school.* American teenagers often use *way* as an intensifier—*That was **way** cool.*

Note that many of these intensifiers are closely related semantically to intensifying adjectives, and a number of them can be formed by simply adding {-ly} to the appropriate adjective.

*She is a **total** incompetent. / She is **totally** incompetent.*

*It was a **real** catastrophe. / It was **really** catastrophic.*

*It was an **absolute** disaster. / It was **absolutely** disastrous.*

*He is a **terrible** fool. / His behavior was **terribly** foolish.*

*It was an **awful** mess. / It was **awfully** messy.*

Like their adjective counterparts, intensifiers like *terribly, awfully,* and *horribly* are not as semantically neutral as other intensifiers. They are usually used to intensify negative or unpleasant meanings—*It's horribly wet out; He's terribly sick; Jennifer looks awfully unhappy. ?She is terribly beautiful* is an odd sentence for many speakers, although it is acceptable to some.

When an intensifier modifies an adjective, it becomes part of an adjective phrase.

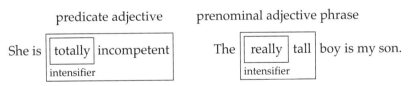

Downtoners

Some adjective modifiers are **downtoners**. Intensifiers and downtoners aren't really distinct categories; they constitute a semantic continuum and as one shades into the other, it is sometimes hard to assign a semantic label. A man who is *really angry* is angrier than a man who is *somewhat angry*. A *very easy exam* is easier than *a pretty easy exam*, but two speakers might reasonably disagree on whether a *pretty easy exam* is easier or harder than *an easy exam*. I would prefer a doctor who is *competent* to one that was *somewhat competent*, but should I prefer a blind date who is *handsome* to one who is *rather handsome*? You'll recognize many of these words and phrases in this section as the same forms that "downtone" noun phrases

*The quarterback is **sort of** clumsy.*

*Your new girlfriend is **kind of** stuffy.*

*Patsy is **rather** tall.*

*Dena is **somewhat** upset.*

*It was a **pretty** nice party.*

*Her mother is **a bit** strict.*

The downtoner *bit* must always be used with the indefinite article—*She is a bit upset*, unless *bit* is preceded by a superlative form, in which case the superlative is preceded by *the*—*He isn't **the** slightest bit jealous; She isn't **the** least bit contrite*. Although this construction can occur in affirmative sentences—*She's the tiniest bit mad*, it most often appears in negatives.

Modification of Comparative and Superlative Forms

Like any other gradable adjective, an inflected comparative form can be modified by an intensifier or a downtoner—*Christine is **somewhat** taller than her brother; Dick is **a lot** nicer than Jane*. Note that the quantifier *a lot* cannot be used with an uninflected adjective—**Dick is a lot nice*. This is evidence that the degree quantifier is modifying the comparative meaning rather than the adjective itself. Comparative *more* and superlative *most* can also be modified by these forms. *More*, which expresses comparative degree, can be modified by a quantifier that also expresses degree—*Elisa is **a lot more** competent than her sister; Alexander is **far more** intelligent than his cousin; She is **so much more** outgoing than Alberto*. The modification relationships in the constructions can be captured by means of nesting boxes.

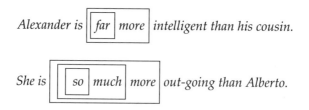

As you can see, in the first diagram *far more* modifies *intelligent* and *far* modifies *more*. The second diagram contains another level of nesting; *so* mod-

ifies *much, so much* modifies the comparative form *more* and *so much more* modifies *outgoing*.

Comparative and superlative adjective constructions can be preceded by a
variety of degree modifiers.

*Jane is **a lot** more fun than Philip.*

*My children are **far** noisier than my sister's.*

*Wendy is **somewhat** taller than Ray.*

*That office is **far** less desirable than this one.*

*Louie isn't **as** competent as his brother.*

Other Degree Modifiers

Too and *enough* also express degree judgments. *Too* indicates that the NP
being modified has an excess of the quality in question; the use of *too* reflects
a negative judgement. *Enough* indicates that the NP has a sufficient amount of
the quality in question. *Enough* always follows the noun being modified.

*The baby is getting **too** fat.*	*The baby is fat **enough**.*
*It's **too** cold in here.*	*It's warm **enough** in here.*
*This house is **too** small.*	*This house is big **enough**.*

Too occurs in predicate adjective phrases but it never modifies prenominal
adjectives—**The too fat baby is my niece; *This is a too cold room.* *Enough* can occur prenominally, although it sometimes sounds odds in this position—*A big
enough house is essential; ?This is a warm enough room.*

Too can, however, precede and modify an adjective when that adjective precedes the entire noun phrase—*This is too big a house; It was too hard an assignment; It was too long a lecture.* In the structure ***too long** a lecture, too long* precedes both the noun head and its determiner; in other words it modifies the
entire NP. Without *too*, the structure is ungrammatical—**long a lecture.*

predicate nominative

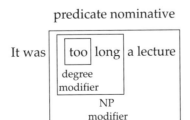

Occasionally *too* is simply used as an intensifier—*You are too kind.* This
occurs most often in negative utterances—*She doesn't look too good* (i.e., *She
doesn't look very good.*).

```
┌─────────────────────────────────────────────────────────────┐
│                     Summary of degree modifiers               │
│                     ━━━━━━━━━━━━━━━━━━━━━━━━━                  │
│                                                               │
│  Intensifiers          Your mom is **very** angry.            │
│                                                               │
│                        This is an **awfully** cold room.      │
│                                                               │
│                        I'm **really** nauseous.               │
│                                                               │
│                        Her apartment is **so** filthy.        │
│                                                               │
│                        Jonah's claims were **totally** ridiculous. │
│                                                               │
│  Downtoners            She's a **rather** strange person.     │
│                                                               │
│                        The baby is **sort of** cute.          │
│                                                               │
│                        Max is getting **a bit** fat.          │
│                                                               │
│                        This cheese is **somewhat** moldy.     │
│                                                               │
│  Other                 The portions are **too** small.        │
│                                                               │
│                        I'm old **enough** now.                │
└─────────────────────────────────────────────────────────────┘
```

Adjective Complements

Predicate adjectives are often followed by prepositional phrases that are clearly working with the adjective in a single grammatical structure. Such prepositional phrases are called **adjective complements**. The relationship of the prepositional phrase to the preceding adjective is semantically rather like the relationship of a direct object to the preceding verb. In a sentence like *Kate is fond of Henry, fond of Henry* is an adjective phrase containing an adjective head *fond* and its complement *of Henry*.

In the following sentences the adjective complements are in boldface.

*Joseph was jealous **of the new baby**.*

*I am glad **of that**.*

*I'm aware **of her problems**.*

*Ted is resentful **of Philip's success**.*

*The children are afraid **of spiders**.*

*She is certain **of her daughter's victory**.*

*Jack is bad **at math**.*

*My father is mad **at our neighbor**.*

*I am pleased **about Kemp's promotion**.*

*Marilyn is mad **about Tom's comment**.*

*I am angry **with you**.*

The predicate adjective **fond** <u>requires</u> a following prepositional phrase—
*Kate is fond is ungrammatical. In the other examples, the phrase is not required
for grammaticality, but the context or the discourse must indicate the complement somehow. The sentence *Jack is bad* without the complement *at math* will
be misinterpreted as a statement about Jack's moral character, unless the rest
of the discourse makes it clear that this is a statement about math skills. *I'm
aware* makes little sense without an overt or covert complement.

Clauses can also function as adjective complements and I will explore these
constructions at some length in Chapter 5.

Use of the Term *Adverb*

Unlike adjectives, adverbs have no characteristic morphology. While {-ly} is
sometimes hailed as an adverb suffix, only a limited number of adverbs actually carry that ending. (There are also a few adjectives that exploit this suffix—
lovely, friendly, fatherly.) As a result, the criteria for establishing adverb status
are somewhat muddy

The term *adverb* is also a bit problematic. Traditional grammars use it to label any structure modifying an adjective, any structure modifying an adverb, and
any structure modifying a verb. Some contemporary grammarians try to avoid
this catch-all term, adverb, by using only semantic terms like *intensifier* or structure terms like *adjunct*. But in fact the traditional labeling system arose precisely
because the same words can take on all three of these modification functions.

"Adverb" modifying an adjective	"Adverb" modifying an adverb	"Adverb" modifying a verb
Irene is **awfully** nosey.	She talks **awfully** fast.	_____
She is **really** nice.	She runs **really** fast.	He **really** enjoyed the film.
You were **extremely** rude.	Tony talks **extremely** fast.	_____
Her dress is **just** beautiful.	She sings **just** beautifully.	I **just** hate this job.
This is **absolutely** awful.	She did it **absolutely** perfectly.	I **absolutely** despise liver.

"Adverb" modifying an adjective (cont.)	"Adverb" modifying an adverb (cont.)	"Adverb" modifying a verb (cont.)
Manny is **rather** tall.	Joe dances **rather** well.	I **rather** like Mitzi.
This is **sort of** suspicious.	He smiled **sort of** sweetly.	I **sort of** enjoyed the party.
The place is **fairly** clean.	I hit the nail **fairly** hard.	She **fairly** sailed out of the room. [British English]

My solution to this terminological dilemma is to use semantic terms like *intensifier* and *downtoner* to refer to those words and phrases that modify adjectives and adverbs and to use the term adverb to refer to words and structures that modify verbs, predicates, and sentences.

Adjunct Adverbs

Adjunct is general term that refers to any item (or person) that functions in an auxiliary capacity. In linguistics it is typically used to describe an optional element, one that is not essential to the acceptability of the utterance. In this section, I'm going to use the term in a restricted sense to refer to a large class of adverbial constructions. Although these adverbs are usually optional, there will be a few constructions in which they are required. (An adjunct is optional only in that it is not required for grammaticality; adjuncts provide crucial information in the discourse.)

Adjuncts are integrated into the sentence or clause in which they appear (Quirk et al., 1972, p. 421). They usually (but not always) appear in the predicate and they usually modify some or all of the VP, although it is not always easy to specify the exact modification relationship. Adjuncts can be stacked up. A given simple sentence can contain only one subject, one direct object (or alternatively one subject complement), one indirect object, but it can contain a number of adjuncts. All of the adverbs discussed in this section are adjuncts. You will see later how adjuncts differ from two other types of adverbs—disjuncts and conjuncts.

INTENSIFYING, DOWNTONING, AND LIMITING ADJUNCTS

Adjunct intensifiers and downtoners are closely related to those that modify nouns, noun phrases, and adjectives. Predictably, when an intensifying adjunct modifies a lexical verb, it simply intensifies the meaning of that verb, while a downtoner downplays it. Most intensifying and downtoning adjuncts co-occur with a limited number of verbs.

Intensifiers often co-occur with psych-verbs, though they can modify other verb types. As you will see, some intensifiers are quite narrowly constrained in terms of context. *Really* is the most versatile intensifying adjunct.

Rick **really** *loves the races.*

I **just** *hate theme parks.*

Albert's criticism bothered me **a lot**.

They **fully** *appreciate her predicament.*

Jack **completely** *ignored her request.*

She needed dental work **badly**.

I agree with you **totally**.

You can't **possibly** *expect me to leave now.* [Occurs only with *can't*]

I don't like her **in the least**. [Occurs only with negatives]

He doesn't like me **at all**. [Occurs only with negatives and questions]

My aunt doesn't mind **in the slightest**. [Occurs only with negatives]

I *don't like him* **a bit**. [As an intensifier, occurs only with negatives]

Downtoners are usually quite flexible. Note that *a bit* can be used as a downtoner when it appears in an affirmative utterance.

I **rather** *enjoyed the play.*

Barbara **sort of** *snickered.*

This will hurt **a bit**.

Stuart was **somewhat** *annoyed by her remarks.*

I was **kind of** *hurt by her behavior.*

Downtoners rarely occur in negative constructions, probably because it is redundant to downtone a quality that has already been negated—**I didn't rather enjoy the play; ??Barbara didn't sort of snicker.* The last sentence is possible if a contrast is implied—*Barbara didn't sort of snicker; she positively guffawed.*

Like the negative particle, some intensifying adverbs have scope and that scope can be manipulated by placing the adverb at different points in the predicate.

I **really** *will slug you.*	[Intensifying *will*, i.e., intention]
I *will* **really** *slug you.*	[Intensifying *slug*]
I *will* **really** *slug you hard.*	[Intensifying both *slug* and *hard*]
I *will slug you* **really** *hard.*	[Intensifying *hard*]

(*Really* can be considered an adjunct in all but the last of the above examples.)
Limiting adjuncts focus the hearer on a narrow or literal interpretation of

the verb. They are often used when the speaker wants to undercut a stronger implication.

*I **merely** spoke to you. [I didn't yell at you.]*

*I **only** tapped him. [I didn't hit him.]*

*I **just** sneezed. [I'm not dying.]*

Note that *just* can function as both an intensifier and a limiter. In *I just <u>hate</u> him*, it's clearly an intensifier and in *I just dislike him [I don't despise him]*, it's a limiter.

Intensifiers and limiters each constitute a small class of adverbs.

LOCATIVES (SPACE ADVERBS)

English contains two different types of space or location adverbs. While adverbs of place and direction might seem very close in meaning, they occur in different environments. Adverbs of place can appear with both stative and dynamic verbs, while adverbs of direction co-occur only with dynamic verbs.

Adverbs of Place

Adverbs of place indicate where someone/thing is located or where an event takes place. Adverbs of place usually answer the question *where?* These adverbs are typically prepositional phrases but can also be single lexical items. Adverbs of place often but not always occur with verbs that reflect states rather than actions. (Although adverbs of place are technically complements rather than adjuncts when they occur with copula *be*, I am including them in this section since they so clearly have the same semantic functions as other locative adverbs.)

*They played croquet **on the lawn.***

*Aunt Sue is sitting **in the bathtub.***

*The bank is **next to the gas station.***

*Your book is **on the table.***

*Zoltan is standing **by his mother.***

*The painting hangs **over the fireplace.***

*Jean works **opposite the police station.***

*Jay is **here.***

*I'll live **anywhere.***

*Jorgen has been **everywhere.***

*Carol is **outside***.

*She has been living **there** a long time.*

Here and *there* can express both anaphora and deixis. The father who yells "Come here" at his child is exploiting only deixis. But the teenager who says to her friend, "I am over at Anne's house. Do you want to come over here?" is exploiting both deixis and anaphora, *Anne's house* being the anaphoric referent for *here*. If a friend says "I'm going to the new club on the beach tonight," and you reply with "I wouldn't be caught dead there," you are exploiting both anaphora and deixis.

Adverbs of Direction

Adverbs of direction indicate just that—the direction in which an entity is going or the path that it takes. Unlike adverbs of place, adverbs of direction must co-occur with dynamic verbs. Adverbs of direction typically include a preposition that inscribes an actual direction in space: *up, down, over, under, around, through, across, into.*

*They waded **into the water**.*

*The horses galloped **across the meadow**.*

*The police walked **around the crime scene**.*

*The snake wriggled **under the log**.*

*The baby crawled **up the stairs**.*

*The beagle climbed **over the fence**.*

*The rock was thrown **through the window**.*

Not all adverbs of direction are prepositional phrases—*We walked **upstairs**; We went **downtown**; They traveled **overland**; They climbed **aboard**.* You can see, however, that these one-word adverbs were originally prepositional phrases, including *aboard*, which used to be *on board*. The forms *here, there, everywhere,* and *anywhere* can function as adverbs of direction as well as adverbs of place— *The baby is crawling **everywhere** now; I'll drive **there** tomorrow. Here* and *there* are often preceded by *over—Gina is coming **over here** later; I'll walk **over there** during my lunch hour.* (Adverbs of place can also be preceded by *over—Jason is over at Janet's house.*)

In adverbs of direction, English speakers can sometimes omit the object of a preposition if it is obvious from the discourse context. A child whose mother has just called her might reply with "But I don't want to come in." It is clear from the context that the child means *in the house*. (**I don't want to come into* would be an ungrammatical response, however.) A boy who is standing in a third floor window might yell to a friend on the street, "Come on up." The boy obviously means "up the stairs." In each of the following sentences, the object of the preposition can be deleted as long as the NP is reasonably clear from the rest of the discourse.

*The train comes **through** ~~town~~ at midnight.*

*Walk **around** ~~the muddy spot~~.*

*You can climb **up** ~~the tree~~ by yourself.*

*A car drove **past** ~~our house~~ late last night.*

*Let's saunter **by** ~~your boyfriend's place~~.*

*Nicole nearly fell **off** ~~the monkey bars~~.*

Place adverbs are far less flexible in this regard. In general the object of the preposition must be expressed in such constructions—**Edwin sat on; *The children played in; *She stood beside*. There are, however, a few contexts in which a conventionally understood object can be omitted, e.g., *Your shirt is hanging out [of your pants]*, and motorcycle racers often talk of *hanging off [the motorcycle seat]*.

Many single-word adverbs and some prepositional phrases can function as both adverbs of place and adverbs of direction Note the contrasting verbs in each set.

*Jared is **ahead**. / Jared ran **ahead**.*

*Camille is **downstairs**. / Camille walked **downstairs**.*

*The kids are **outside**. / The kids have gone **outside**.*

*The canoe is **downstream**. / The canoe floated **downstream**.*

*She lives **across the street**. / She walked **across the street**.*

*They live **aboard their boat**. / They went **aboard the boat**.*

In a few cases, clearly related prepositional forms can be used to distinguish between position and direction. In these cases the semantic difference has been **lexicalized**, i.e., the difference in meaning is expressed by different lexical items.

*Joe danced **on** the table. / Maggie leapt **onto** the table.*

*Nancy sat **in** the tub. / Hank stepped **into** the tub.*

It is possible for a locative utterance to be ambiguous. In *My brother fell downstairs*, two different interpretations are possible depending on whether my brother fell down the stairs or was downstairs when he fell.

Sometimes adverbs of direction literally name directions—*We traveled **west***. Sometimes they indicate moving toward a goal—*The kids walked **to the store**; They ran **toward the lights**; They headed **for the woods***. (Some linguists consider *goal* to be a separate semantic category but that will not concern us here.) In other cases, adverbs of direction simply indicate a path—*She drove* **across the bridge**; *They strolled* **through the garden**. All direction adverbs can be preceded by other modifiers—*Robin walked* **straight** *into the house; The children walked* **directly** *to school; We drove* **straight** *east*.

Meanings of Spatial Prepositions

Each spatial preposition has a range of related meanings. While the core meaning of *over* inscribes direction ⌢, other nondynamic meanings have evolved from this (Lakoff, 1987, pp. 418–430). In *There was snow all over the sidewalk, over* suggests "covered"; in *The lamp hung over the table, over* suggests "above." Sometimes *over* indicates physical contact—*They walked over the bridge* and sometimes it doesn't—*They flew over the Rockies*.

Metaphor has played a significant role in broadening the meanings of prepositions. Linguist George Lakoff and philosopher Mark Johnson (1980) have written extensively on the role of metaphor in language. They have pointed out (p. 59) that, while the core meaning of the preposition *in* is "inside a container," this meaning has been extended metaphorically in sentences like *Lucien is in a difficult situation; Pilar is in trouble;* and *Kirsten is in love.* Does it even make sense to label *in trouble* and *in love* adverbs of place? One might be able to make a case for *in trouble* but *in love* strongly suggests a state rather than a location. We see the same semantic progression with *under*.

The baby is under the table.

These students are under his authority.

Jack is under Jill's spell.

Farouk is under the weather.

The more metaphorical and idiomatic the construction, the harder it is to choose an appropriate grammatical category for the prepositional phrase.

Direct Object Versus Prepositional Constructions

As you saw in Chapter 1, there is often a subtle difference in meaning between locative prepositional phrases and simple NPs, which have a locative meaning. While such NPs are usually considered direct objects, they are semantically related to adverbs. Compare the following pairs of sentences.

They climbed up the mountain. / They climbed the mountain.

She swam across the English Channel. / She swam the English Channel.

Megan hiked through the valley. / Megan hiked the valley.

The first sentence in each pair contains an adverb of direction, which describes some sort of path. The second sentence in each pair communicates the notion that this path has been completely traversed. As linguist Beth Levin (1993, p. 44) has pointed out, the prepositional phrase usually has a "partitive" interpretation, while the NP has "holistic" interpretation, i.e., *They climbed the [whole] mountain.* Locative direct objects sometimes suggest that the subject has accomplished a feat. One might make the *Guinness Book of Records* for climbing a mountain, but lots of people climb up mountains.

This contrast between direct objects and directional prepositional phrases occurs in other contexts as well. In *Mary poked her brother,* it is clear that physical contact was made, while this is less clear in *Mary poked at her brother. At* often occurs in constructions in which the intent of the agent isn't realized or the action has an inconclusive result. (Goldberg, 1995, pp. 63–64).

I slapped at the mosquito. / I slapped the mosquito.

Pat kicked at her attacker. / Pat kicked her attacker.

The archeologist chipped at the rock. / The archeologist chipped the rock.

Batman shot at his adversary. / Batman shot his adversary.

Locative Inversion

Sometimes intransitive verbs allow **locative inversion**. This occurs when a sentence initial locative adverb is followed directly by the verb, i.e., the subject and verb are inverted. Locative inversion often has an exclamatory character—*Here comes trouble! There goes the most obnoxious employee in the office.* It can also be used to present someone in a social situation—*Here is my old English teacher. I'd like you to meet her.* Occasionally it is used to introduce unexpected participants or items into the discourse (Givón, 1993b, p. 209). This is especially true in traditional narratives like fairy tales, which is why the last two examples in the following set sound a bit archaic. These examples contain both exclamatory and presentation types of locative inversion.

Here is my wife Judy.

Here comes Jay.

There goes my hope for a promotion!

Behind my boyfriend stood a large grizzly bear.

In the woods lived an evil witch.

In the carriage sat the most handsome man Cinderella had ever seen.

A sentence like *Into the room walked my ex-husband!* introduces an unexpected participant and at the same time expresses surprise.

Locative inversion occurs only with intransitive verbs and copula *be.* While *Down the street walked Art* is fine, **On the table put she the books* is completely ungrammatical. But even intransitive verbs are highly constrained in this regard. Adverbs of direction seem more amenable to locative inversion than adverbs of place. *Around the corner came Nell* is far more acceptable than *?On the table danced Nell*. But even adverbs of place can trigger locative inversion when the verb is stative—*In the corner sat a wizened old man*.

As you may recall from Chapter 1, locative inversion represents **marked** (i.e., non-prototypical) word order. Marked word order always has a special communicative function and that is certainly the case in these examples.

TEMPORAL ADVERBS

English has at least four different types of adverbs related to time. Like locative adverbs, temporal adverbs take a variety of forms—single words, prepositional phrases, and complex clauses (which will be discussed in Chapter 5).

Adverbs of Point or Boundary in Time

Adverbs of point or boundary in time indicate when an event occurs or a state endures and, as a rule, they answer the question *when*? Such adverbs are often prepositional phrases but they can also be single lexical items or phrases. Adverbs of time vary in how they constrain the time frame. Some express a very specific time—*You must turn in your research paper **at 5:00 P.M. on January 7***. Some bound the time frame at one end but not the other; in *You must turn in your research project **before noon on January 7***, the time frame is bounded at the far end (noon of January 7) but not at the near end (anytime before that.) There are also time adverbs that bound the time frame on both sides—*You must turn in your research project **between January 7 and January 9***. Some are simply vague—*Turn in your research project **later***.

Summary of adverbial constructions expressing a point or boundary in time

Specific time frame	David finished his test **at 3 P.M.**
	Mary Ann lived in Indiana **in 1985**.
	I washed the car **yesterday**.
	My supervisor was sick **this morning**.
	Steve went to Paris **last week**.
	She lost her job **a year ago last Tuesday**.
	Ms. Rogers is sitting in your office **right now**.
Time frame bounded on one side	You must finish your exam **before noon**.
	This offer is good **until March 15**.
	We will talk **after dinner**.

Summary of adverbial constructions expressing a point or boundary in time (cont.)	
Time frame bounded on two sides	I should arrive **between five and six o'clock.**
	She lived here **sometime between 1992 and 1994.**
Vague time frame	My mother was promoted **recently.**
	I will do the dishes **later.**
	I plan to visit Mr. Kuno in Japan **someday.**
	I haven't seen Paul **lately.**

As you can see, some time adverbs are deictic and some are not. Deictic adverbs like *tomorrow, yesterday, today, last Tuesday,* and *a year ago* are all interpreted relative to the time of speaking. On Monday, yesterday is Sunday and tomorrow is Tuesday; but on Tuesday, yesterday is Monday and tomorrow is Wednesday. Cyclical time adverbs like days of the week and months of the year are also deictic. While *Beth is arriving Tuesday* may seem to express a straightforward time frame, there are countless future Tuesdays and the hearer will automatically pick the one following the time of speaking. Adverbs that express recurring events are not deictic, however. If I tell you that "In the Alaskan bush the mail plane comes on Tuesdays," you don't need to know the time of speaking to interpret this utterance; presumably the mail plane comes every Tuesday.

Now and *then* are both deictic, and *then* is anaphoric as well. The time frame in a sentence like *Jason was working in Scotland then* is impossible to interpret unless that time frame has been established elsewhere in the discourse—*We lived in Northumberland in 1970s; Jason was working in Scotland then. Now* always refers to an event which is occurring or imminent—*I am doing the dishes now; I'll fix your computer now. Then* typically refers to a future or past time relatively distant from the time of utterance—*The rainy season will end in a month; I will fix the roof then,* although there certainly are occasions when *then* refers to the immediate future—*The game ends in one minute; I'll take out the garbage then.*

Adverbs of time can sometimes be modified by limiters—*The baby was born **just** an hour ago; Beth arrived **only** last night.* Adverbs expressing vague time frames can also be modified by intensifiers and downtoners—*Alan came **a bit** early; They moved into this house **very** recently; Mary Pat arrived **somewhat** later.*

Since the present perfect typically involves present time in some way, adverbs that specify a particular past time cannot co-occur with this construction. A speaker cannot say "Rosie has been to Russia in 1990" or "I have been to the dentist yesterday." If I say "I have been to the library this morning," it must still be morning. The present perfect does appear with adverbs that <u>include</u> present time—*I have washed four loads of clothes **today**; Martin has read two chapters **so far**; Georgia has been here **since noon**; I've seen Maggie twice **this week**.* It also co-occurs with adverbs that reflect the recent past—*My great aunt has been* sick **recently**; Silas has **just** arrived; I haven't seen Renee **lately**. (*Lately* often occurs in negatives and questions.)

Adverbs of Duration

Adverbs of duration specify how long an event or state lasts. They typically answer the question *how long?* and usually take the form of prepositional phrases, noun phrases, or clauses. Remember that unlike the simple past tense, the perfect typically expresses a time frame with duration. It is not surprising then that adverbs of duration constitute one of the most important strategies for constraining the time frames communicated by the perfect, although they can appear in other constructions as well.

*Mary and John have lived in Canada **for twenty years**.*

*He has been attending the University of New Mexico **since January**.*

*My neighbors had been fighting **for hours** [when the police arrived].*

*I worked there **a few weeks**.*

*We lived in that cabin **from June to September**.*

*Claudia will be here **for six days**.*

*He is going to stay here **indefinitely**.*

*Evelyn is going to stay **awhile**.*

Adverbs of Frequency

Adverbs of frequency specify the frequency with which an event occurs. They typically answer the question *how often?* Nouns referring to time units can often be transformed into adverbs of frequency by adding an {-ly} suffix—*hourly, daily, weekly, monthly, yearly* (but not **minutely*). Adverbs of frequency can range from common occurrences—*usually, continually* to few or zero occurrences—*seldom, rarely, never*.

*I had the flu **five times** last year.*

*Liz blinked **twice**.*

*Lyle travels **frequently**.*

*My sister has visited Paris **many times**.*

*Martha washes her car **annually**.*

*Peter **always** cleans his plate.*

*My cousin **seldom** visits her father.*

*Do you come here **often**?*

*Connie **rarely** attends these events.*

Adverbs of frequency can be modified by both intensifiers and limiters—*Betsy* **very** *seldom cleans her room; I have been to Poland* **just** *twice.*

Occasionally the position of an adverb in a sentence will affect its semantic role. The sentence *Kirsty once dated Herman* indicates that Kirsty dated Herman at some unspecified period of time in the past. But in *Kirsty dated Herman once,* the adverb indicates frequency. Sometimes a given construction will have two possible interpretations. In *Brett stole a lot, a lot* might be a direct object NP, i.e., Brett stole a lot of stuff, or it might be an adverb of frequency, i.e. Brett stole often.

More than one temporal adverb can occur in the same predicate. Adverbs of frequency commonly co-occur with adverbs of point/boundary in time— *The baby has fallen twice this morning.* They can also co-occur with adverbs of duration—*She frequently coughs for hours.*

Time Relationship Adverbs

There are some time adverbs that don't fall into any of the above categories. These adverbs usually communicate a time frame which is relative to some other time frame and the semantics are sometimes quite complex. (Some grammarians call these aspectual adverbs because they communicate information about the relative time frame.) None of these adverbs comfortably answers the adverbial questions *when? how long?* and *how often?*

Galina **first** *visited Budapest when she was a teenager.*

Isabel **finally** *turned in her test paper.*

I **still** *don't like liver.*

I don't drink coffee **anymore**.

Scott has lost his keys **again**.

Judy hasn't finished the project **yet**.

I have **already** *filed my income tax form.*

The adverb *first* communicates the fact that Galina has visited Budapest more than once and, in conjunction with a clause which expresses a point in time, indicates the time frame of the initial visit. *Finally* doesn't indicate an actual time frame but suggests that it took Isabel an excessive amount of time to turn in her paper. *Still* suggests an unspecified duration and underscores the fact that circumstances have not changed, while *anymore*, which co-occurs with a negative verb, suggests that circumstances have changed. (In some dialects, *anymore* can be used in an affirmative sentence to mean "these days"—*People just throw their trash out the window anymore.*)

Again reflects an activity that has occurred an unspecified number of times but more than once, while *yet*, which usually occurs with a negative verb, suggests a time frame that is still open.

Constraining the Time Frame

In Chapter 3, you saw that tense and even aspect constrain time only in very general ways. Without modification, both past and future go on indefinitely. Temporal adverbs provide the tools for focusing in on smaller pieces of this enormous canvas.

Obviously, the nature of the discourse will determine to what degree a time frame will be manipulated by adverbs. Historical narratives tend to be highly constrained. The following passage is from *Undaunted Courage: Meriwether Lewis, Thomas Jefferson and the Opening of the American West* (Ambrose, 1996). (Boldface added.)

> **By June 30**, the iron frame was put together and the skins . . . had been prepared. **In the morning**, the sewing together of the skins over the frame would begin. **Meanwhile**, the portage was within two days of completion. **Soon** the expedition would be rolling up the river **again**. (p. 245)

This brief paragraph contains five temporal adverbs, each of which places some portion of the narrative in a different time frame. ("[W]ithin two days" is a temporal expression but not technically an adverb.)

Of course time is always an important element in a biography, a history, or a personal narrative. But even in conversation, speakers are constantly manipulating temporal adverbs. Consider this exchange from Patricia Cornwall's novel *From Potter's Field* (1995). (Boldface added.)

> "Mr. Gault," I said. "Do you have any idea where your daughter is **now**?"
>
> "Well, she **eventually** went out on her own **four or five years ago when Luther passed on**. We **usually** hear from her **at Birthdays**, **Christmas**, **whenever the mood strikes**."
>
> "Did you hear from her **this Christmas**?" I asked.
>
> "Not directly **on Christmas day**, but **a week or two before**." (p. 307)

ADVERBS OF MANNER

Adverbs of manner indicate the manner or style in which the subject of the sentence acts or is acted upon. Adverbs of manner are often formed by simply adding the {-ly} suffix to an adjective form—*boldly, loudly, obnoxiously, coldly, gracefully, recklessly, quickly, carelessly,* etc. Adverbs that are derived in this way are typically gradable—*They danced very gracefully; She drove really recklessly.* There are also a few uninflected one-word adverbs of manner that are gradable—*She runs really fast.* A prepositional phrase headed by the preposition *like* or *with* can be used to construct an adverb of manner—*He drives like a maniac; She writes with great flair.* (As you will see in Chapter 5, clauses can also function in this way.) Adverbs of manner answer the question *how?* but it is important to distinguish them from adverbs of means, which also answer this question.

*The little boy sobbed **noisily**.*

*They **surreptitiously** entered the vault.*

*She skis **like a professional**.*

*He replied **angrily**.*

*They danced **with grace**.*

*He scrubbed the kitchen **thoroughly**.*

*The Girl Scouts walked **single file**.*

*Lourdes cooks beans **Cuban-style**.*

*Our friends are acting **like idiots**.*

*The clothes snapped **briskly** in the breeze.*

*The limb hit the window **with great force**.*

*The baby's aunt **accidentally** frightened him.*

*The backhoe can dig a basement **efficiently**.*

As you can see, adverbs of manner most often occur with agent subjects but they can also occur with patient, causer, and even instrument subjects. Sentences containing experiencer subjects seldom occur with adverbs of manner, in large part because such sentences reflect private, internal states, and it's hard to attribute manner to a state. Sentences like *She thought longingly about her children* are certainly possible, however.

In Chapter 3 you examined the structure of **pseudo-passives**, constructions that are active in form and passive in meaning. Almost all pseudo-passives contain adverbs of manner and they often depend on these adverbs for grammaticality.

Cotton washes well.

These shirts iron easily.

Tangerines peel nicely.

This software loads quickly.

If the adverbs are removed, these sentence lose their acceptability for most speakers—*?Cotton washes; ??These shirts iron; ??Tangerines peel; ??This software loads*. If a contrasting context is provided, grammaticality can often be restored—*Cotton washes but wool doesn't; This software loads but that other disk is defective.*

ADVERBS OF MEANS

Adverbs of means indicate by what means or method an action is carried out. When an agent, causer, or instrument appears in a position other than subject, it is usually an adverb of means. The *by* prepositional phrase of a passive is always an adverb of means, since the agent/causer/instrument of the active always becomes the object of *by* in the corresponding passive. However, as you will see in the following examples, not all agent/causer/instrument *by* prepositional phrases occur in the passive. *With* prepositional phrases are often (but not always) instruments. Adverbs derived from adjectives with the suffix {-ly} can also function as adverbs of means.

*The armadillo was hit **by a bus**.*

*Ben was fired **by his boss**.*

*The dog was frightened **by the thunder**.*

*This garment was made **by hand**.*

*Paulette always travels **by train**.*

*The mobster obtained the money **by illegal means**.*

*He flew **Air France**.*

*The mole was removed **surgically**.*

*Analyze this sentence **grammatically**.*

*She repaired the computer **with a hammer**.*

*He swayed them **with his great charm**.*

*These photos were taken **with a telephoto lens**.*

A passive sentence can contain two adverbs of means, an instrument and an agent—*The mole was removed **with a laser by my family doctor**; The computer was repaired **with a hammer by my assistant**.* In such cases the *by* prepositional phrase will always contain the agent.

Note that an adverb of means need not literally be an agent or an instrument; it can also be a process, a method, or even a mode of behavior—*surgically, grammatically, by illegal means, with his great charm.*

Adverbs of manner and adverbs of means do not co-occur with copulas. **She is assertive quietly* is ungrammatical. (As you will see later, however, sometimes {-ly} forms can modify adjectives—*She is quietly assertive*.) Stative verbs rarely occur with adverbs of manner and means. You will occasionally hear a sentence like *They own that property **illegally***, but such constructions are rare. In the sentence *Dave wants this car **badly***, *badly* is acting as an intensifier rather than an adverb of manner.

Sometimes adverbs of manner shade into adverbs of means. In fact some grammarians include both types in a single category called **process adverbs**

(Quirk et al., 1972, pp. 459–61). Some grammarians would argue that *She got the goods illegally* contains an adverb of manner, while *She got the goods by illegal means* contains an adverb of means; yet, the two utterances are very close in meaning.

ADVERBS OF REASON/PURPOSE

Adverbs of reason/purpose indicate why or to what purpose something occurs. They usually answer the question *why*? These two semantic categories are often grouped together because there is a great deal of semantic overlap.

He did it for love.	[reason]
I searched the room for evidence.	[reason, purpose]
We ran for cover.	[purpose]
Pete carefully prepared for the race.	[purpose]
She stayed married for the sake of the children.	[reason, purpose]
The program failed because of a software error.	[reason]
The circuit breaker tripped due to a short in a wire.	[reason]

Reason/purpose constructions can often be paraphrased with a clause containing *in order to*; *He did it in order to obtain love*; *We searched the room in order to obtain evidence*.

Note that in *She stayed married for the sake of the children*, the prepositional phrase *for the sake of the children* closely resembles a benefactive. However, the noun head in a benefactive is always animate, while the noun head *sake* is inanimate. In *She did it for the children, for the children* is indeed a benefactive phrase. This illustrates the problems inherent in syntactic labeling. One could certainly argue that *for the children* is an adverb of purpose, the purpose being to benefit the children. Traditionally, however, benefactives have been treated as nominal constructions rather than adverbial.

Adverbs of purpose/reason are most often clauses, so I will discuss these constructions more thoroughly in Chapter 5.

ADVERBS OF RESULT

Occasionally, a prepositional phrase will indicate a result.

The jailers starved their prisoner to death.

Their taunting drove the child to tears.

The little girl cried herself to sleep. [i.e., *into* sleep]

Adverbs of result have a lot in common with other constructions that express results, including object complements—*Their taunting drove the child crazy*.

There are some constructions in which a prepositional phrase is locative but at the same time expresses a strong result—*The audience booed the actors off the stage; She laughed him out of the room; Grandma scared the children away from the garden.* In each of these examples the prepositional phrase indicates where the direct object went as a result of the activities of the subject, e.g., The audience booed and as a result the actors went off the stage.

ADVERBIAL PROFORMS

Since the term **pronoun** contains the root **noun**, it isn't appropriate to use this label to refer to words that substitute for other parts of speech. Linguists have coined the all-purpose term **proform** for a small word that substitutes for another word or construction. (A pronoun is simply one type of proform.) Just as pronouns are noun substitutes, **adverbial proforms** are adverb substitutes. Adverbial proforms are ubiquitous in *wh* questions and, as you will see in Chapter 5, they also occur in dependent clauses of a particular type. Adverb proforms can participate in any kind of adjunct construction except limiters. In the following examples the function of the proform is indicated in brackets.

Where did he hide?	[adverb of place]
When are you coming?	[adverb of time]
How often has he fallen?	[adverb of frequency]
How long can you stay?	[adverb of duration]
Why has she quit her job?	[adverb of reason]
How does Fanny dance?	[adverb of manner]
How can this situation be remedied?	[adverb of means]
How well does she speak Russian?	[degree modifier within adverb of manner]
How much does he love her?	[degree modifier within intensifier]

As you can see, the proform *how* often acts as a degree modifier within a larger adverbial construction. Like the other interrogative words, modifier *how* moves to sentence initial position in a question but it brings with it the form that it modifies. *How* can also be used to modify any quantifier that expresses a nonspecific quantity.

How many books has Inga sold?

How little does he know?

How much snow is there?

SOME OTHER ADJUNCT CATEGORIES

There are a great many other constructions in English that appear adverbial in nature. It is difficult to catalog all of the possible semantic categories, so I'll list just a few of them below.

Adverbs of accompaniment usually occur with the preposition *with*—*I walked with my mother; Signe played with her friends; Lu partied with her roommates.* We can also include in this category constructions like *They ate chicken with lemon sauce* and *I like strudel with vanilla ice cream.* On the other hand, in *They ate chicken with their fingers*, the *with* prepositional phrase is clearly an adverb of means. Our interpretation of these sentences depends a lot on what we know about the world; we recognize fingers and forks as perfectly reasonable instruments for eating chicken, but it's impossible to construe lemon sauce as an tool in this context. But *lemon sauce* <u>is</u> an adverb of means in *He won her heart with his wonderful lemon sauce.*

There is a small set of verbs that take **adverbs of remuneration** (payment). They usually appear as *for* prepositional phrases—*The realtor will sell you this house for $150,000; I bought this for very little; My dad works for peanuts.*

Adverbs of source indicate the source or place of origin of someone or something—*Hamish is from New Zealand; Jamie borrowed this book from his mother; Helen stole the stereo from her neighbor; Susan bought that car from Bob; He got the money from his partner.* There is a great deal of semantic overlap between adverbs of direction and adverbs of source. Usually adverbs of direction co-occur with dynamic verbs and adverbs of source with stative verbs—*Solange came from France yesterday* versus *Solange comes from France.*

Concessive adverbs indicate that one circumstance is surprising in light of another. While such adverbs are usually clauses, which will be discussed in Chapter 5, occasionally concessive adverbs appear as prepositional phrases—*Joe was a graceful dancer* **in spite of his size**, *Farah became an accomplished pianist* **despite her arthritis**.

PROBLEMS IN CATEGORIZING ADJUNCTS

There is some amount of overlap in the semantic categories discussed in the adjunct section, and there are a number of other adverbial constructions for which conventional semantic labels don't exist. How, for example, should we treat *Mary Ann hid the presents* **from Trevor** and *The doctors isolated the infected child* **from the family**? Is this an adverb of direction or do we need a separate "concealment" category? Should we create a special "material/ingredient" category for constructions like *This cake was made* **with thirty egg whites** and *These tiles are made* **from cement**?

There is a large set of verbs all of which communicate some kind of social interaction and all of which can be followed by a *with* prepositional phrase.

Tristan flirted with Isolde.

Gracie joked with George.

Alice corresponded with Gertrude.

Charlotte argued with the merchant.

The coach consulted with the umpire.

The fact that all of these sentences are about communication of some sort and that the participants are not necessarily in proximity suggests that more than "accompaniment" is at stake. Yet another semantic category may be in order.

Creating semantic categories for all the possible adjuncts in English is a daunting task. It's not surprising that linguists disagree about what criteria should be used to create these categories and where the semantic boundaries should be drawn.

MOVABILITY OF ADJUNCTS

While adjuncts rather naturally follow the verb, they can occur in other positions in English sentences. As a class, adjuncts can occupy three positions—sentence initial, before the lexical verb, and somewhere after the lexical verb. Temporal adverbs are particularly flexible. Many of them can occur at the beginning of a sentence as well as at the end.

Next week, my girlfriend will be here. / My girlfriend will be here next week.

Tomorrow we'll go to the park. / We'll go to the park tomorrow.

For three years, Marsha lived alone in the woods. / Marsha lived alone in the woods for three years.

On rare occasions, Toby washes his truck. / Toby washes his truck on rare occasions.

Some one-word temporal adverbs can occur before the lexical verb—*The train is now arriving; Alicia often arrives late; Bill occasionally washes the dishes; Henrietta seldom drinks. Never, seldom* and *rarely* can occur in sentence initial position only if the subject and auxiliary are inverted—*Never have I eaten so much fudge; Seldom have I been so well treated; Rarely have we been invited to their home.* As you have already seen, subject/auxiliary inversion is often exclamatory and that is certainly the case here. *Never* does not appear in sentence final position.

Locative adverbs are less flexible than temporal adverbs and adverbs of direction are less flexible than adverbs of place. *In the yard, the kids were playing badminton* is far more acceptable than *??Into the yard he drove his car*. In general, however, locative adverbs are most likely to occur in the predicate.

While adverbs of manner and adverbs of means usually occur after the VP, a single-word adverb can sometimes be found before the lexical verb, even in a passive—*She **secretly** dug the hole; The mole was **surgically** removed; They have* **surreptitiously** *transferred those funds.*

One-word adverbs of manner are quite flexible in terms of word order. Those ending in the {-ly} suffix can usually occupy all three of the positions discussed above.

Quietly she entered the library.	*Gracefully they danced across the floor.*
She quietly entered the library.	*They gracefully danced across the floor.*
She entered the library quietly.	*They danced across the floor gracefully.*

On the other hand, prepositional phrase manner adverbs almost always follow the lexical verb—*She plays tennis like a professional; He lectures with great enthusiasm.* **Like a professional she plays tennis* is ungrammatical for most speakers.

ADJUNCTS AND THE SCOPE OF NEGATION

Scope of negation affects the movability of some adjuncts. As you have already seen, the negative particle usually negates everything that follows it. Moving an adverb to sentence initial position removes it from the scope of negation. In *The hikers didn't go into the cave*, the entire proposition *go into the cave* is negated. While I can move the prepositional phrase in an affirmative utterance without impairing grammaticality (*Into the cave the hikers went*), moving it in a negative utterance produces a marginally acceptable sentence (*??Into the cave the hikers didn't go*). A problem arises in this case because the verb is within the scope of negation but the locative prepositional phrase is not.

Adverbs of manner are especially strange in this regard. When an adverb of manner follows the negative particle, it is usually just the adverb that is negated. In *She didn't enter the library quietly, quietly* is the only lexical item within the scope of negation, i.e., she entered the library, but not quietly.) In *Larry isn't working very hard*, the verb *working* is not negated; Larry is working but not very hard. In *Susie didn't hit her brother on purpose*, the assumption is that Susie did indeed hit her brother, but not on purpose. When we hear *Ed doesn't dress as well as Karl*, we assume that Ed does dress, but not as well as Karl. If I say that "My sister didn't perform well last night," only *well* is within the scope of negation; my sister did perform and she performed last night, but not well. We see the same phenomenon with a few temporal adverbs. If you heard someone say "Soohee didn't get up until noon," you would assume that Soohee did get up, but not before noon.

Certain adverbs of frequency are intrinsically negative and do not co-occur with the negative particle. *Billy seldom cleans his room* is perfectly acceptable, but **Billy doesn't seldom clean his room* is ungrammatical, as is **Billy doesn't rarely clean his room*. Many speakers would also reject *Susan doesn't hardly eat*, although this usage is common in some dialects.

English speakers often use stress to clarify cases in which the scope of negation may be misunderstood. In *Santiago didn't borrow your car <u>yesterday</u>*, *yesterday* is stressed to indicate that it is the focus of the negation; Santiago did indeed borrow your car, but not yesterday. Constructions other than adverbs can be stressed in the same way. I might say "I didn't loan your car to <u>Santiago</u>." Here only Santiago is within the scope of negation; I did loan your car to someone, but not Santiago.

THE STACKING AND COORDINATION OF ADJUNCTS

As a rule, only adjuncts from the same semantic category can be coordinated with *and—Mary Anne walked over the bridge and through the woods; He danced gracefully and with great feeling*. Attempts to coordinate different semantic adverbial categories usually yield unacceptable utterances—**Mary Anne walked to the park and at noon; *He danced gracefully and across the floor*. However, any number of adjuncts from different categories can be stacked up without coordination—*Mary Anne walked to the park at noon; He danced gracefully across the floor*. **I hit the latch carefully and with a hammer* is very odd, but the deletion of *and* makes it perfectly acceptable.

A surprising number of adjuncts can be used in a single sentence.

> **Last night** *they argued* **loudly for an hour in the dining room***.*
>   [time]   [manner]   [duration]   [place]

When adjuncts of different types are stacked up in the predicate, there is a loosely conventional order. Adverbs of duration and adverbs of frequency usually precede adverbs of time—*I walked for two hours today; I woke up five times last night*. In these cases the more inclusive time frame goes last. Locative adverbs usually precede adverbs of time—*We played volleyball in the park yesterday*. Adverbs of manner typically precede adverbs of time—*You behaved like a baby last night; The kids whispered loudly during the movie; Josie has been behaving badly this week*.

But these conventions are easily violated if a speaker wishes to focus on a particular adjunct—*I worked last night for four hours*. Moving the adverb of duration to the end of the sentence focuses the hearer on the issue of duration. In fact, moving any adverb to the end of the sentence typically puts the focus on that adverb. In *Patricia put the jar on the shelf carefully* the adverb of manner is underscored, while it does not receive focus in *Patricia carefully put the jar on the shelf*.

Summary of adjuncts

Intensifier	Nikki **really** loves baseball.
Downtoner	I **rather** dislike monster movies.
Focuser	I **merely** touched the painting.
Place	Jenny lives **in an apartment**.
Direction	Andrew drove **across the lawn**.
Time (point/boundary)	Charles will arrive **at noon**.
Duration	They stayed **for hours**.
Frequency	Mary Jane sneezed **twelve times**.
Time relationship	Dena doesn't like you **anymore**.
Manner	He drives **with great skill**.
Means	Agnes cut the grass **with a scythe**.
Reason/purpose	She did it **for revenge**.
Result	Chuck polished it **to a bright shine**.

Adjective Phrases Revisited

Although adverbs and adjectives have different grammatical functions, they have many things in common. Both express modifying relationships; some adverbs are derived from adjectives; both categories contain intensifiers and downtoners; adverbs and adjectives can themselves be modified by the same set of intensifiers and downtoners; prepositional phrases can function in an adjectival or adverbial capacity. Clearly, these two systems overlap in a number of ways.

ADJUNCT FORMS THAT MODIFY ADJECTIVES

When present and past participles function as adjectives, they don't really lose their verbal qualities and they can sometimes be modified by adverbs of manner and temporal adverbs. Consider the following sentences.

*The **sweetly** smiling child kicked me.*

*The **recently** discovered galaxy was full of stars.*

*I am appalled by their **rapidly** deteriorating marriage.*

*The **newly** married couple left for Trinidad.*

*My **often** abused transmission finally blew up.*

*This is a **rarely** seen species.*

*The interviewer rejected the **carelessly** dressed candidate.*

*Place the pasta in **lightly** salted water.*

Newly is interesting because it never occurs as an adjunct in the predicate—*The couple was married newly,* even though it carries the adverbial {-ly} ending and expresses the meaning "very recently." Some participial prenominal adjectives can appear only when accompanied by modifiers. *This is a seen species* and *The discovered galaxy was full of stars* are both ungrammatical. You have already seen that a *read manuscript* is ungrammatical but a *seldom read manuscript* is fine.

Occasionally, even prototypical adjectives can occur with adjunct modifiers.

*Ms. Ramsay was sitting in her **always** tidy living room.*

*Davy was one of those **quietly** obnoxious people.*

*Jane's **often** nervous laughter is distracting.*

ADJECTIVES THAT FUNCTION AS ADJUNCTS

Up until now we've used the term *adjunct* exclusively in terms of adverbial constructions. However, adjectives can function in very much the same way. You already know that copulas require some sort of a complement, usually a predicate nominative or a predicate adjective. Sometimes intransitive verbs are followed by adjectives that modify the subject in much the same way that predicate adjectives do.

(a)	(b)
*Charley sleeps **nude**.*	*The river froze **solid**.*
*Mary arrived **drunk**.*	*The box broke **open**.*
*They emerged from the building **alive**.*	*A door slammed **shut**.*
*Cassie walked into the room **mad**.*	

Constructions like these pose a number of problems. Clearly the adjectives in these sentences are not required for grammaticality; they are not complements in the technical sense. Furthermore, all of these verbs are typical intransitive verbs; none are copulas. Yet, each of the adjectives in column (a) modifies the subject by indicating what state it is in and each of the adjectives in column (b) modifies the subject by specifying a resultant state. The term **adjunct adjective** is sometimes used to describe such forms because the adjective is an optional construction. In addition, some of these adjectives do seem to have an adverbial quality. For example, *Mary arrived drunk* might be paraphrased as *Mary arrived **while she was drunk*** and *Cassie walked into the room mad* might be paraphrased as *Cassie walked into the room **while she was mad***; in each case the boldface clause in the paraphrase is an adverb of time (Culicover, 1988, p. 53).

In Chapter 1, I discussed object complements that co-occur with verbs that are typically monotransitive.

*Pandora broke the box **open**.*

*Cyril tied the rope **tighter**.*

*The cook wiped the counter **clean**.*

*The agents shot the kidnapper **dead**.*

In each of these sentences the adjective reflects a state that results from the action of the verb. Some grammarians call these adjectives adjuncts rather than object complements because they are not required for grammaticality.

There is another construction that seems structurally related to the last set of examples but it has some odd characteristics. Take a look at the following sentences.

*Justin cried himself **sick**.*

*Minnie drank herself **unconscious**.*

*Trudy talked herself **hoarse**.*

These, too, look like object complement constructions, except that none of these verbs are complex transitive and *cry* and *talk* are actually intransitive. In each case the verb is followed by a reflexive pronoun and, while that pronoun looks like a direct object, it's not doing the things reflexive objects normally do: an individual can't *cry himself, talk herself,* or *drink herself*. These reflexives have been appropriately called "fake objects" (Goldberg, 1995, p. 192). In each of these sentences the adjective is actually describing the state that the subject achieves as a result of the verb. I will label these adjectives adjuncts because all of the them can be paraphrased as temporal adverbial clauses—*Justin cried **until he became sick**; Minnie drank **until she became unconscious**; Trudy talked **until she was hoarse**.*

Disjuncts

Disjuncts are a separate category from adjuncts. *Disjuncts* are so labeled because they don't modify structures within the sentence and they generally stand apart at the beginning of the sentence. In other words, disjuncts are to some extent "disjoined" from the rest of the utterance. Some linguists call disjuncts **sentence modifiers** but this label overstates the modification relationship. As you will soon see, style disjuncts don't modify the sentence at all. (Don't confuse this use of the term *disjunct* with *disjunction* in formal logic and semantics.)

ATTITUDE DISJUNCTS

English speakers can use an adverb to express an attitude toward the proposition contained in the sentence. In an utterance like *Foolishly, Joan quit school,* the proposition is <u>Joan quit school</u> while *foolishly* is an "editorial" comment made by the speaker, i.e., the speaker thinks that Joan's action was foolish. Typically, attitude adverbs occur first in the utterance and are followed by a pause (represented by a comma in written text); occasionally they occur last in the utterance and are preceded by a pause.

***Unfortunately**, you have not finished your homework.*

***Luckily**, they were saved by a hiker.*

***Incredibly**, he passed the bar examination.*

*The storm did little damage, **surprisingly**.*

***Strangely enough**, she never discovered the truth.*

***Amazingly**, Maria married Arnold.*

***Curiously**, she never asked him about the money.*

Sometimes attitude disjuncts follow the subject—*She **foolishly** forged her mother's signature; He **stupidly** loaned his boss some money.* In these cases the disjunct is not marked by pauses.

Attitude disjuncts can be post-modified, usually by *enough—Oddly enough, she didn't mind; Strangely enough, Janice stayed.* Occasionally they can be negated—*Not surprisingly, she caught cold.*

Editors, style manuals, and composition teachers proscribe most attitude disjuncts. The *Publication Manual of the American Psychological Association* (1994, p. 41) argues that "Hopefully, this is not the case" is incorrect and should be replaced by "I hope that this is not the case." But in casual speech, attitude disjuncts, including *hopefully*, are extremely common.

STYLE DISJUNCTS

When a speaker exploits a style adverb, s/he is indicating in what mode the sentence is being uttered, i.e., the speaker is being frank, truthful, honest, etc. In the film version of *Gone With the Wind*, when Rhett Butler says to Scarlett O'Hara, "Frankly, my dear, I don't give a damn," he indicates his discourse style, i.e., he is being frank. One might paraphrase a style adverb as "I am speaking to you _____ly," although not all style adverbs end in {-ly}. Style disjuncts don't modify the content of the sentence in any way.

> **Confidentially**, *I can't stand my boss.*
>
> **Truthfully**, *I don't think she did it.*
>
> *I* **honestly** *can't help you.*
>
> **In strictest confidence**, *my daughter-in-law has been fired.*
>
> **Seriously**, *don't tell anyone.*

Sometimes the same form can function as both an adverb of manner and a disjunct. Consider the contrasting meanings in the following sentence pairs.

> *I didn't speak to him, honestly. / I didn't speak to him honestly.*
>
> *Frankly, she rarely talks to the kids. / She rarely talks to the kids frankly.*
>
> *Truthfully, Ned never spoke. / Ned never spoke truthfully.*

In each case the adverb of manner modifies the verb that precedes it, while the disjunct has no impact whatsoever on the grammar of the sentence.

POINT OF VIEW DISJUNCTS

Sometimes speakers will indicate that they are speaking from a particular point of view or perspective. In a sentence like *Politically, the speech was a disaster*, the adverb *politically* indicates that, from the point of view of politics, the speech was a disaster. Viewpoint adverbs provide the context (social, geophysical, philosophical, etc.) in which the utterance is to be understood.

> **Ethnically**, *New York is a very diverse city.*
>
> **Geographically**, *the Falklands are somewhat isolated.*
>
> *The government is corrupt* **morally**.
>
> **In terms of student aid**, *this school is outstanding.*

EPISTEMIC DISJUNCTS

Epistemic adverbs function very much like epistemic auxiliaries. They convey the speaker's assessment of the possibility or probability that a proposition is true. Like the various types of speaker comment adverbs discussed above, they are usually, but not always, sentence initial.

> **Maybe** *Alicia will arrive on time.*
>
> **Perhaps** *it won't rain tomorrow.*

Surely, *she won't reveal your secret.*

Professor Lee will **undoubtedly** *be angry.*

Supposedly, *my sister has a great new job.*

Summary of disjuncts

Attitude	**Stupidly**, she left the letter in the rain.
Style	**Frankly**, I can't stand the man.
Point of view	**Politically**, the event was a great success.
Epistemic	**Perhaps** tomorrow will be sunny.

Conjuncts

Conjuncts are adverbs that help us organize discourse. Like conjunctions, conjuncts join elements of an utterance together. As you will see in Chapter 5, conjunctions typically conjoin sentences and elements within sentences. Conjuncts, on the other hand, conjoin larger units of discourse. You will see below that conjuncts are typically used only in the context of two or more sentences.

SEQUENCING CONJUNCTS

In discourse, events normally proceed forward in time (Schiffrin, 1987, p. 250) and we often use conjuncts to organize events serially. Conjuncts are especially evident in relatively formal discourse. They are used to organize steps in a process, events in a sequence of events, and points in an argument.

> **First** *we place the acid in the test tube.* **Next** *we heat it over a low flame.* **Finally** *we pour the acid into the beaker.*

> **In the first place**, *the treaty has inadequate inspection provisions.* **Second**, *we do not have the resources to monitor compliance. And* **third**, *this government cannot be trusted.*

In the following passage from *The Blind Watchmaker*, Richard Dawkins (1996) uses repeated instances of *then* to express temporal organization. (Boldface added.)

> The computer starts by drawing a vertical line. **Then** the line branches into two. **Then** each of the branches splits into two sub-branches. **Then** each of the sub-branches splits into sub-sub-branches and so on. (p. 51)

Of course we also organize informal discourse in temporal terms, although casual speech is less tightly structured than highly formal discourse. The following is a segment of an actual conversation (Schiffrin, 1987). (Except for the first instance, boldface is in the original.)

> So **first**, I played with the b- the twins, who're two and half. And uh. I went on the beach with them. **Then** when they went ho- off eh for their, nap, I:- **then** I gave the younger son uh . . . attention. So it was quite hectic on Saturday . . . and **then** we babysat Saturday night. (p. 251)

Sometimes a sequencing conjunct reflects a parallel time frame.

> *Out on the range the wranglers were trying to round up all the stray cows. It was cold and windy.* **Meanwhile**, *back at the ranch, Roy and Dale were repairing fences.*

ADDING AND REINFORCING CONJUNCTS

Adding and **reinforcing conjuncts** add material to the discourse and often reinforce what has been said before.

> *You really insulted me yesterday.* **Furthermore**, *you insulted my boyfriend by calling him a fraud.*

> *This morning I had a radiator leak and a flat tire.* **On top of it all**, *someone sideswiped me on the expressway.*

> *Jolene stole the records from the file cabinet.* **What is more**, *she deleted my computer files.*

The following passage from Elmore Leonard's novel *Out of Sight* (1996) exploits a commonly used, informal reinforcing conjunct. (Boldface added.)

> "**Like I said**, I walked away from prison myself one time . . ." (p. 71)

RESULTING CONJUNCTS

As the label implies, **resulting conjuncts** communicate the results of events in the preceding discourse.

> *Marcel didn't study for his finals.* **Consequently**, *he failed out of school.*

> *Beryl wasn't wearing her seat belt.* **As a result**, *she was thrown from the car.*

> *Tom always treats me badly;* **therefore**, *I'm not inviting him to my party.*

In speech, *so* is frequently used in this context, sometimes across two or more speakers, as in the following passage from Tony Hillerman's novel *Sacred Clowns* (1993). (Boldface added.)

"I don't like that Blizzard theory at all" Janet said. . . . " Collectors know about these things. . . . They'd know that Tano Pueblo still had its Lincoln Cane. And **so** they'd know that the one they'd bought was a fake. . . ."

"**So** they couldn't brag about it. Or show it off," Blizzard said. (p. 305)

Sometimes *so* is used to communicate a resulting <u>conclusion</u> on the part of the speaker. The following passage is from Leonard's *Ought of Sight*. (Boldface added.)

"He said the reason he came to Florida was to see you. **So** I guess you spent some time together." (p. 143)

Then often appears in contexts in which one speaker reaches a conclusion based on something another speaker has said. The following dialogue between a father and his adult daughter also appears in Leonard's novel. (Boldface added.)

"He's still married though, huh?"

"Technically. They're separated."

"Oh, he's moved out?"

"He's about to."

"**Then** they're not separated, are they?" (p. 18)

Because is sometimes used to mark previously mentioned results. The following passage is from Richard Dawkin's *The Blind Watchmaker*. (Boldface added.)

This is what *cumulative* evolution is all about, although, because of our high mutation rate, we have speeded it up here to unrealistic rates. **Because of this**, Figure 4 looks more like a pedigree of *species* than a pedigree of individuals. (p. 59)

TRANSITIONAL CONJUNCTS

Transitional conjuncts are used when a speaker wants to change the subject. They are rarely used in edited English since there are more formal ways of signaling topic changes in written discourse, i.e., paragraphing, subtitles, chapter divisions, etc. Conjuncts like the ones below usually occur in the middle of a conversation and can signal fairly dramatic topic changes.

By the way, have you seen Sylvia's new baby?

Incidentally, I won't be able to come to the wedding.

Oh, did you remember to take out the garbage?

A speaker who wants to move to a different but related topic might choose *as for*—*Mr. Borden is a nice guy. **As for** his daughter Lizzie, she's a bit strange.*

CONCESSIVE CONJUNCTS

As we saw above, the term *concessive* describes a relationship between two circumstance in which one circumstance is surprising in light of the other. English has a small inventory of concessive conjuncts.

*I didn't study very hard. **Nevertheless**, I got an A on the exam.*

*Marilyn is always sweet to Herman. **In spite of that**, he doesn't like her.*

*I'm wearing a down coat; **even so** I can't get warm.*

But can be used concessively, even in contexts where one speaker is responding to the comments of another. In the following passage two characters in Leonard's *Out of Sight* discuss a failed prison break. (Boldface added.)

"The only thing to stop anybody from leaving is a sign that says Off Limits. Man, once I was pumped up—listen, they would've had to . . . chain me to a wall to keep me there."

"**But** you didn't make it," Foley said. (pp. 60–61)

SOME OTHER CONJUNCTS

The previous list of conjuncts is by no means exhaustive. English contains **summation conjuncts** (*in conclusion, thus, to summarize,* etc.), **equating conjuncts** (*likewise, correspondingly, similarly*), **restating conjuncts** (*in other words, rather*), and a number of other types.

Since conjuncts often appear in subordinate clauses, I will revisit this issue again in Chapter 5.

CONJUNCTS IN DISCOURSE

Some of the conjuncts discussed previously are used regularly in conversation. This is especially true of the "little" words—*so, then,* and *but* and transitional conjuncts like *by the way*. But conversation tends to be a somewhat disorganized affair with multiple participants, abrupt shifts in topic, and interruptions. Speakers don't expect their conversations to be altogether orderly and don't necessarily worry about providing smooth transitions. But the rules of formal, edited English require that a text be tightly organized and in discourse of this sort, conjuncts are used frequently and systematically. In a two-page sub-section of a popular linguistics book, the authors exploit five very different conjuncts. (This passage is highly edited; boldface added.)

So far we have given a provisional account of grounding. . . . We have argued, **moreover**, that most of our conceptual system is metaphorically structured. . . . **Thus**, we do not need an independent definition for the concept BUTTRESS. . . . **Against this**, the *abstraction* view claims that there is a single . . . concept BUTTRESS. . . . It denies, **however**, that either concept is understood in terms of the other. (Lakoff and Johnson, 1980, pp. 106–7)

Summary of conjuncts

Sequencing	**Next** I stirred the egg whites briskly.
Adding and reinforcing	**Furthermore**, you lied to me.
Resulting	**Consequently**, she didn't impress me.
Transitional	**By the way**, I like your new car.
Concessive	**In spite of her opposition**, I got the job.

Summing Up

Adjective and adjective phrase constructions are relatively straightforward in English. The adverbial system, however, is complex and heterogeneous. No other part of speech takes so many different forms and has so many different semantic functions. Grammarians have had difficulty creating coherent and exhaustive categories for adverbs and, while the adverbs discussed above represent some of the most important semantic categories, the list is by no means complete. You will also find that grammarians disagree on the syntactic category as well. Some include intensifiers and downtoners and others include the negative particle *not*. These differences will not concern us.

5

Clauses: Coordination and Subordination

Thus far we have examined relatively simple grammatical structures. Our NPs have contained determiners, adjectives, and noun heads, at most. Our most complicated adverbial constructions have been prepositional phrases. But English speakers readily create far more complex sentences:

> *Nancy didn't like what Sid said to her while they were dancing and she told him so.*

> *Did you know that the man living downstairs thinks that the world is flat, despite the fact that he is a science teacher?*

Linguists are fond of saying that any human language contains an infinite number of possible sentences. The reason for this extraordinary potential is the **recursive** quality of language; the same basic structures can be repeated over and over again in a given sentence.

Clauses

Recursive processes depend a great deal on **clauses**. A clause is any structure that contains its own verb. A clause that can stand on its own is called an **independent clause**, thus any sentence is technically an independent clause. A coordinated sentence like *Popeye sang the blues and Bluto danced a jig* contains two independent clauses. A **subordinate** or **dependent clause** is one that cannot stand alone as a grammatical entity. In a sentence like *I wanted **the Marlins to win**, the Marlins to win* is a subordinate clause. When a structure contains a subordinate clause, the containing structure is often called a **matrix clause**. If the matrix clause also contains the "main verb" of the sentence, it is the **main clause**. (Sometimes one subordinate clause is contained within another subordinate clause; in this case the containing matrix clause is not the main clause of the sentence.)

I wanted	the Marlins to win
main verb	subordinate clause

This terminology will seem more natural when we actually begin to examine clause structure.

Subordinate clauses will usually contain a **subordinator** (sometimes called a **complementizer**), one or more small function words or special suffixes that signal that the following verb is not to be construed as the main verb of the sentence. As you will see below, the most common subordinators are *that, for,* {-ing}, infinitives, and proforms beginning with *wh.* Clauses can perform a great many grammatical functions—subject, direct object, indirect object, subject complement, object complement, adjective phrase, adverb, and some others that I have not yet discussed. Once you have mastered the structures discussed in the previous chapters, clauses are relatively simple. In general, they recapitulate the structures of the simple sentence.

Conjoining

Recursion occurs in two different contexts. We can always <u>add</u> one structure to another by **conjoining** two or more elements with a **conjunction**. Most grammarians recognize three conjunctions in English—*and, or,* and *but,* although it is not altogether clear that these three forms really constitute a coherent grammatical category.

CONJUNCTION *AND*

Conjunction *and* can be used to conjoin a variety of structures, from single lexical items to sentences, i.e., independent clauses. Normally conjunction *and* only joins the same structural types. When three or more items are conjoined in edited English, *and* is used only between the last two. (This constraint does not apply in spoken English.)

Conjoined NPs (regardless of function)	*Jack and Jill went up the hill.*
	Jack, Jill, Goldilocks, and the three bears went up the hill.
	I like broccoli and liver.
	Marina has been to Spain, Morocco, and Finland.
	I gave the deans and the vice-presidents a big raise.

Conjoined verbs	*Caroline* **was and is** *the most competent member of the family.*
	They **ate and drank** *everything in sight.*
Conjoined modals	*I* **can and will** *help you.*
Conjoined predicates	*Jamie* **got up and ate breakfast.**
	Casey **hit the ball, ran toward first base, and was tagged out.**
Conjoined adverbs	*They walked* **far and fast.**
	Ginger dances **smoothly and gracefully.**
Conjoined intensifiers	*My boss got* **more and more** *upset.*
Conjoined prepositions	*The kids ran* **in and out** *of the door.*
	The couple strolled **up and over** *the hill.*
Conjoined adverbial prepositional phrases	*Nora walked* **down the stairs and out the door.**
	Grandma lives **up the street and around the corner.**
Conjoined adjectives and adjective phrases	*He was* **short and blond.**
	She was **very angry and very loud.**
Conjoined sentences	**Crystal washed the car and Art mowed the lawn.**
	Elvira exercised, Mike slept, and the kids read comic books.

Most, but not all, grammatical categories can be conjoined with *and.* Prenominal adjectives are typically stacked rather than coordinated—*a beautiful old photograph,* although some can be coordinated quite comfortably—*an old and valuable locket; a mean and nasty person.* Since predicate adjectives cannot be stacked, they must be coordinated—*The child was tall and strong.* Articles cannot be conjoined under any circumstances and conjoined demonstratives are usually unacceptable—*??I want this and that book.* Conjoined genitive determiners are also problematic—*??This is his and her house; ??This is her and my project.* One reason conjoined demonstratives and genitives are marginal is that we have separate lexical items for these functions, e.g., *those, their, our.* However, conjoined demonstratives and genitive determiners are reasonably acceptable if the speaker points to the referents while speaking, since the pointing gesture underscores the fact that the speaker wishes to separate out the participants. Conjoined genitive NPs are perfectly acceptable, although the genitive marker generally appears only on the second NP—*Carol and Bob's house; my aunt and uncle's car.*

Typically, *and* is an additive conjunction; it adds information by adding a word or construction of the same type. But the additive relationship between the two (or more) coordinated constructions is often determined by social convention. If I tell you that *The kids ate spaghetti and meatballs,* you will assume that the meatballs were in (or on) the spaghetti, but you would not make the same assumption in the case of *The kids ate spaghetti and salad. Trish bought a table and chairs* suggests a (matched) set, but *Trish bought some chairs and a table* does not. The phrase *horse and carriage* means that the horse pulls the carriage but *horse and rider* clearly suggests a very different relationship. When two items are routinely coordinated in discourse, they sometimes take on a conventional order—*bread and butter; fish and chips; black and white; law and order; you and I.* In most of these cases the conventional order can be violated—*I'll have butter and bread,* but the ordering constraint on *you and I* is exceptionally strong. **I and you should fix this faucet* is unacceptable in all dialects, but some speakers do say "Me and you should fix this faucet."

In a few cases frequently coordinated items have taken on the status of idioms, and in such constructions the order is never reversed.

*After the fight, Joe's arm was **black and blue**.*

*Mary's friends left her **high and dry**.*

*The solution is **cut and dried**.*

*I packed a few **odd and ends**.*

*I love **rock and roll**.*

*The union **rank and file** voted no.*

*The CEO **wined and dined** the client.*

***By and large**, they were well behaved.*

Wined and dined is especially interesting because this predicate <u>requires</u> coordination for grammaticality; the CEO cannot *dine* a client nor *wine* one. *By and large* violates the usual rules of coordination, since it conjoins two entirely different parts of speech—a preposition and an adjective, and its meaning can in no way be deduced from its lexical content.

As you saw in Chapter 3, when *and* conjoins predicates or sentences, it often suggests the temporal sequence of events. Since there are constraints on "excessive" conjoining in edited English, speakers exploit *and* far more freely than writers do. The following passages were recorded when subjects in a linguistics experiment were asked to describe events that they had just seen in a short film (Beaman, 1984). Each instance of *and* reflects the temporal organization of the episode in question. (Boldface added.)

So one of the boys whistles to [the man], **and** stops him, **and** gives him his hat back. (p. 55)

As they passed he turned to look at her, **and** his hat blew off. (p. 57)

And then he gets down out of the tree, **and** he dumps all his pears into the basket, **and** the basket's full, **and** one of the pears drops to the floor, **and** he picks it up, **and** he takes his kerchief off, **and** he wipes it off, **and** places it in the basket which is very full. (p. 59)

In the final example, you can also see two examples of *and* used in a resulting sense; "he dumps all his pears into the basket and [as a result] the basket's full, and [as a result] one of the pears drops to the floor." Of course temporal sequencing and the expression of results are not incompatible semantic functions, since causes invariably precede results.

Sometimes *and* can be used in a conditional sense, i.e., if A then B.

Come any closer and I'll scream.

Do that again and you'll be punished.

Put the merchandise back and I won't call the police.

Note that in each of these examples, the subject of the initial clause is a covert *you*, even though the first two sentences are not classic imperatives. (The first speaker is <u>not</u> demanding that the hearer come closer.) Such sentences can be paraphrased as conditional *if* clauses—*If you come any closer, I'll scream.*

With certain verbs *and* has a reciprocal meaning. In Chapter 3, I discussed transitive reciprocal verbs, e.g., *Alia resembles Julia*. Some intransitive verbs take on a reciprocal meaning when subject NPs are coordinated with *and*. *Brenda and Cathy argued* means that Brenda argued with Cathy and Cathy argued with Brenda. There are a number of verbs that express this kind of reciprocity when the subject NPs are conjoined.

Ward and June fought.	*Hannah and her sister embraced.*
Paul and Paula eloped.	*My aunt and her husband met at the races.*
Tom and Jerry wrestled.	*Archie and Veronica joked.*

Language is often used **iconically**, i.e., the actual <u>form</u> of a word or construction signals meaning. Onomatopoeic expressions like the nouns *bow wow* and *choo choo* in child speech are classic examples of this and so is the use of vowel elongation to signal intensification—*Luba is sooo smart; Dick is reeeally tall*. Similarly, we often use coordinated structures to communicate the notion "more" on some continuum; more words reflect more of some other quality—*Nori talked and talked and talked and talked* (more activity); *The bees stung Leah again and again and again* (more frequency); *The kite flew higher*

and higher (more direction); *She became more and more agitated* (greater intensification).

CONJUNCTION *OR*

Like *and*, *or* is extremely flexible grammatically. It, too, can conjoin a variety of structures but, as a rule, a given instance of *or* conjoins only the same
types of structures.

Conjoined NPs	*Have you seen* **Ken or Brian?**
Conjoined VPs	*Little Bo Peep* **has lost or misplaced** *her sheep.*
Conjoined predicates	*Marnie will* **clean the house or fix the meal.**
Conjoined PPs	*The baby always throws her bottle* **under the bed or behind the dresser.**
Conjoined prepositions	*Should we walk* **around or through** *that puddle?*
Conjoined adjectives	*My partner is* **naive or dumb.**
Conjoined modals	*I* **may or may not** *attend the lecture.*
Conjoined sentences	**Mary Jane's sleeping or she's not at home.**

Conjunction *or* has two somewhat different meanings in discourse. When
your host says "Do you want tea or coffee?" he presumes that you will choose
one beverage or the other, but not both. Not surprisingly, this *or* is called **exclusive or**. Occasionally *or* is used in a context that does not force a choice. An
application which reads, "You may apply for this grant if you are Hispanic or
female," does not imply that a Hispanic woman is ineligible; it's okay to be
both Hispanic and female. This is called **inclusive or** and it is common in bu-
reaucratic language. In everyday discourse, however, we usually interpret *or*
to be exclusive and when speakers want to underscore inclusivity, they will often resort to the *and/or* convention—*You may have pie and/or ice cream*. This strategy is especially common in written texts.

There are some interesting idioms containing *or* or its negative counterpart
nor.

In this graduate program you either **sink or swim.**

We saw neither **hide nor hair** *of him.*

As the only linguist in the group, she felt like she was neither **fish nor fowl.**

Things happen here without **rhyme or reason.**

*She'll finish the project **sooner or later**.*

***Put up or shut up**.*

Or often co-occurs with the **correlative** term, *either* and you will probably find that many of the earlier examples sound better when *either* is included.

Little Bo Peep has either lost or misplaced her sheep.

My partner is either naive or dumb.

Either Mary Jane is sleeping or she's not at home.

The function of *either* is to explicitly correlate one structure to another and to underscore the fact that there is an alternative. *Either* always precedes the first of the two structures being coordinated. In *Either Betty or Todd will go*, the NPs *Betty* and *Todd* are being coordinated; in *He will either sink or swim*, the lexical verbs are being coordinated; in *Either you give me your candy bar or I will tell the teacher*, two sentences are being coordinated. Correlative *either* is not necessary for grammaticality in any of these examples. (Correlative *either* is semantically related to determiner *either* as in *Either dress will be fine*.)

Neither and *nor* are the negative counterparts of *either* and *or*.

Neither Sandy nor Gene knew the outcome.

I neither saw her nor called her last night.

Jane neither can nor will help you.

While *either . . . or* indicates that one alternative or the other is viable, *neither . . . nor* indicates that neither alternative is viable. In most cases a *neither . . . nor* utterance can be paraphrased by an utterance in which two negative propositions are coordinated by *and*—*I didn't see her and didn't call her last night; Jane can't and won't help you.*

While *neither* is not required for grammaticality in sentences containing *nor*, the first of the coordinated structures must contain some sort of negative word.

*Teresa received **no** help **nor** support from her sisters.*

*He did**n't** study for his exam **nor** did he write his term paper.*

***None** of the spectators offered help **nor** did they call the police.*

Note that when two independent clauses are conjoined in this way, the word order of the second is affected, i.e., the subject and the operator are inverted.

CONJUNCTION *BUT*

But is normally categorized as a conjunction, but it behaves quite differently from *and* and *or*. *But* is highly constrained in the kinds of structures it can coordinate. It does not conjoin nouns or noun phrases, one of the most common functions of the other two conjunctions; it occasionally conjoins modal auxiliaries—*She can but won't help me*; it sometimes conjoins verbs—*She likes but fears her teacher*; and it readily conjoins predicate adjectives—*They are poor but happy*. Most often *but* conjoins predicates and independent clauses. (As you saw in Chapter 4, it is also used as a conjunct to organize larger pieces of discourse.)

Tim saw the prowler but didn't confront him.

He eats bacon but he doesn't really like it.

I like Meg but I can't stand her brother.

But always suggests some sort of contrast and it is sometimes used concessively to indicate that the second item is odd or unexpected in light of the first—*I eat very little but I'm gaining weight*. A sentence like *?I eat very little but I'm not gaining weight* is strange precisely because the second sentence is <u>not</u> unexpected given the content of its predecessor. I have a friend who routinely makes jokes based on this unconventional use of *but:*

"It's hot but it's humid."

"He's stupid but he's incompetent."

"These tools are cheap but they're flimsy."[1]

Because *but* typically expresses contrast, you will usually find a negative construction in contrast with an affirmative one, as in these actual fragments of conversation (Schiffrin, 1987). (Boldface in original.)

Henry: Now I don't want you to think that I'm biased, **but** this is the way I was brought up. (p. 157)

Debby: And were you born in *North* Philadelphia?

Ira: No. I was born in uh in—*South* Philadelphia, **but** I moved to North Philadelphia when I was a year old. (p. 159)

Jan: I can read Latin **but** I can't speak it. (p. 161)

COORDINATION AND QUESTIONS

Speakers of English tend to process coordinated items as single structures. It's impossible, for example, to construct a *yes/no* question using only one element within a coordinated phrase, although echo questions of this type are fine. Consider the following sentences.

Betsy wants candy or popcorn.	*Milan gave the job to Phil and Miriam.*
Betsy wants candy or what?	*Milan gave the job to Phil and who?*

*What does Betsy want   *Who did Milan give the job to
candy or?*   Phil and?*

In normal yes/no question formation, the entire coordinated structure must be replaced by the *wh* word—*What does Betsy want? Who did Milan give the job to?*

ELLIPSIS AND GAPPING

Coordinated constructions often reflect **ellipsis**. In general the term ellipsis refers to any omission of a word or words; in fact, the dots that are used to indicate omitted material in a quoted text are called *ellipses*. Linguistic ellipsis occurs when material is omitted from a construction but can be recovered by looking at the previous linguistic context. In *Lenore can't ski but Lydia can*, we know that the missing element after *Lydia can* is *ski* because we are able to recover it from the syntax of the previous clause. Often, deleted material is signaled by a short function word.

Sylvia may come and she may not [come].

Michelle told me she would fix the furnace and she did [fix the furnace].

*Liang bought a leather briefcase and now Lisa wants **one*** [a leather briefcase].

*I was looking for a nice yellow belt and I found **one*** [a nice yellow belt].

*Sue skipped school yesterday and Charlene did, **too*** [skipped school].

*Kenny should clean his room and Robbie should, **too*** [clean his room].

*Daniel will help with the kids and **so** will I* [help with the kids].

*Teresa really dislikes romance novels and **so** does Alec* [dislike romance novels].

*I don't like Pat's attitude and I told him **so*** [that I didn't like his attitude].

In the above examples, *one* replaces missing NPs, while *too* replaces the missing elements of the predicate, i.e., everything after the operator. If there is no operator in the first clause, periphrastic *do* must appear in the second—*I like ice cream and Kemp **does**, too*. *So* also replaces missing elements of the predicate but it functions in two distinct ways. It often behaves very much like *too*, replacing everything after the operator, although *so* also forces subject/operator inversion in the second predicate—*Iris can program computers and so can Franny.* *So* can also replace a clausal direct object construction. In *I hate Pam's boyfriend and I told her so*, *so* stands for the entire proposition "I hate Pam's boyfriend," i.e., *I hate Pam's boyfriend and I told her [that I hate her boyfriend].* *So* usually occurs with communication verbs, although psych-verbs are possible—*Bev thinks that her office mate is an idiot and I know so.* (Direct object clauses will be discussed in detail shortly.)

Ellipsis can operate across separate sentences and even across speakers. Consider this scene from Patricia Cornwall's novel *From Potter's Field* (1995), which features a first person narrator and a second speaker.

(a) "I'm not crying," I said.

(b) "You're about to."

(c) "No, I'm not." (p. 173)

In (b), the second speaker deletes the word *cry*, which is recoverable from the narrator's first sentence, (a); in (c), the narrator maintains the deletion of *cry* and also deletes *about to*, which is recoverable from (b).

Gapping is somewhat similar to ellipsis but it is a less common and more highly constrained phenomenon. It occurs when the lexical verb is deleted from the second of two coordinated structures—*Chuck ordered beer and Mary Jane wine; Lu Anne likes bulldogs and Judith poodles.*

Embedding

Recursion can also be accomplished by embedding. While coordination involves placing structures side by side, **embedding** is accomplished by placing one structure inside another. We have already seen examples of genitive structures embedded inside other genitive structures and modifiers embedded inside other modifiers. Similarly, subordinate clauses can be embedded within a matrix clause. For example, a *that* clause can function as the direct object of a verb. In the following sentence, the boxed clause is the direct object of *know* and it is embedded within the main clause.

direct object

I know | that Bob told Eve something |

The direct object of a verb within a *that* clause can be another *that* clause. In the following sentence, the larger box represents the direct object of *know*, while the smaller box represents the direct object of *told*. (The labels above the nesting boxes refer to the structures of the main clause, while the labels below the boxes refer to structures embedded within those larger structures.)

direct object

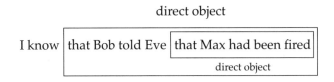

I know | that Bob told Eve | that Max had been fired |
direct object

The following sentence contains yet another embedded direct object clause.

direct object

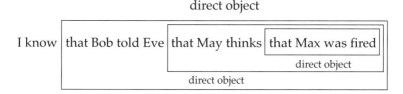

This embedding process can be repeated over and over to produce (theoretically) an infinitely long sentence. But after a certain number of embedded clauses, a sentence becomes hard to process, in large part because the hearer simply can't recall all the earlier clauses—*I know that Bobby told Evelyn that Max said that Joan had heard that Marsha felt that everyone knew that she was a loser.* Technically a sentence with two, three, twenty, or fifty such clauses is possible. The limitation here is human memory, not the grammar of the language.

You will notice that I often use the terms "higher" and "lower" in referring to clause structures. This terminology originated in generative grammars in which embedded structures are lower on a tree diagram than the structures that contain them. In the following example the subject *Megan* is lower in the diagram than the subject *she*, while the verb *knows* is higher than the verb *hates*.

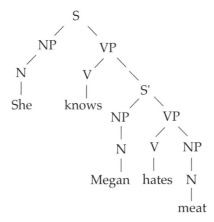

This terminology has become so standard that even syntacticians who do not use tree diagrams exploit it.

Nominal Clauses

As a class, clauses can perform most of the functions that simple NPs perform; such clauses are called **nominal**, meaning that they are noun-like. There are, however, constraints on individual types of nominal clauses, e.g., only one clause type can function as an indirect object or an object complement and only a few types can function as the objects of prepositions. Nominal clauses take a number of different shapes and I will categorize them in terms of their subordinators, i.e., those words and affixes that signal subordinate clause status.

Nominal clauses are usually embedded within the main clause or another embedded clause.

THAT CLAUSES

In *that* clauses the subordinator is the function word *that*. This *that* has no semantic content and is unrelated to deictic demonstrative *that* and relative pronoun *that*, which will be introduced later in this chapter. Nominal *that* clauses can function as subjects, direct objects, and predicate nominatives, structures with which you are already familiar.

Apart from its subordinator, a *that* clause looks exactly like a main clause. Its verb phrase is finite (i.e., it reflects tense) and it can contain the full range of verbal morphology and auxiliaries. A *that* clause can contain any verb form that a main clause can except for the imperative. In each of the following sentences, the subordinate direct object clause contains something beyond a simple, tensed verb.

*I think **that Victoria <u>is going to</u> be sick**.*	semi-auxiliary
*I believe **that it <u>may</u> rain tomorrow evening**.*	modal auxiliary
*Sergio knows **that Tina <u>has</u> <u>written</u> to Selma**.*	perfect
*I wish **that we <u>were</u> go<u>ing</u> on vacation**.*	progressive
*She thinks **that the garden <u>was</u> destroy<u>ed</u> by voles**.*	passive
*I demand **that Yishai <u>leave</u>**.*	subjunctive

The tense of the main verb and the tense of the verb in the clause need not be the same—*We know that she lied; We now think that she was an informant.*

That *Clauses as Direct Objects*

The number of verbs that can take *that* clauses as direct objects is limited.[2] They include psych-verbs, e.g., *know, believe, think, hope, wish, assume, guess*; some sensory verbs, e.g., *hear, see, feel* (although these verbs do not denote literal sensory perceptions, as you will see later); and verbs that denote various ways of communicating, e.g., *say, argue, note, insist, demand, agree, suggest, indicate, write*. Sentences like *I hear that Melinda is doing well* and *The coach thinks that Sammy is an excellent athlete* are typical.

subject		direct object
The coach	thinks	that Sammy is an excellent athlete

Like any clause, a direct object clause has its own internal structure. This is a classic example of recursion, structures within structures.

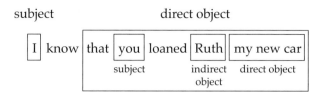

Mandative subjunctives <u>require</u> a *that* clause direct object—*I move **that the meeting be adjourned**; I demand **that she leave**; We insist **that the client accept this offer**.*

Direct object *that* clauses are common in all kinds of discourse. The following examples come from Tracy Kidder's book *House* (1985), a nonfiction narrative, and a Joyce Carol Oates collection of short stories, *Will You Always Love Me?* (1997). (Boldface added.)

> He'd realize **that in the fall he would not be playing soccer**. (Kidder, p. 154)
>
> "I assume **that primarily we're on the same team**." (Kidder, p. 37)
>
> She knew **that she admired her stepdaughter**. (Oates, p. 184)
>
> Sharp-eyed, Mrs. K has noticed **that Mrs. D. has another time glanced surreptitiously at her wristwatch**. (Oates, p. 229)

In most cases a direct object *that* clause can be replaced by a single pronoun.

> *I know **that my best friend cheated on the exam**. / I know **something**.*
>
> *Judy believes **that Amelia will be found**. / Judy believes **it**.*
>
> *I realized **that my best friend was lying**. / I realized **something**.*

There are, however, a few verbs that can take clausal direct objects but cannot take simple NPs or pronouns. *I insisted that Lindy leave* is fine but **I insisted it* is ungrammatical. A simple NP direct object is possible only when the verb is *insist on—I insisted on real butter; She insisted on it*. (*On* is a verb particle here.) The same phenomenon occurs with *think*. By itself, *think* typically takes only a clausal direct object—*I think that Andrew will attend*. Occasionally people say "I thought it, but I didn't say it" or "Think snow!" but these are unusual constructions. (Cognate direct objects are possible with *think—I think terrible thoughts all the time; Think good thoughts*.) As a rule, a nonclausal direct object requires the multi-word verb *think about—I think about Mary all the time; I am thinking about my children*.

Theoretically, a direct object *that* clause can become the subject of a corresponding passive. Unfortunately, the main verbs involved in these constructions are usually stative and don't passivize well. However, if the subject is an indefinite pronoun, passives are often possible.

Everyone knows **that Simon did it**. / **That Simon did it** *is known by everyone.*

Anyone can see **that Romeo loves Juliet**. / **That Romeo loves Juliet** *can be seen by anyone.*

Everyone assumed **that Susanna would be chosen**. / **That Susanna would be chosen** *was assumed by everyone.*

When a *that* clause appears in direct object position, the subordinator *that* can readily be omitted. Normally hearers will process the first verb that they hear as the main verb of the sentence. Upon hearing the sentence *I know that my doctor has the answer,* the hearer will automatically process *know* as the main verb, thus *has* is subsequently processed as a subordinate verb. Since the first verb has already been processed as the main verb, a subordinator isn't really necessary—*I know my doctor has the answer.* More often than not we omit the subordinator in a *that* clause. The following examples are also from Tracy Kidder and Joyce Carol Oates. (Boldface added.)

"I know **they have some dreams hidden in the work**." (Kidder, p. 251)

"I decided **I would talk to him**." (Kidder, p. 159)

He thought **Ned looked down on him**. (Kidder, p. 147)

"I wish **these issues were perfectly clear**." (Kidder, p. 195)

. . . she would not have said **she knew Ednella Crystal, really**. (Oates, p. 184)

Harry believed **he heard her being sick in the bathroom**. (Oates, p. 84)

He claims **he never saw her**. (Oates, p. 84)

That *Clauses and Ditransitive Verbs*

As you saw in Chapter 1, ditransitive verbs take both direct and indirect objects. There are a few ditransitives that can co-occur with *that* clause direct objects.

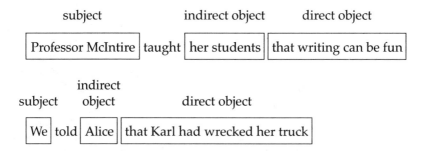

subject		indirect object	direct object

| Professor McIntire | taught | her students | that writing can be fun |

	subject	indirect object	direct object

| We | told | Alice | that Karl had wrecked her truck |

In ditransitive constructions containing a clausal direct object, the indirect object must precede the direct object construction; a prepositional indirect object is impossible—*We told that Karl had wrecked her truck to Alice; *Professor McIntire taught that writing can be fun to her students.*

That clause direct objects

I know **that my senator lied**.

Margaret believes **that Charlie is honest**.

We taught the kids **that canals are dangerous**.

The teacher admitted **that the exam was too easy**.

I demand **that Jan leave**. [subjunctive]

I insisted **that Mildred be informed**. [subjunctive]

Tony can see **that his father is uncomfortable**.

I hear **that they have broken up**.

Clauses in which *that* is deleted

She thinks **Sam is nice**.

I told her **I wouldn't go**.

I wish **she would leave**.

The child admitted **she broke the window**.

I see **you've bought a new car**.

That *Clauses as Predicate Nominatives*

When they follow copulas, *that* clauses occur as predicate nominatives.

subject		predicate nominative
My concern	is	that he'll never learn responsibility

Structurally such sentences resemble the direct object clauses discussed above. But a *that* clause always embodies a proposition involving states, actions, agents and patients, etc. A proposition is by its very nature an abstraction. Since a predicate nominative must always have the same referent as the subject of the sentence, the subject, too, must reflect this abstract quality. As a result, the subjects of such sentences always contain abstract noun heads like *plan, idea, no-*

tion, belief, hope, etc. When a *that* clause functions as a predicate nominative, the copula is almost always *be.*

That clause predicate nominatives

The plan was **that Linda would leave first.**

Her hope is **that the exam will be easy.**

The presumption was **that Jerry had never received the money.**

His defense is **that he wasn't even in the neighborhood.**

My belief is **that they'll never find the real culprit.**

Because *that* clauses embody propositions (not people), they never function as indirect objects.

That Clauses as Verb Complements

There are some structures that look vaguely like indirect object plus direct object constructions except that the higher verbs are uniformly monotransitive and have deontic force.

Joanie warned Henry **that she was an expert pool player.**

Rebecca alerted the family **that the basement was flooded.**

My colleagues convinced me **that I should not apply.**

In these sentences, the NP following the main verb, not the clause, is the direct object. That NP can be made the subject of a corresponding passive— *Henry was warned by Joanie that she was an expert pool player; The family was alerted by Rebecca that the basement was flooded.* But even though the NP is the direct object of the preceding verb, the clause is required for discourse coherence. If the clause is omitted from one of the above sentences, its content has to be recoverable from the preceding conversation or the context. In a sentence like *Joanie warned Henry,* the hearer must be able to ascertain the content of the warning or a great deal of meaning is lost. I will call a nominal clause that follows an NP direct object and is required by the verb a **verb complement.** Like any other nominal clause, the verb complement has internal structure.

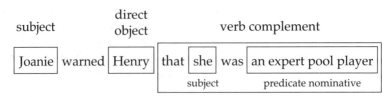

The verbs that take *that* clause complements are "communication" verbs of a very particular type. They all indicate that the subject is imparting information to the direct object and the clause expresses the content of that information. However, unlike the ditransitive communication verb *to tell*, verbs that take clausal complements are more or less deontic; they always express the fact that the subject has affected or is attempting to affect the behavior of the direct object in some way.

That clause verb complements

Edwina convinced her daughter **that she would like her new school**.

Delila assured Samson **that she wouldn't touch his hair**.

The officer advised us **that the road was closed**.

I cautioned my students **that they might find the exam difficult**.

Beth persuaded Jo **that Amy had not stolen the manuscript**.

The officer warned us **that there were mud slides ahead**.

That *Clauses as Subjects*

That clauses also function as subjects of sentences.

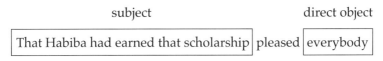

And of course the subject clause itself has internal structure.

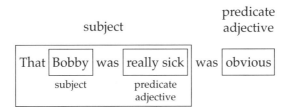

That clause subjects co-occur with a very limited number of verbs. Most stative copulas can take *that* clause subjects and so can verbs that suggest emotional states or personal reactions.

That the election was rigged *seemed clear.*

That my niece has been arrested for shoplifting *bothers me.*

That I had been chosen *thrilled my parents.*

A subject *that* clause can readily be replaced by a single pronoun—*It seemed clear; **This** bothers me.*

When a *that* clause functions as the subject of a sentence, the subordinator *that* cannot be deleted. **Habiba had earned the scholarship surprised everybody* is completely ungrammatical. Since hearers will process the first verb encountered as the main verb of the sentence, the subordinator is necessary to alert them that next verb is <u>not</u> the main verb.

A subject *that* clause expresses a proposition and, since propositions don't carry number, there is no singular/plural contrast with clausal subjects. Nominal clause subjects always take singular verbs, singular being the fall-back (default) number when a subject has no intrinsic number—*That the boys want our old chairs **pleases** me; That Eileen hasn't found a job **is** surprising.*

That clause subjects

That Pam and Andy had wrecked my car really annoyed me.

That Orville dislikes Wilbur seems clear.

That Randy was elected bothers me.

That everyone agreed was amazing.

That she is guilty is indisputable.

That Marcie had told Neta the results was surprising.

Extraposition of That *Clauses.*   Actually, English speakers don't often place *that* clauses in subject position, even though such sentences are entirely grammatical. More often we move such clausal subjects to the end of the sentence, replacing them with the pronoun *it.* (See the discussion of *cataphoric it* in Chapter 1.) Note the pattern in the following sentences.

> ***That Jason lies** really bothers my mother.* / ***It** really bothers my mother **that Jason lies.***

> ***That Samantha resigned** surprised everyone.* / ***It** surprised everyone **that Samantha resigned.***

> ***That our boss had been convicted** was shocking.* / ***It** was shocking **that our boss had been convicted.***

This process is called **extraposition**. In the first sentence of each pair, the subject is a *that* clause. In the second sentence of each pair, the grammatical subject is the pronoun *it*, which stands in for the "semantic" subject, the content of the *that* clause. In other words, the pronoun *it* simply holds down the subject position for the semantic subject, which appears at the end of the sentence. Normally, *it* has **anaphoric** reference, i.e., it refers to an entity that has already been introduced into the discourse. Here, however, *it* has **cataphoric** reference; its referent is a clause that appears later in the utterance.

grammatical subject   extraposed clause

| It | was astonishing | that the burglary had not been discovered |

While extraposed subject clauses are common in all kinds of discourse, they are ubiquitous in formal edited English. The following examples all come from *The New York Review of Books* (1997, June 12). (Boldface added.)

It is conceivable **that some of the skeptics will turn out to be right about the big-bang theory**. (Weinberg, p. 20)

It is not surprising **that his patriotism should have taken this bloodcurdling form**. (Ignatieff, p. 32)

It was almost inevitable **that Younghusband would become a soldier**. (Bernstein, p. 45)

Long or complex subject clauses are especially prone to extraposition. This phenomenon is sometimes called **heavy NP shift**, and it occurs in other syntactic contexts as well. The following passage is from an instruction manual for yoga (Hittleman, 1964). (Boldface added.)

It is gratifying to note **that more and more companies are realizing the value of brief exercise periods**. . . . **It** would seem obvious **that the efficiency of the worker will increase if he** [sic] **has the opportunity to either avoid or release the onset of . . . fatigue**. (p. 143)

In general, *that* clause subjects seem easier for the hearer to process when they have been extraposed.

But what about a sentence like *It seems that Donna has quit her job*? While *that Donna has quit her job* may look like a predicate nominative (it follows a copula), it is not. If the pronoun *it* in the above sentence were a personal pronoun, it would have anaphoric reference but this *it* is clearly cataphoric. We find exactly the same phenomenon with copula *to appear*—*It appears that the Dean is angry*. Both these sentences reflect extraposition, despite the fact that the non-extraposed versions are ungrammatical—**That Donna has quit her job seems; *That the Dean is angry appears*.

Even direct object clauses are sometimes extraposed.

*I took **it** for granted **that you would help me**.*

*The ski instructor made **it** obvious **that she considered me hopeless**.*

*I hate **it** **that my daughter smokes**.*

(In the last example, note that the *that* clause directly follows cataphoric *it*. This is a case of "vacuous" or empty extraposition, i.e., the extraposition of the clause doesn't really change the structure of the sentence.)

When a sentence includes an object complement, the direct object *that* clause <u>must</u> be extraposed. A sentence like *Susan made her position clear* is perfectly acceptable, but **Susan made **that she didn't like me** clear* is ungrammatical. Extraposing the direct object restores grammaticality—*Susan made it clear **that she didn't like me***. There is a small set of complex transitive verbs that take extraposed *that* clause objects.

> *She made **it** obvious **that she didn't enjoy the food.***
>
> *He considers **it** a miracle **that they weren't killed.***
>
> *I think **it** wonderful **that people have walked on the moon.***

(Some speakers may find the last example a bit unnatural.)

Factive and Non-Factive Constructions

In Chapter 3 we saw that epistemic modality is frequently communicated by auxiliaries and in Chapter 4 we saw that it can be communicated by adverbs as well. Epistemic modality is also commonly expressed in sentences containing *that* clause constructions. *That* clauses always contain propositions and these propositions can be treated as factual or speculative by the speaker. In some cases the speaker presupposes that the proposition articulated in the clause is a fact; these are called **factive** constructions—*It is odd that Jenny didn't come; I regret that I didn't get the job.* In other cases, however, the proposition is treated epistemically; these are **non-factive** constructions—*It is possible that she will have to repeat the fifth grade; I believe that the safe is empty.* It is the matrix predicate which determines whether a clause is factive or non-factive.

Factives	Non-factives
It's tragic that those puppies died.	It's possible that he'll be fired today.
It's exciting that you're going to Ireland.	Is it true that you hate chocolate?
It amuses me that Carol had to sell her Corvette.	I suppose that Bruce ate all the cookies.
He regrets that she resigned.	He alleges that she assaulted him.
I resent that you told him.	

Factives (cont.)	Non-factives (cont.)
That she is still here is significant.	I imagine that Ivy has already told him the news.
That she was the embezzler surprised me.	That she will succeed is unlikely.
	That the Cubs will lose is inevitable.

As you can see, both factive and non-factive constructions can contain cataphoric *it* and extraposed subjects.

INFINITIVE CLAUSES

Infinitive clauses are those in which the verb occurs in its infinitive form—*to sleep, to run, to be,* etc. Infinitives, as the name suggests, are not finite; they do not carry tense. Since modal auxiliaries always occur first in the VP and since modals have no infinitive forms, modals never appear in infinitive clauses. You will find semi-auxiliaries, perfect, progressive, and passive constructions in such clauses, however.

I would hate to <u>have to</u> apologize.	semi-auxiliary
Merle wants Adam to <u>have</u> finish<u>ed</u> by noon.	perfect
I want you to <u>be</u> clean<u>ing</u> your room by 8 A.M.	progressive
Harold hopes to <u>be</u> select<u>ed</u> by the committee.	passive

Infinitive Clauses as Direct Objects

Infinitive clauses frequently take on nominal roles, and they are very common in direct object position.

*I hope **to be a physician someday**.*

*Toby would love **to run a marathon in under three hours**.*

*Jesse plans **to attend UCLA**.*

*I like **to jog in the early morning**.*

*Lee remembered **to shave**.*

*She longs **to be in Paris**.*

*I want **Xi to attend the conference**.*

*I would hate **for my father to know about this**.*

*The host would like **for you to leave**.*

Like any other clause, an infinitive clause has internal structure.

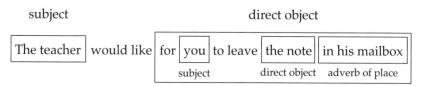

But infinitive clauses have one unusual characteristic. Look closely at the direct object clause in the following example.

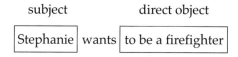

You may remember that in Chapter 1 I made much of the fact that English is a subject dominant language. At that time I carefully noted that, with the exception of the imperative, the main verb of the sentence must have a subject. However, a verb in an infinitive clause can be subjectless, as in the sentence above. This verb is subjectless in much the same way that an imperative verb is subjectless; although there is no **overt** subject, the hearer can determine the **covert** (unexpressed) subject from the grammatical context. In this case the subject of the embedded clause is the same as the subject of the main clause.

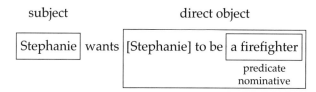

The predicate nominative *a firefighter* refers back to the covert subject of the clause, [*Stephanie*].

The term **equi** (from the Latin word for *equal*) is used to characterize any construction in which an overt NP in one clause and a covert NP in another are identical. In *Stephanie wants to be a firefighter*, the equi is **subject controlled**; this means that the content of the lower, covert subject is determined by the content of the higher subject. If the subject of the infinitive clause is different from that of the higher verb, the subject must be explicitly stated, i.e., **overt**—*Stephanie wants her son to be a firefighter*.

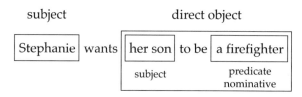

The verbs that take infinitive clauses as direct objects are all psych-verbs. Most of these verbs can take simple NP direct objects as well—*Stephanie wants a vacation. Long* and *hope*, however, always take clausal direct objects—*I long to hike the Grand Canyon; I hope to do well on the bar exam*. Only when they are followed by the particle *for* can these verbs take simple NP objects—*I long for peace; I am hoping for a new car*.

As you will see in the examples below, occasionally a clausal direct object containing an overt subject will have two subordinators, *to* and *for*. *For* precedes the <u>subject</u> of the infinitive clause. Which higher verbs require *for* in the clause is rather arbitrary; no particular semantic criteria exist. *Like* can take *for* in its infinitive clause but does not require it—*I would like **for** Beth **to** come* or *I would like Beth **to** come*. For many speakers, however, the verb *hate*, requires both subordinators—*I would hate **for** her **to** see you*.

Infinitive clause direct objects

Covert subject in clause

William wants **to go to Morocco**.

Elizabeth planned **to take her boyfriend to dinner**.

I would like **to be elected to the Board of Directors**.

She hopes **to have left by June**.

I would hate **to be moving in this weather**.

Overt subject in clause

Jack wants **his children to eat a better breakfast**.

Barb planned **for her parents to take a trip**.

John would like **Sue to be elected**.

I would hate **for the kids to move so far away**.

Infinitive Clauses as Predicate Nominatives

Infinitive predicate nominatives behave very much like *that* clause predicate nominatives. As in the case of *that* clauses, the infinitive clause states a proposition, and the subject to which it refers must be abstract.

Infinitive clause predicate nominatives

Covert subject in clause

My dream was **to become a dentist.**

Stuart's fantasy was **to climb Denali.**

Their plan was **to break into the apartment quietly.**

Her strategy was **to make herself indispensable.**

Overt subject in clause

David's plan was **for Jill to give Ann the information.**

The best idea would be **for her to tell the truth.**

The best thing would be **for the kids to stay here.**

As you can see, predicate nominative infinitive clauses can contain covert subjects, but here the covert subject is not necessarily the same as the higher subject. The pronoun *I* does not actually appear in *My dream was to become a dentist*, yet *I* is clearly the covert subject of *become—My dream was [I] to become a dentist. I* derives from the genitive *my* in the subject NP.

predicate nominative

My dream was [I] to become a dentist

The same phenomenon occurs in a number of the sentences in the preceding chart, i.e., the covert subject of the infinitive actually derives from a genitive in the higher subject. Sometimes the covert subject of an infinitive predicate nominative is simply indefinite—*The best thing would be to tell her the truth.*

predicate nominative

The best thing would be [for someone] to tell her the truth

Infinitive Clauses as Verb Complements

In a sentence like *The teacher wanted **Sarah to join us,*** the boldface clause is the direct object of *wanted* and we can easily replace the entire clause with a pronoun—*The teacher wanted something; What did the teacher want? Sarah* is the overt subject of that direct object clause.

direct object

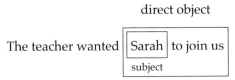

The teacher wanted │ Sarah │ to join us

subject

But a sentence like *The teacher persuaded Sarah to join us* requires a different analysis. Here *Sarah* is the covert subject of *join*, but she is at the same time the overt direct object of *persuaded*. The infinitive clause that follows *Sarah* is a **verb complement**.

direct   verb
object   complement

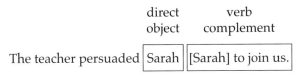

The teacher persuaded │ Sarah │ │ [Sarah] to join us.

How do we know that *Sarah*, rather than the entire clause, is the direct object of *persuade*? In more general terms, how do we know that *persuade* behaves differently from *want*? One piece of evidence lies in the passive; note that I can make *Sarah* the subject of a passive with *persuade*—*Sarah was persuaded by the teacher to join us*. This operation is impossible when the main verb is *want*— **Sarah was wanted by the teacher to join us*.

There is a second piece of evidence that demonstrates that *I want Sarah to join us* and *I persuaded Sarah to join us* require two different analyses. Pronouns can be reflexivized only when their antecedents occur in the same clause. A sentence like **Mary didn't want the man to hurt herself* is ungrammatical precisely because it violates this rule; *Mary* occurs in the matrix clause and *herself* in the embedded clause. *Mary didn't want the man to hurt himself* is fine because both *the man* and *himself* occur in the embedded clause.

subject   direct object

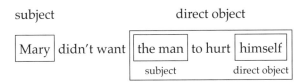

│ Mary │ didn't want │ │ the man │ to hurt │ himself │

subject   direct object

Now consider *Harry persuaded himself to attend the party*. *Himself* must be co-referential with *Harry* since there isn't any other masculine NP in the sentence. If these two NPs are co-referential, they must be clause mates. If these two NPs are clause mates, *himself* must be the direct object of *persuade*; no other grammatical relationship is really possible.

direct
subject   object   verb complement

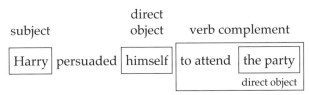

│ Harry │ persuaded │ himself │ │ to attend │ the party │

direct object

A third test that illustrates the difference between infinitive direct objects and infinitive verb complements involves a passive construction within the embedded clause. A clause is a somewhat autonomous structure; what happens grammatically within the clause has a very limited effect on the rest of the sentence. For example, in cases in which the infinitive clause is a direct object, it is possible to change an active infinitive clause into a passive construction without a significant change in meaning:

*They wanted **the priest to read the eulogy.** / They wanted **the eulogy to be read by the priest.***

*I wanted **the doctor to examine my daughter.**/ I wanted **my daughter to be examined by the doctor.***

Notice, however, what happens when the NP after *persuade* becomes the subject of a passive within the clause.

*I persuaded **the doctor to examine my daughter.** / I persuaded **my daughter to be examined by the doctor.***

The effect of adding the passive is dramatic. Clearly, these two sentences do not mean the same thing; in the first example I am persuading the doctor to do something and in the second I am persuading my daughter to do something. This semantic disparity occurs because the covert subject of the infinitive clause is <u>also</u> the direct object of the main verb. Here equi is **object controlled**, i.e, the direct object of the higher clause is also the covert subject of the lower.

subject		direct object		verb complement
I	persuaded	the doctor		[the doctor] to examine my daughter

subject		direct object		verb complement
I	persuaded	my daughter		[my daughter] to be examined by the doctor

In all of the examples above, the main verb is followed by two required structures, a simple NP direct object and an infinitive complement, which takes as its covert subject that same direct object NP.

Verb complements typically follow verbs that have deontic force.

We forced Antoine to share his chocolate.

The professor persuaded Hilda to drop the course.

The guard ordered the intruders to leave.

Don't urge Lawrence to play his accordion.

Many of the same deontic <u>communication</u> verbs that take *that* clauses as verb complements also take infinitive complements.

Dr. Einstein warned the students to leave the lab.

I advised the tourists to avoid the local restaurants.

Patsy cautioned the hikers to be careful.

The agent advised us to pay by check.

A few normally ditransitive verbs co-occur with infinitive clauses—*She asked Nina to leave; I told Harold to hand me the wrench.* There are two possible analyses here. One identifies the NP following the ditransitive verb as the indirect object and the following clause as the direct object, with equi being controlled by the indirect object.

                   indirect

subject   object   direct object

| I | told | Harold | [Harold] to hand me the wrench |

But this analysis overlooks the fact that *told* has deontic force here, something it lacks in a typical ditransitive construction like *I told Harold the truth* or *I told Harold that it was snowing.* In *I told Harold to hand me the wrench, told* is reporting a directive. Whenever a normally ditransitive verb occurs with an infinitive clause, it takes on this deontic quality.

I asked my fiancé to leave.

Faye asked Melinda to drive.

Lucas told Sophia to drink her milk.

In each of the above examples, the speaker reports an attempt to affect the behavior of another (although the outcome is unspecified). For this reason a verb complement analysis seems more plausible than an indirect object analysis.

                   direct

subject   object   verb complement

| I | told | Harold | [Harold] to hand me the wrench |

Only "communication" verbs exhibit this pattern. Other ditransitive verbs like *give, hand,* and *offer* don't take verb complements.

The verb *promise* poses an interesting problem. In all of the infinitive verb complements discussed so far, equi is controlled by the higher direct object—*I asked Patricia [Patricia] to leave.* But note what happens with *promise,* another deontic communication verb. In *I promised Patricia to leave,* the equi is controlled by the higher <u>subject</u>—*I promised Patricia [I] to leave*. Infinitive verb complements offer the grammarian a host of complications like this one.

In the following chart, the direct object of the higher verb is italicized.

Infinitive verb complements

(a)   Darlene forced *me* **to move the car.**

        He persuaded *us* **to leave.**

        I won't allow *the kids* **to stay there late.**

        They permit *the homeless* **to sleep in the park.**

        They coaxed *the rabbits* **to leave the garden.**

        They won't let *the dog* **sleep on the furniture.** [bare infinitive]

        The teacher made *my daughter* **sit in the corner.** [bare infinitive]

(b)   I told *Rene* **to do the dishes.**

        She asked *Penny* **to calibrate the machine.**

        I warned *the students* **to fill out the form correctly.**

        The police ordered *the demonstrators* **to disperse.**

(c)   I saw *my partner* **steal the money.** [bare infinitive]

        She heard *the neighbors* **argue.** [bare infinitive]

        I felt *the building* **shake during the earthquake.** [bare infinitive]

(d)   She considers *her sister* **to be a success.**

        We helped *him* **to defeat his opponent.**

        Sheila helped *Scott* **fix the roof.** [bare infinitive]

All of the main verbs in section (a) pattern like *force;* none of them can take a clausal direct object and each is followed by an direct object NP, which is itself followed by the complement clause. A sentence like *Darlene forced to move the car* is ungrammatical. While it may appear that verbs in category (a) can take simple NP direct objects, there is always an underlying complement clause—*Darlene forced me [to do something]; They coaxed the rabbits [to do something]*. Many of the verbs in (a) reflect coercion or persuasion—*force, make, persuade, coax* and all are strongly deontic.

The verbs *make* and *let* <u>require</u> that the following infinitive be **bare**, i.e., that it occur without *to*—*I made them give up; She let her students take a make-up exam*. Non-native speakers who have more or less mastered the infinitival complement construction often make mistakes in cases where a bare infinitive is required, e.g., *She made her students to write an essay.*

All of the main verbs in set (b) express communication of some sort. They pattern grammatically like those in (a), and they, too, have deontic force. But, unlike most of the verbs in set (a), these verbs are silent on whether or not behavior was actually affected—*I forced Derek to leave* versus *I told Derek to leave.*

The main verbs in section (c) are sensory and are not the least bit deontic. Note that these infinitives are all bare. Sensory verbs that take infinitive complements contrast sharply in meaning with those that take *that* clause objects. In *I have heard that you are running for office*, the verb *hear* is not being used literally; the information contained in the clause may have been acquired by a means other than hearing—someone sent me a fax; I read it in the newspaper; your publicist wrote me a letter. The same holds true for an utterance like *I see that you don't like Jerry.* My conclusion may be based exclusively on the fact that I heard you screaming at him; the evidence need not be visual. But when an infinitive clause follows a sensory verb, it expresses an event that was literally heard, seen, or felt—*I heard Seth fall; Maneck saw Don leave; I felt the floor shake.*

As with the other verbs that take infinitival complements, the NP following a sensory verb behaves like a direct object grammatically, e.g., it can occur as the subject of a passive with the sensory verb—***The neighbors** were heard to argue; **My uncle** was seen to steal the money.* Nevertheless, the bare infinitive clause is required for coherence. *I felt Jennifer move* does not entail *I felt Jennifer.*

Category (d) is a garbage can. Since neither *consider* nor *help* falls into the general semantic categories discussed previously, I'll simply lump them together. The complement of *help* can occur with a bare infinitive or a full infinitive—*We helped him change his tire; Brian helped me to understand my childen better.* When *consider* is followed by a verb complement, it behaves semantically very much like complex transitive *consider.* In *Nancy considers this project **to be her most successful**,* the verb complement clause could easily be replaced by an object complement NP—*Nancy considers this project **her most successful**.*

Dual Structure Infinitive Clauses

There is a third type of infinitive clause in English that shares characteristics with both direct object clauses and infinitive complement clauses. Consider the following sentences.

The lawyer found her to be uncooperative.

Everybody expected Stella to marry Stanley.

The police believe Lizzie to be guilty.

The doctor assumed Portia to be cured.

The teacher proved Jimmy to be the culprit.

The generals declared the war to be over.

In many ways these infinitive clauses resemble direct objects. For one thing, in each case the infinitive clause can be loosely paraphrased with a *that* clause, and *that* clauses which appear directly after the verb are typically direct objects (or predicate nominatives)—*The generals declared that the war was over; Everybody expected that Stella would marry Stanley.* Furthermore, each clause can be replaced by a simple pronoun—*The police believe this; The teacher proved it.* A passive within the infinitive clause doesn't really affect the meaning of the sentence. *I expect the students to choose Trevor* and *I expected Trevor to be chosen by the students* are basically synonymous. All of this suggests that the entire infinitive clause is functioning as the direct object of the higher verb.

On the other hand, the NP following the higher verb can become the subject of a passive with that verb. This suggests that the infinitive clause is functioning as a verb complement.

She was found to be uncooperative (by the lawyer).

Stella was expected (by everyone) to marry Stanley.

Lizzie is believed to be guilty (by the police).

The war was declared to be over (by the generals).

(Such sentences sound best when the agents are omitted.)

Constructions like these have two potential structures. In one an infinitive clause with an overt subject is the direct object of the higher verb, while in the other a direct object NP is followed by a verb complement with a covert subject.

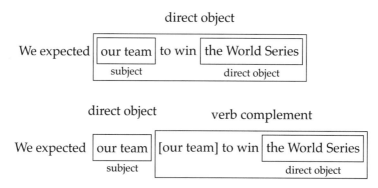

When a direct object NP is followed by a complement clause, both structures are required for coherence. Without their respective infinitive complements, *found* in *The lawyer found her to be uncooperative* and *expected* in *Everyone expected Stella to marry Stanley* take on a completely different meaning—*The lawyer found her; Everyone expected Stella.* This fact is dramatically illustrated in the sentence *I believe this politician to be a liar.* If the infinitive complement is deleted, the sentence becomes *I believe this politician,* which clearly contradicts the original utterance.

Many of the verbs in the dual structure category are complex transitive. In these cases the infinitive complement clause performs much the same function as an object complement.

The jury found Patty guilty. / *The jury found Patty to be guilty.*

The President appointed him Ambassador. / *The President appointed him to be Ambassador.*

They declared Susan the winner. / *They declared Susan to be the winner.*

Dual structure infinitive clauses

Everyone expected **Lonnie to fall**.

Mathematicians have proved **this equation to be unsolvable**.

The kids believe **Dee to be the graffiti artist in the neighborhood**.

The inspector found **the wiring to be faulty**.

NASA declared **the launch to be a success**.

They assumed **Isabella to be the winner**.

Infinitive Clauses as Subjects

Infinitive clauses can also function as subjects.

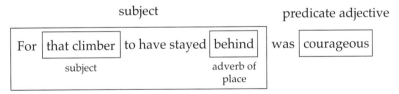

An infinitive subject clause can itself have an overt or covert subject. This poses an interesting problem since there is no "higher" subject from which to extract the covert subject of the clause. However, covert subjects can often be recovered from the previous discourse. If you are grousing about a course with a friend and say, "To require six exams in this course is really stupid," your friend will undoubtedly interpret the covert subject of *to require* as the teacher of the class in question. If Elaine has just saved a drowning child, you might say "To have done that took real courage," and your hearer will know that the covert subject of *to have done* is Elaine. Sometimes the covert subject of a subject infinitive clause is simply an indefinite *anybody*—*To be stalked by a mountain lion must be a terrifying experience.*

Infinitive clause subjects

Covert subject in clause

To have this kind of house takes money.

To have stolen that software was dumb.

To be a CPA isn't easy.

To join this sorority requires four nominations.

To know her is to love her.

Overt subject in clause

For Ken to win would be wonderful.

For her to have said that was inexcusable.

For Laurie to be honest is crucial.

For those rescuers to succeed will take a miracle.

Note that in those examples in which the infinitive clause has an overt subject, that subject is preceded by subordinator *for*. *For* is always required when an infinitive clause that contains a subject is itself a subject. When *for* is omitted in such a sentence, the sentence is ungrammatical—**Ken to win would be wonderful; *Laurie to be honest is crucial.* Hearers tend to process the first NP they hear as the subject of the main clause and the *for* alerts them that the first NP is not the main subject.

Extraposition of Infinitive Clauses.   Like *that* clauses, subject infinitive clauses are frequently extraposed. In fact you will probably find that many of the examples in the prevoius section actually sound better with extraposed subjects.

It takes money **to have this kind of house.**

It was dumb **to have stolen that software.**

It is crucial **for Laurie to be honest.**

It will take a miracle **for those rescuers to succeed.**

Here, too, extraposition is especially likely if the subject clause is long and/or complex.

For my sister to have offered her boyfriend my baseball card collection *was outrageous.*

*It was outrageous **for my sister to have offered her boyfriend my base-ball card collection**.*

On those infrequent occasions when an infinitive clause occurs as the direct object of a complex transitive verb, the direct object clause must be extraposed.

*I find **it** impossible **to be nice to Jethro**.*

*Marla considers **it** important **to be prompt**.*

*My son thinks **it** unnecessary **to bathe daily**.*

Infinitive Clauses Are Problematic

Infinitive clauses have proven to be a knotty problem for syntacticians. There is disagreement on how some of the constructions discussed above should be treated and there are other infinitive clause structures that seem to require a different analysis altogether. Consider the infinitive clauses in the following sentences.

Kim began to sweat.

The baby started to cry.

Rebecca tried to unlock the door.

Liam condescended to speak to me.

Amy tends to annoy her sisters.

Note that none of these clauses can take an overt subject—*Kim began Claudia to sweat; *The baby started Benny to cry; *Rebecca tried Stefan to unlock the door. Began* and *start* seem to have an aspectual dimension but the others do not. *Condescend* and *try* require animate subjects. while *begin, start,* and *tend* don't— *It began to rain; This paint tends to peel.*

Reams of paper have been devoted to discussions of these structures and there is no real consensus as to how they should be treated. English syntax poses many challenges and the analysis of the infinitive clause is one of the big ones. You will find that there are a great many different approaches to the various infinitive clauses in English. The analysis presented above is designed to fit infinitive clauses into the basic sentence patterns of Chapter 1 whenever possible.

ING CLAUSES

In nominal *ING* clauses, the subordinator is the {-ing} suffix. This subordinating {-ing} should not be confused with the {-ing} of the progressive; unlike the progressive suffix, subordinator {-ing} can be attached to stative verbs—*She* *was unhappy about **being** tall; I enjoy **seeing** snow on the mountains.* ING clauses are non-finite (i.e., they don't carry tense). They don't contain modal auxiliaries (since modals have no participle forms) but they do contain semi-auxiliaries, the perfect, and the passive. Since they carry the {-ing} subordinator, they don't contain the progressive.

*Jackie hates **<u>having to</u>** take clarinet lessons.*	semi-auxiliary
*Tom liked **<u>having been</u>** Grandma's favorite.*	perfect
*The baby enjoys **<u>being cuddled</u>**.*	passive

Some grammarians call *ING* constructions of this type **gerunds**. This term is problematic, however. As David Crystal points out in his *Dictionary of Linguistics and Phonetics* (1997a, p. 279), "the traditional notion of **gerund** [is] where the word derived from a verb is used as a NOUN, as in *smoking is forbidden*." But this traditional definition of a gerund is a bit misleading. While *smoking* is acting as the subject of the sentence in *Smoking is forbidden,* it never loses its verbal qualities; it can take a direct object and an adverb like any other verb—*Smoking cigars in your office is forbidden.* The entire clause, *Smoking cigars in your office* is functioning as the subject of the sentence, but *smoking* is quite verb-like.

subject

This confusion over the status of *ING* constructions arises because they can range from very nominal in character to very verbal. A few *ING* forms have become so nominalized that they can take the plural marker—*shootings, beatings, feelings, (sand)castings, hearings, shavings,* etc. These forms have become full-fledged nouns. In *His loud yelling bothers me, yelling* is preceded by a genitive determiner and an adjective, modifiers that are typically associated with nouns. In *The shooting of the cow was accidental, shooting* is modified by the article *the* and an *of* prepositional phrase, both of which typically accompany nouns. It is not unreasonable to think of the *ING* forms in these contexts as a "verbs used as nouns" and these constructions can appropriately be called gerunds. The following *ING* clauses are all on the nominal end of the scale.

ING nominal construction	Nominal markers
Her drinking disturbs me.	*ING* form preceded by genitive determiner
He was ticketed for **dangerous driving**.	*ING* form preceded by preposition and adjective

ING nominal construction (cont.)	Nominal markers (cont.)
I can't stand **their incessant criticizing**.	*ING* form preceded by genitive determiner and adjective
The first warning has been issued.	*ING* form preceded by determiner and postdeterminer

When an *ING* form occurs in a very nominal construction, its subject must take the genitive form, as in *Bill's accidental shooting of that cow created a furor*.

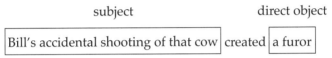

However, in the sentence *Bill's accidentally shooting that cow last week created a furor, shooting* is clearly acting as verb, not a noun; it takes both a direct object and an adverb. When the {-ing} construction is highly verb-like, the genitive form is not necessarily required for grammaticality. *Bill accidentally shooting that cow last week created a furor* is fine for many speakers.

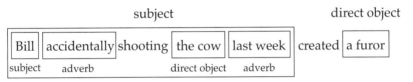

ING *Clauses as Direct Objects*

Like infinitive direct object clauses, *ING* clauses follow psych-verbs—*I enjoy riding the subway; Natalie remembers giving you that file*. Like infinitive direct object clauses, *ING* direct object clauses exhibit equi. In a sentence like *Susan hates driving at night*, the covert subject of *driving* is *Susan*.

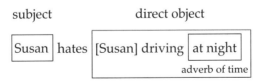

As you saw previously, when the *ING* clause contains an overt subject, the subject can be marked with a genitive form—*I dislike Nancy's using my car; I don't remember his being there*. Prescriptive grammarians demand that the subject of the *ING* verb be a genitive form, but many educated speakers use the uninflected form or (in the case of pronouns) the object form instead—*I dislike Nancy using my car; I don't remember him being there*. In fact, for some speakers, there is a real difference in meaning between a genitive form and an unmarked form or object pronoun in an *ING* clause. Compare *I hate Cal's driving* and *I*

*hate **Cal driving**.* Many people would argue that in the first example the speaker hates the way Cal drives, while in the second example the speaker expresses displeasure over the fact that Cal is driving. When prescriptivists argue that the genitive is always required before an *ING* form, they ignore dramatic counterexamples like *I don't want **him** doing that.* Clearly, **I don't want **his** doing that* is completely ungrammatical.

Many speakers use an uninflected subject NP in a clausal subject—*Jim losing all that money really upset his wife,* and some are even comfortable with an object pronoun in this position—***Him** losing all the money really upset his wife.*

The covert subject of an *ING* clause in direct object position can have indefinite reference if the *ING* form is nominal enough. In a sentence like *I enjoy racing, racing* can be construed as having an indefinite subject (*I like to watch anyone/anything racing*) or it can be analyzed as exhibiting equi (*I like [I] racing*). But in the case of the highly verbal form *riding* in *John hates riding a bicycle during rush hour,* speakers will automatically interpret the covert subject of *riding* as *John.*

Direct object *ING* clauses are fairly easy to identify. Like other direct object clauses, they can often be replaced by a pronoun or a simple NP—*Susan enjoys **eating in restaurants**. / Susan enjoys **it**. / Susan enjoys **this activity**.*

ING direct object clauses

Covert subject in clause

I hate **eating liver**.

Tucker loves **swimming in the ocean**.

She enjoys **giving money to the poor**.

The kids admitted **breaking the window with rocks**.

Lisa doesn't remember **being there**.

Overt subject in clause

I dislike **Eric('s) wearing my clothes**.

Maeve resented **her mom('s) telling those stories**.

Do you remember **my/me loaning you that book**.

As you saw earlier in this chapter, there are some verbs that can take *that* clause objects but not simple NP objects, e.g., *insist, think*. To take simple NP objects, these verbs must be followed by particles, *insist on, think about*. These same verbs also require particles when they are followed by *ING* object clauses.

In each of the following categories, note how the main verb patterns relative to the direct object type.

That clause direct object	NP direct object	*ING* clause direct object
I **insisted** that she leave the puppy at home.	The children **insisted on** ice cream.	Maggie **insisted on** doing the dishes.
Everyone **thinks** that you should help.	I **think about** my problems constantly.	Jiggs has **thought about** selling his truck.
I **dreamed** that I was an astronaut.	I **dreamed about** my grandmother.	I **dream about** owning a sports car.
Deb **complained** that her soup was cold.	Deb **complained about** the service.	Deb **complained about** having to wait.

Infinitive and ING *Clauses Compared.*   Often direct object infinitive and *ING* clauses are quite close in meaning—*I prefer to eat lunch before noon. / I prefer eating lunch before noon.* Sometimes, however, the semantic differences are striking.

I regret **to inform you of an accident.**	[Regretting precedes informing.]
I regret **informing you of the accident.**	[Informing precedes regretting.]
Linda forgot **to tell Neil about the file.**	[Forgetting precedes (not) telling.]
Linda forgot **telling Neil about the file.**	[Telling precedes forgetting.]
Tim remembered **putting the books away.**	[Putting precedes remembering.]
Tim remembered **to put the books away.**	[Remembering precedes putting.]

Direct object infinitive clauses usually refer to an event that has not yet occurred or to a nonrealized event—*She wants to be a singer; I had hoped to leave tomorrow; I would hate for my candidate to lose. ING* clauses, on the other hand, often signal an actual event. Contrast *I wanted to go to Paris* with *I enjoyed going to Paris*. Although both contain a past tense main verb, only the *ING* clause refers to a trip that actually took place.

ING *Clauses as Predicate Nominatives*

ING predicate nominative clauses behave very much like infinitive predicate nominative clauses. The copula is almost always *be* and the subject of the main verb is always an abstraction. The covert subject of such a clause is sometimes derived from a structure in the higher subject—*Her vice is [she] eating pizza; The problem we face is [us] finding adequate space; The issue for **Sergio** is [Sergio] locating his natural mother.* Sometimes the covert subject is simply indefinite—*The biggest nightmare is [anyone] shopping on Christmas Eve.* Of course, clausal predicate nominatives can also have overt subjects —*The problem is Marcia having angered the boss; The difficulty is Nan's demanding a raise.*

ING predicate nominative clauses

The issue is **merchants selling illegal fireworks**.

The trick has been **arriving on time**.

Pat's problem is **yelling at people**.

Her concern is **Hector('s) drinking when he drives**.

Sometimes the copula *be* plus an *ING* predicate nominative clause looks a great deal like a progressive construction—*Mary's favorite activity is fishing in the Everglades* versus *Mary is fishing in the Everglades*. The semantics of the first example rules out a progressive analysis, however; *fishing* requires an agentive subject and the noun head *activity* doesn't qualify. The second example can't be analyzed as a copula plus predicate nominative since *Mary* can't possibly have the same referent as *fishing in the Everglades*.

ING *Clauses as Verb Complements*

You have already seen that when bare infinitive clauses follow sensory verbs, they function as verb complements—*I felt the baby **kick**; I heard Pamela **shout**.* When an *ING* clause follows a sensory verb, it behaves in the same way except that the action is interpreted as repeated or ongoing. In *I saw Bobby hit Billy,* bare infinitive *hit* can refer to a single act, but in *I saw Bobby hitting Billy, hitting* clearly refers to repeated action. *Hit* is a punctual verb and the {-ing} morpheme affects the meaning of *hit* in this non-finite clause in the same way that the progressive affects its meaning in a finite clause. When the clausal verb is not punctual, the {-ing} indicates that the action is ongoing—*I felt the baby moving; I heard Pamela shouting.* It is only after sensory verbs that the {-ing} subordinator carries this "progressive" meaning. In *ING* verb complement clauses equi is object controlled.

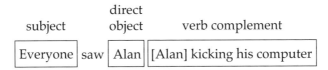

Because the NP *Alan* is the direct object of *saw*, it can become the subject of a corresponding passive—*Alan was seen kicking his computer.*

ING *Clauses as Subjects*

ING clauses can also function as subjects—*Chewing gum in class is rude; Hiking up a mountain during a hail storm is painful.*

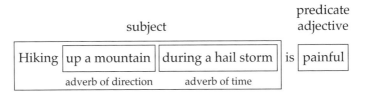

Subjectless *ING* clauses in subject position usually have indefinite reference. *Taming lions is dangerous* means that for <u>anyone</u> taming lions is a dangerous endeavor. Sometimes, however, a more explicit subject is clear from the situation, the discourse, or the grammatical context. If I have just given a lecture and say,"Speaking to a large audience is so stressful," my hearer will assume that *I* is the covert subject of *speaking*. Sometimes a covert subject appears overtly in another construction in the sentence.

*Cleaning the bathrooms every day wore **Nate** out.*

*Sleeping in a strange bed is stressful for **my daughter**.*

*Looking good is important to **Elmer**.*

*Getting up every morning at six was hard on **Gayle**.*

ING subject clauses

Covert subject in clause

Dancing is fun.

Walking in the rain gives me asthma.

Telling stories to children is Theo's job.

Naming that baby Morticia was cruel.

ING subject clauses (cont.)

Looking healthy is important.

Drinking wine in the morning is very decadent.

Overt subject in clause

Sue('s) playing cards every afternoon upsets her mother.

His losing all that money bothers me

Jen('s) being so tall amazed me.

Their lying about the money was really stupid.

RELATIVE TENSE IN NON-FINITE CLAUSES

As you have seen, neither infinitive nor *ING* clauses carry tense. They do, however, express what some linguists call **relative tense** (Comrie, 1985, pp. 56–82). This means that the time frame expressed by the main verb is usually extended to the non-finite verb. In *It bothered me to hear Denny curse*, both the bothering and the cursing took place in the past. In *It bothers me to hear Denny curse*, both the bothering and the cursing encompass present time; Denny is either cursing at the moment or is a habitual curser. The same pattern occurs in *I hated Janet's wearing my shirts* versus *I hate Janet's wearing my shirts* and *Fern forced Tyrone to leave* versus *Fern is forcing Tyrone to leave*.

It is, however, possible to express past time in a non-finite clause even when the main verb is present. As we saw in Chapter 3, the perfect is sometimes used with modal auxiliaries to express past time, and it can perform the same function in a non-finite clause—*It bothers me to **have** seen such an awful accident; I resent Howard's **having** borrowed my hammer.*

WH NOMINAL CLAUSES

The same *wh* forms that appear in information seeking questions also occur in nominal clauses—*who, what, which, where, when, why, how.* (I will treat *how* as a *wh* word even though it is spelled with an initial *h*.) In such clauses the *wh* word is both a proform and a subordinator. Until now all of our subordinators (except possibly the genitive and the {-ing} after a sensory verb) have been semantically empty. This is not true of *wh* words because they do have referents, even though those referents are not specified in the sentence.

*I know **who Justine is dating**.*	[Justine is dating someone.]
***What he said** shocked the reporters.*	[He said something.]
*I saw **what she did**.*	[She did something.]

Wh clauses differ from interrogatives in that the operator in the *wh* clause does not move. (Because *wh* questions require subject-auxiliary inversion, non-native speakers of English sometimes use subject-auxiliary inversion in *wh* direct object clauses, too, as in "I don't know how old is the baby.") The *wh* word usually occurs first in the clause regardless of its function. In the following sentence *what* is moved out of normal direct object position and appears at the beginning of the clause.

I heard **what** Geoff said [ ]

↑ – – – – – – – – –

Wh clauses can perform all the normal nominal functions.[3] They can act as subjects, direct objects, indirect objects, subject complements, object complements, and also as the objects of many prepositions. *Wh* words within nominal clauses take on a variety of functions—subject, direct object, indirect object, object complement, subject complement, determiner, adverb, and object of a preposition.

Wh *Clauses as Direct Objects*

Wh clauses often function as direct objects. Like any other clause, the *wh* clause has internal structure.

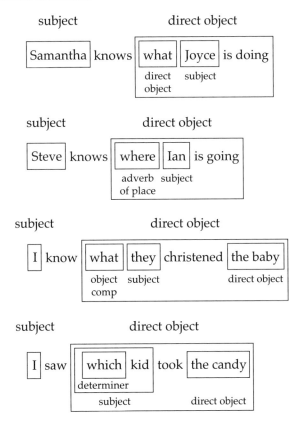

If the *wh* word is the object of a preposition, the speaker has two options. In conversation, most speakers follow the rule of thumb discussed above; the *wh* word, i.e., the object of the preposition, appears first in the clause and the preposition is left stranded in its normal position.

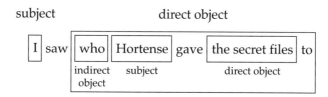

Formal edited English usually requires that the preposition precede its object, which makes the preposition, not the *wh* word, the first word in the clause.

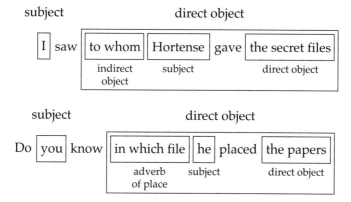

While I often write sentences of this type, I very rarely utter them.

As you saw above, *wh* words in *wh* clauses usually have a specific, but un-specified, referent. If I say "I know who Yvette is dating," *who* refers to a specific individual. There are, however, a number of *wh* compounds all of which have nonspecific reference. These compounds always take the same shape, a standard *wh* proform followed by {-ever}—*whoever, whatever, wherever, whenever, whichever, however.* In *I resented what Butch said, what* has specific reference, but in *I resent whatever Butch says, whatever* does not. In the following examples, none of the *wh* words has specific reference.

> *I will go **wherever** they send me.*
>
> *Barney will eat **whatever** you have in the house.*
>
> *I always like **whoever** Alessandra dates.*
>
> *Read **whichever** book appeals to you.*
>
> *You can prepare the turkey **however** you like.*

In the following summary chart, the grammatical function of each itali-cized *wh* word or phrase is indicated.

Wh direct object clauses

Marsha reported *what* **Mehmet had said.**	[direct object]
I saw *what* **Charlie gave Bianca.**	[direct object]
I know *who* **is stealing her tools.**	[subject]
Did Bruce know *who* **we gave the money to?**	[indirect object]
I saw *where* **the kids hid.**	[adverb of place]
I understand *why* **she might dislike it.**	[adverb of reason]
I don't know *when* **she left.**	[adverb of time]
I now understand *how* **they fixed it.**	[adverb of means]
Do you see *how* **he stands?**	[adverb of manner]
Do you know *how long* **they stayed?**	[adverb of duration]
Has anyone told you *how often* **this happens?**	[adverb of frequency]
I saw *which* **toy she took.**	[determiner]
I can't imagine *whose* **money that is.**	[determiner]
I will eat *whatever* **you fix.**	[direct object]
I don't know *whether* **the defendant is guilty**.	[no function]

Note that most of the verbs that can take *wh* clause direct objects can also take *that* clause direct objects and the same semantic categories are represented—mental state verbs, some sensory verbs, and communication verbs.

The *wh* word *whether* is an atypical subordinator. The function of *whether* within the clause is to communicate two alternative possibilities. Sometimes the possibilities are spelled out in the clause—*I don't know whether Fergus likes me or not* and sometimes they are implicit—*I wonder whether Annette speaks Polish*. *If* behaves in exactly the same way in *I don't know if Farouk is attending or not*. The subordinators *whether* and *if* have no real grammatical function within the clause.

Clauses containing *whether* and this kind of *if* are typically direct object clauses following certain psych-verbs, verbs of speculation, and verbs of inquiry.

Do you know whether Tammy has moved or not?

She doesn't care whether I live or die.

I wonder if Janice will come or not.

Cynthia asked whether Moira had been invited.

I can't decide whether to wear the blue jacket or the red one.

Wh *Clauses as Predicate Nominatives*

When *wh* clauses function as predicate nominatives, they occur in the same environments that characterize infinitive and *that* clause predicate nominatives.

Wh predicate nominative clauses

The issue is **what she told her boss.**

The problem is **where we will put the visitors.**

The question is **why he told her at all.**

Wh *Clauses as Indirect Objects and Object Complements*

While *that* clauses, infinitive clauses, and *ING* clauses never function as indirect objects or object complements, *wh* clauses do. However, in the case of indirect object clauses, this occurs only when the *wh* word is nonspecific *whoever* or *whichever* and very occasionally *whatever. Who* never appears in a *wh* indirect object clause; *I will give the silver dollar to whoever gets the highest grades* is fine but **I will give the silver dollar to who gets the highest grades* is ungrammatical.

Wh indirect object clauses

He gave **whoever answered the door** the subpoena.

I will offer my services **to whoever I like.**

I will tell **whichever reporter arrives first** my story.

Give the free lunch **to whatever group needs it most.**

The most common *wh* forms in object complements are *whoever* and *whatever*, but *what* can also occur in these structures. *Wh* object complement clauses are somewhat unusual, however.

Wh object complement clauses

You may name the puppy **whatever seems suitable.**

Paint the room **whatever color you like.**

Wh object complement clauses (cont.)

This makeup artist can make you **whoever you want to be**.

They named the baby **what they were told to name her**.

Wh *Clauses as Subjects*

Wh clausal subjects occur in a very limited environment; they most often precede copulas and verbs that communicate a psychological reaction—*shock, bother, disturb, please, thrill, elate*. As with direct object clauses, the *wh* word in a *wh* subject clause can take on almost any function.

Wh subject clauses

Who gave me the report is confidential.

Who I loaned my car to is none of your business.

Who Mary's admirer is remains a mystery.

What Louise said pleased me.

What this machine does is to stamp the packages.

Which house they sold isn't relevant.

When they left isn't clear.

Why he screamed was a mystery.

How long we are staying is Gertrude's decision.

Which suspect is guilty hasn't been determined.

Whether she participates or not is immaterial.

Whatever he said shocked his parents.

Whoever told you this lied.

Sometimes *wh* clause subjects are followed by infinitival predicate nominatives in which the *to* is optional—**What Sam did** *was [to] offend the boss;* **What this policy does** *is [to] protect you from flood and fire.*

Extraposition of Wh *Clauses.* Subject *wh* clauses can be extraposed fairly readily and many sound better extraposed.

It's none of your business **who I loaned my car to**.

It hasn't been determined **which suspect is guilty**.

It is immaterial ***whether she participates or not.***

It isn't clear ***when they left.***

Direct object *wh* clauses containing *when* are routinely extraposed, even though the extraposed clause often follows the cataphoric *it* directly.

*I hate **it when my brother interrupts me.***

*I enjoy **it when my students seem enthusiastic.***

*Mom doesn't like **it** a bit **when you whine.***

Clauses as Adjective Complements

As you saw in Chapter 2, predicate adjectives can be followed by complements, e.g., *George is not fond of broccoli.* Such complements can be clauses as well as phrases. *That* clauses often function as adjective complements.

That clauses as adjective complements

I was happy **that the auditor didn't find any discrepancies.**

Ginny is certain **that the project will be a success.**

Lena was unaware **that the job had been filled.**

I am pleased **that you are going to work here.**

Don't confuse the above constructions with those in which a subject has been extraposed, e.g., *It is crucial that you tell the truth.* These always contain cataphoric *it*.

Infinitive clauses can also function as adjective complements.

Infinitive clauses as adjective complements

Bert was anxious **to help us.**

I would be happy **to travel with you to Madagascar.**

She was afraid **to tell them the truth.**

Gregory was eager **to dance the macarena.**

I am sorry **to give you bad news about your exams.**

> ### Infinitive clauses as adjective complements (cont.)
>
> Ed is ready **to leave**.
>
> Maria is eager **for Paul to arrive**.
>
> This will be easy **for Tina to fix**.
>
> Reiko's parents were happy **for her to go**.

Those infinitive clauses that contain a subject require the subordinator *for* as well as *to*. **Maria is eager Paul to arrive* is ungrammatical.

In the chart above, all those adjective complements with covert subjects reflect subject controlled equi.

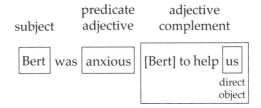

Now consider this pair of sentences made famous by linguist Noam Chomsky.

John is eager to please. / John is easy to please.

It should be clear that while the covert subject of *please* is *John* in the first sentence, this is not the case in the second. In *John is easy to please* the covert subject of the clause is an indefinite *somebody*, while *John* is the <u>direct object</u> of *please*. In other words, *It is easy for someone to please John*.

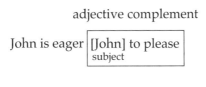

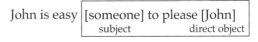

When a predicate adjective that expresses "ease" or "difficulty" is followed by an infinitive complement, the structure is often called a **tough construction** because the adjective reflects the relative "toughness" of the activity expressed by the infinitive clause. Tough constructions always reflect the structure of *John is easy to please*.

This cabinet will be tough to move.

This computer will be easy to fix.

Hilda is difficult to talk to.

She is hard to work with.

Those kids are impossible to discipline.

There are a number of other predicate adjectives that pattern in exactly the same way but don't reflect "toughness," e.g., *Birds are fascinating to watch; Motorcycles are fun to ride; Sharks are interesting to study.*

Predicate adjectives that pattern like *eager* require an animate subject, while those patterning like *easy* do not.

The kids were eager to help.	*These shirts are easy to iron.*
The dog was happy to see them.	*That system is hard to repair.*
Ingrid was glad to loan us the money.	*This floor is tough to clean.*
Nigel is anxious to leave.	*Caroline is hard to convince.*

The degree modifiers *too* and *enough* are often used in conjunction with infinitive adjective complements. Note that *enough* always <u>follows</u> the adjective it modifies.

Emily is too sick to work.	*She's old enough to drink.*
Alan is too upset to help us.	*Luke is tall enough to reach the sink.*

Too and *enough* reflect ends of the same semantic continuum—*She's old enough to be here* versus *She's too old to be here.* Everything between *old enough* and *too old* is an "acceptable" age.

While *that* clauses and infinitive adjective complements typically follow the predicate adjective directly, *ING* clauses are found after prepositions—*Tony is unhappy **about Mike's leaving**; I am furious **over the corporation demoting my sister***. In these sentences the prepositional phrase itself is the adjective complement and the clause is the object of the preposition.

ING clauses in prepositional phrase adjective complements

Susan wasn't aware **of Jill('s) having been subpoenaed.**

I am angry **about Anthony('s) quitting school.**

Dave was sorry **about Rachel('s) having had an accident on her bike.**

Gretchen is afraid **of her kids getting into bad company.**

Note that all of the prepositional clauses above can be loosely paraphrased with a *that* clause—*Susan wasn't aware that Jill had been subpoenaed; I am angry that Anthony is quitting school*, etc. Furthermore, many complement clauses can be paraphrased with a non-clausal prepositional phrase—*They are certain that she is guilty* versus *They are certain of her guilt*. Complement phrases, complement clauses, and complement prepositional clauses function semantically in much the same way.

Wh clauses can on occasion function as complements of predicate adjectives—*Doris wasn't certain **who was coming to the party**; I wasn't sure **whether Mabel would be there***. More often, however, a *wh* clause functions as the object of the preposition in prepositional phrase adjective complements. In the sentences in the following chart, the adjective complement is a prepositional phrase in which the object of the preposition is a *wh* clause.

Wh clauses in prepositional phrase adjective complements

Regina was afraid of **what might happen to her house**.

Ted was worried about **who would feed the cats during the trip**.

They were sorry about **what their dog had done to my rug**.

Evie is unhappy about **who was chosen**.

Postnominal Modification

English has a number of postnominal modifying constructions. One of the most common is the **relative clause**. A relative clause is a *wh* clause that always follows an NP; the relative proform, always a *wh* word or *that,* has the same referent as the preceding NP. In *The guy who borrowed your car isn't reliable, who* and *the guy* refer to the same individual. The relative proform always has a grammatical function within the clause and at the same time acts as a subordinator.

English contains two distinct types of relative clauses, each of which has a different effect on the preceding NP.

RESTRICTIVE RELATIVE CLAUSES

The primary job of a restrictive relative clause is to restrict the possible referents of the preceding NP, thus making the referent more accessible to the hearer.

*Give the man **who is waiting at the door** the package.*

*The repairperson **who fixed your computer** was totally incompetent.*

*The dress **that Jeanne bought for the wedding** is stained.*

*I really like the house **that Peter bought last month**.*

*The steak **which you brought me** is cold.*

In a sentence like *The kids **who are playing on the doorstep** are too noisy,* the restrictive relative clause tells us <u>which</u> kids are being referred to; it's not the kids who are sitting in the living room or the kids who are hiding in the attic; it's the kids who are playing on the doorstep.

Since restrictive relative clauses restrict the possible referents of the NP, such clauses do not occur with proper nouns because proper nouns already have unique reference. In a sentence like *The John Doe who is in my statistics class is an idiot,* John Doe is not technically a proper noun. (See Chapter 2.) The presumption here is that there is more than one John Doe and the relative clause restricts the reference to the one in my statistics class. Because of this restricting function, restrictive relative clauses are usually used in cases in which the preceding NP has more than one potential referent (although there are exceptions to this generalization, as you will see shortly). If I know that a friend has two daughters, I might say "The daughter who lives in Cleveland just finished medical school, and the daughter who lives in Tucson is unemployed."

Relative clauses can modify NPs in any position and the clause is embedded in the nominal structure. In other words, if the clause modifies a direct object NP, then the relative clause is part of the direct object.

direct object

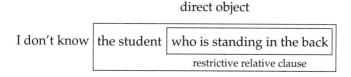

Like any other clause, a restrictive relative clause has internal structure and the *wh* word typically comes first in the clause, regardless of its grammatical function within the clause.

restrictive relative clause

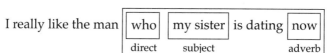

Restrictive relative clauses can modify indefinite pronouns:

*I don't know anyone **who can fix this**.*

*No one **that I know** would say such a thing.*

*This is somebody **who has a grudge**.*

*Anybody **who would do that** is a creep.*

They can also modify personal pronouns, but only when the pronouns are used as indefinites—*He **who dies with the most toys** wins*. Indefinite personal pronouns are fairly rare in Modern English. On rare occasions *you* is used with a restrictive relative clause, as in *You who's holding up the line, move along*.

Although *who* and *which* both function as relative proforms, the most ubiquitous relative proform in English is *that*. In Old English the only relative proform was the invariable word *þe* from which relative *that* is derived (at least in part). Although *who/whom* and *which* existed in Old English as interrogatives, they were not used as relative pronouns until the Middle English period. (This usage was modeled on Norman French, which used its interrogative pronouns as relative pronouns.) In casual conversation *that* is routinely used with both human and inanimate noun heads, despite the complaints of prescriptivists.

I hate the coat that my mother bought me.

The car that Nori bought is a lemon.

The dentist that you're seeing just lost his license.

Do you know the people that live there?

While formal edited English requires *whom* when the relative pronoun functions as an object (including object of a preposition), even highly educated speakers of English use *who* in all positions in conversation—*I know the woman who you offered that job to; I met the guy who you had that big fight with.* This usage is actually quite natural; *I know the woman to whom you offered that job* sounds stilted in informal social contexts.

Where, when, and *why* can also be used as relative proforms in very limited circumstances. *Where* must follow an NP that indicates a place, *when* must follow an NP that indicates time, and *why* typically follows the NP *the reason*.

*The town **where I was born** no longer exists.*

*Do you remember the time **when we danced until dawn**.*

*She won't tell me the reason **why she did it**.*

The indefinite *wh* proforms (*whoever, whatever, wherever,* etc.) do not occur as relative pronouns.

Inanimate NPs pose an interesting problem for relative clause formation. In Old English, the *wh* interrogative pronouns had only one genitive form *hwæs*, the source of Modern English *whose*. Ever since the *wh* forms took on the function of relative pronoun in Middle English, *whose* has been used with both animate and inanimate nouns, as in this passage from Shakespeare's *Hamlet*. (Boldface added.)

"I could a tale unfold **whose** lightest word / Would harrow up thy soul" (Act I, Sc. v, line 15).

Unfortunately, prescriptivists eventually proscribed the use of *whose* with inanimate nouns and this proscription created a real gap in the grammatical system. The only solution in contemporary edited English is a somewhat awkward periphrastic genitive construction.

> *I bought a book the cover **of which** was torn.*
>
> *Did you see that house the roof **of which** was missing?*
>
> *Ivana has a tree the bark **of which** is dark red.*

Inanimate *whose* does endure in speech, however, and you will often hear sentences like *My doctor gave me some pills whose side-effects were terrible* or *That's the school whose roof blew off in Hurricane Andrew.*

Restrictive relative clauses	Function of italicized or covert proform
I know the lawyer *that* **was just indicted**.	subject
I need someone *who* **can fix this**.	subject
I don't like the new salesman **they've hired**.	direct object [covert]
Do you know the people **she loaned her car to**?	indirect object [covert]
The names *which* **Sherry called Bobby** were shocking.	object complement
I don't like the person *that* **my son has become**.	subject complement
The place *where* **my sister lives** is rundown.	adverb of place
The woman **on** *whose* **porch you are sitting** is my aunt.	genitive determiner
The house **in** *which* **I grew up** has been razed.	object of preposition (PP functioning as adverb of place)

Deleting the Relative Proform

Relative proforms that don't function as the subject of the clause are routinely deleted in many types of discourse. The following examples are from Elizabeth George's novel *In the Presence of the Enemy* (1997). (Boldface added.)

Slowly, Luxford replaced the graph **he'd been holding**. (p. 406)

He had to admit that she'd shown an uncharacteristic mercy in leaving him to sleep the binge off instead of awakening him and forcing him to engage in the conversation **he'd been so insistent upon having with her**. (p. 138)

"Mr. Chambers, I don't need to tell you how serious a situation **you're in**." (p. 495)

An omitted relative proform can always be recovered because it has the same referent as the preceding NP.

Extraposition of Relative Clauses

Restrictive relative clauses are sometimes extraposed in conversation. While such constructions are not acceptable in edited English because the modifying clause is too far from its noun head, they do occur in casual discourse.

*A student **who had failed physics** came in for counseling. / A student came in for counseling **who had failed physics**.*

*The baby **that Jane adopted** is beautiful. / The baby is beautiful **that Jane adopted**.*

*Alexander gave a book **that he had found at a garage sale** to Katrina. / Alexander gave a book to Katrina **that he had found at a garage sale**.*

As is often the case with extraposition, extraposed relatives frequently occur when the clause itself is long and/or complex—*He is going out with a woman next weekend **that he met on a boat during a trip to Tahiti**.*

Infinitive Restrictive Clauses

While the prototypical restrictive clause is finite (i.e., it carries tense), infinitive clauses also restrict NPs. Some restrictive infinitive clauses have overt subjects and others covert subjects.

Infinitive restrictive clauses

Colleen needs someone **to play with**.

The dog wants some water **to drink**.

Nancy has no one **to talk to**.

I want some boxes **to store these antiques in**.

Here is a toy **for you to give to the baby**.

I need a firm mattress **for my father-in-law to sleep on**.

While many of these infinitive clauses can be loosely paraphrased with a conventional relative clause, e.g., *Colleen needs someone who she can play with; I have no one that I can talk to,* such paraphrases overlook a significant semantic dimension of these infinitival relatives. Unlike *wh* relatives, infinitive relatives focus on the real world function of the NP being modified. Colleen needs someone, and that person's function is playmate; the water is for drinking; the boxes are for storage; and the mattress is for sleeping. Semantically these structures resemble adverbs of purpose.

Discourse Functions of Restrictive Relative Clauses

Restrictive relative clauses are ubiquitous in discourse. While they routinely restrict the referents of the preceding NPs, they also have broader discourse functions. When a speaker believes that a referent is familiar to a hearer but knows that the referent has not yet been introduced into the immediate discourse, s/he will often use an NP plus relative clause to introduce that referent (Givón, 1993b, p. 108). Such constructions typically feature an NP containing a definite determiner like *the* or *that.*

I lost the book that I borrowed from you last week.

That plumber who Latisha hired is really good.

Do you know that exchange student who's living with the Wilsons?

Presumably the hearer already knows that the speaker borrowed a book, that Latisha has hired a plumber, and that there is an exchange student living at the Wilsons. The function of the relative clause is simply to bring that knowledge into consciousness and to then use that knowledge to restrict the potential referents of the preceding NP.

But sometimes a relative clause follows an NP containing the indefinite article *a,* and, as you saw in Chapter 2, the indefinite article indicates that the NP encodes new information. In this context a relative clause will be more descriptive than restrictive if the NP has definite reference. An utterance like *Mia has a son who is extremely handsome* is possible even if Mia has only one son. Here the function of the restrictive clause is to provide descriptive information; this sentence could even be paraphrased as *Mia has an extremely handsome son.* In *Mr. Brady wants to marry a woman who really likes children,* the primary function of the clause is to restrict the possible referents of the non-specific NP, *a woman.* But in *Ms. Brady is a woman who really likes children,* the relative clause characterizes Ms. Brady. The following quotations from Elizabeth George's *In the Presence of the Enemy* (1997) contain both restrictive and descriptive relative clauses. The purely restrictive clauses follow NPs containing the definite article, while the descriptive clauses are those in which the preceding NP contains the indefinite article. (Underlining and boldface added.)

... the school was run by the Sisters of the Holy Martyrs. The Sisters were <u>a</u> group of women **whose mean age appeared to be seventy**. (p. 1)

A twentyish boy with the eyes of a frog, he was wearing the grease-splotched overalls of his profession and <u>a</u> baseball cap **that had the word *Braves* scrolled across the front.** (p. 394)

<u>The</u> clerk **from whom Stanley had ordered the coffee** stood there with two plastic cups of it. (p. 395)

"He put those glasses in the car. He's been waiting for <u>the</u> moment **when you'd stumble on them.**" (p. 410)

Note that the first example would be rather odd if the relative clause were omitted—*The Sisters were a group of women.* Most of us know that nuns are women. The purpose of the relative clause construction in the original sentence is to provide the descriptive comment about age, and without it the sentence is almost reduced to a tautology.

OTHER RESTRICTIVE POSTNOMINAL MODIFIERS

In English, there are a number of constructions that do not have all the features of relative clauses but nevertheless restrict the possible referents of the NPs they follow. Consider the following sentences:

*The woman **chosen for the post** used to be my dentist.*

*I don't know those kids **playing in the backyard**.*

*The gloves **lying on that chair** belong to my aunt.*

*The bratwurst **in the refrigerator** is spoiled.*

*I know many people **from Indonesia**.*

In each case the structure in boldface plays the same role that a restrictive relative clause would—*the woman **who was chosen for the post***; *the kids **who are playing in the backyard***; *the gloves **that are lying on that chair***, etc.

Early transformational grammarians hypothesized that such structures were **"reduced" relative clauses**, i.e., structures in which the relative pronoun and the verb *be* have been omitted.

The tree house ~~which was~~ built by my children was destroyed in the storm.

The woman ~~who is~~ sitting over there was my fifth grade teacher.

The motorcycle ~~which is~~ in the garage is Pete's.

This process reduces the relative clause in the first example to a past participle clause and the relative clause in the second example to an *ING* clause.

While most contemporary grammarians would reject the notion that these structures actually derive from full relative clauses, I will exploit this idea briefly because it's useful in understanding certain postnominal constructions.

Using the reduced relative clause model, a construction like *the people who are sitting on the porch* can be reduced to *the people sitting on the porch* and *the chairs that are in the living room* can be reduced to *the chairs in the living room*. In the last example it is important to realize that, although the prepositional phrase *in the living room* looks like an adverbial phrase, it is not. Consider the sentence *The chairs in the living room are being re-covered*. While *in the living room* expresses a location, is not an adverb indicating where the chairs are being reupholstered; on the contrary, this prepositional phrase is indicating <u>which</u> chairs are being reupholstered, i.e., the chairs in living room, not the ones in the den.

subject

| The chairs | in the living room | | are being re-covered. |

postnominal modifier

In Chapter 4, we saw examples of postnominal modifiers after indefinite pronouns—*She is wearing something **blue**; Nobody **decent** would say such a thing*. These constructions can also be analyzed as reduced relative clauses—*She is wearing something ~~which is~~ blue; Nobody ~~who is~~ decent would say such a thing*. In essence, whatever is left over after a relative clause is reduced takes on the function of the clause. In *Something here smells bad, here* retains the semantics of a locative adverb, but its grammatical function is that of postnominal modifier.

While the reduced relative clause strategy is useful for understanding the postnominal constructions discussed above, it has its limitations. Consider the following sentences:

*The woman **with the smirk on her face** is my boss.*

*Students **with strong academic records** will be accepted by the program.*

*A man **resembling my boyfriend** robbed a convenience store last night.*

*Anyone **knowing the code** should punch it in.*

*Those campers **seeing the crash** should call the FAA immediately.*

None of these modifying structures can readily be replaced by a relative clause—**the woman who is with the smirk on her face; *a man who is resembling my boyfriend; *anyone who is knowing the code*. (The last three examples are problematic because each contains a stative clausal verb, which is rendered progressive in a full relative clause.)

Because there are so many holes in the reduced relative clause analysis, I will simply label all of the phrases and clauses discussed in this section as **restrictive postnominal modifiers**. Restrictive postnominal modifiers are typically *ING* clauses, past participle clauses, and prepositional phrases. Occasionally lexical adjectives and adverbs take on this function.

Restrictive postnominal modifiers

The child **standing in the hall** wants to see the principal.

Any student **having the measles** must report to the school nurse.

Do you know the girl **being treated by the paramedics**?

The coat **trimmed in red** is mine.

The lamp **broken during the argument** has been repaired.

The papers **on your desk** are blowing all over.

I really enjoy the students **in my morning class**.

Many brides wear something **blue**.

Everyone **there** enjoyed the party.

The people **here** are very snobbish.

Sometimes a prepositional phrase in the predicate is a postnominal modifier and sometimes it is an adverb. This functional flexibility can produce grammatical ambiguity as in *The police arrested the students in the park*. Here *in the park* might be an adverbial prepositional phrase indicating where the arrests took place or it might be a restrictive postnominal modifier indicating <u>which</u> students were arrested, i.e., the students in park, as opposed to the students in the administration building.

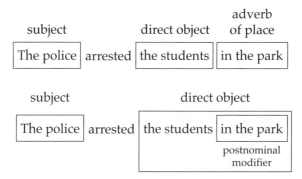

NON-RESTRICTIVE RELATIVE CLAUSES

Non-restrictive relative clauses perform a very different function from restrictive relative clauses; they simply provide additional information about the NP and are never crucial in identifying the referent(s). While non-restrictive relative clauses are subordinate clauses, i.e., they can't stand alone, they are not embedded within the NP. Unlike restrictive clauses, they can co-occur with proper nouns and they don't co-occur with indefinite pronouns. The fact that non-restrictive clauses provide additional information and are not embedded is underscored by the pauses that surround these clauses in discourse; these pauses are reflected by commas in written texts.

> *Jerry Seinfeld,* **who is a stand-up comedian,** *had his own T.V. show.*
>
> *My oldest sister,* **who is an accountant in New York,** *handles my taxes.*
>
> *George is visiting Cecilia,* **who is living in Spain.**
>
> <u>*Absalom, Absalom,*</u> **which Faulkner published in 1936,** *was his most difficult novel.*

Although the material provided by non-restrictive relative clauses is "additional," it is not superfluous or irrelevant. Sometimes a non-restrictive clause will provide very important information as in *These batteries, which should be changed monthly, will ensure that your smoke detector can be heard all over the house.*

Non-restrictive relative clauses almost never exploit the proform *that* after human NPs and only occasionally after inanimate NPs. A sentence like *?My new couch, that was just delivered yesterday, is already torn* is marginal for many speakers.

Unlike restrictive relative clauses, non-restrictive relative clauses can refer back to structures other than NPs. Because the referents of these clauses are structures rather than people, the relative proform is always *which*.

Diana loves that purple dinosaur, **which many kids do.**	[refers to preceding predicate]
I know you're mad, **which you have every right to be.**	[refers to predicate adjective]
Today is Sunday, **which means I can sleep in.**	[refers to entire sentence]
Aaron lied to his parents, **which really bothered them.**	[refers to entire sentence]

Non-restrictive modifiers sometimes take the shape of past participle clauses.

> *My Uncle Bob,* **called Bubba by his friends,** *is a corporate vice-president.*
>
> *Ms. Grundy,* **just named teacher of the year,** *has been fired.*
>
> *My brother,* **known by everyone as the best player on the team,** *was benched all season.*

When a non-restrictive structure is an NP rather than a clause, it is usually called an **appositive**. Like non-restrictive relative clauses, appositives refer to the same entity as the NP they follow.

Non-restrictive relative clause	Appositive
My daughter, **who is a surgeon in Texas**, has been awarded a big grant.	My daughter, **a surgeon in Texas**, has been awarded a big grant.
Dr. Keller, **who is a well-known chemist**, made an amazing discovery.	Dr. Keller, **a well-known chemist**, made an amazing discovery.
Ward, **which is an old counter-culture community**, is fascinating.	Ward, **an old counter-culture community**, is fascinating.

Discourse Functions of Non-Restrictive Relative Clauses and Appositives

Non-restrictive relative clauses and, even more commonly, appositives allow us to introduce unfamiliar people into discourse by using a common NP or a proper noun followed by explanatory material, as in this passage from Sister Helen Prejean's narrative *Dead Man Walking* (1994). (Boldface added.)

"We hired a man, **an electrician, who filled out a civil service application for the job**. Frank Blackburn, **the warden at Angola at the time**, interviewed the prospective candidate for the job in some depth." (p. 104)

Appositives and non-restrictive relative clauses are especially common in newspapers, because a journalist is constantly introducing unfamiliar individuals and entities into the discourse. The following passages are from an article published in *The Miami Herald* (Kolata, 1997, p. 30A). (Boldface added.)

... it is unlikely that irradiated meats could be available before next summer, said Jacque Knight, **a spokeswoman for the Department**.

The American Meat Institute, **which represents meat processors**, said the agency's action was a "victory."

... the irradiation of meats ... could destroy bacteria such as E. coli, **a strain that infected hamburger meat processed by Hudson Foods**.

Dr. Michael Jacobson, **director of the Center for Science in the Public Interest, a consumer advocacy organization based in Washington**, said he would prefer that the meat industry use other methods.

Note that the last example contains an appositive embedded within an appositive.

Both non-restrictive relative clauses and appositives are also extremely common in contexts in which a speaker or author seeks to explain and define. They are ubiquitous in textbooks, reference books, and manuals. Consider the following passages from *The Complete Book of Bicycling,* a manual for bicycle owners written by Eugene A. Sloane (1988). (Boldface added.)

> More common than bursitis is tendinitis, **an inflammation of the tendons and ligaments**. (p. 159)

> Cartilage, **which separates the major bones of the knee**, prevents bone-to-bone contact. (p. 159)

> Vigorous cycling helps to clear away cholesterol deposits, **which can lead to clogged and hardened arteries**. (p. 137)

Of course non-restrictive relative clauses and appositives occur in highly informal discourse as well. In the following passages from *God Bless John Wayne* (1996), novelist Kinky Friedman uses non-restrictive clauses to introduce characters to his readers and at the same time provide information about them. (Boldface added.)

> Ratso was my flamboyant fleamarket friend **who sometimes served as a rather weather-beaten Dr. Watson to my postnasal Sherlock Holmes**. (p. 11)

> Ratso, **who'd accompanied me on practically all of my forays into crime solving,** was now a registered guest of the NYPD. (p. 198)

> I thought of Ratso's dad—his adoptive father—**Jack Sloman, who'd died quite recently in Florida**." (p. 29)

RESTRICTIVE APPOSITIVES

There is another construction that resembles both restrictive and non-restrictive relative clauses. These are the so-called **restrictive appositives**. The most common type of restrictive appositive is a *that* clause preceded by an abstract NP. The following examples will give you a sense of the structure.

> *The fact **that they had lied** bothered me.*

> *I couldn't accept the idea **that Eva was leaving us.***

> *The theory **that the world is flat** has been disproved.*

> *I reject the notion **that he would deceive us.***

> *He harbored the hope **that his briefcase would be returned.***

> *We didn't believe the story **that they had been kidnapped by pirates.***

These clauses differ from normal relative clauses in that the subordinator is always *that,* never a *wh* word, and this subordinator has no grammatical role within the clause. Subordinator *that* can always be deleted in a restrictive appositive if the preceding NP is in the predicate—*I couldn't accept **the idea Eva was leaving us**; He harbored the hope **his briefcase would be returned**.* The deletion of *that* when the clause is part of subject NP is problematic for many speakers—*??The fact **they had lied** bothered me*; *?The story **they had been kidnapped** didn't ring true.*

Like restrictive relative clauses, restrictive appositives restrict the possible referents of the NP. In *The fact that the file is missing has been noted,* the clause tells us <u>which</u> fact is at issue. However, unlike restrictive relative clauses, restrictive appositives occur with a very limited set of NPs. And unlike non-restrictive appositives, these clauses are not set off by pauses in speech (or commas in text).

Restricted appositives are sometimes extraposed in casual discourse.

> *The idea **that he could get into Harvard** is absurd.* / *The idea is absurd **that he could get into Harvard**.*

> *Her notion **that children will eat only what they need** is silly.* / *Her notion is silly **that children will eat only what they need**.*

When restrictive clauses of any type are extraposed, no cataphoric *it* is required, since the preceding NP remains to function as the subject.

Infinitive clauses can also function as restrictive appositives and they, too, follow a small group of abstract nouns.

> *The plan **to drive to Tucson** sounds reasonable.*

> *She had an opportunity **to speak to the Director**.*

> *The girls made an attempt **to help the injured horse**.*

> *Malik expressed a desire **to study dance**.*

The first example could be paraphrased as *The plan, which is to drive to Tucson, sounds reasonable.*

Infinitive restrictive appositives are not commonly extraposed.

Adverbial Clauses

Adverbial clauses are extremely heterogeneous in form. They include clause types that don't appear in other constructions. Because of their heterogeneity, it is much easier to group adverbial clauses by semantic type rather than grammatical form. Not all adverbial clauses are embedded structures. As you will see, some are contained within the predicate of a higher clause, but others simply stand apart from the sentence. The following discussion focuses on the types of adverbs discussed in the adjunct adverb section in Chapter 4.

LOCATIVE ADVERBS

Locative adverbial clauses are not especially common in English discourse and they take a limited number of forms. As a rule, adverbs of space contain the subordinators *where* or *wherever*. *Where* suggests that the place referred to in the clause is specific—*I am going where the sun shines all winter. Wherever* refers to an indeterminate place—*I will go wherever you send me.* It is sometimes hard to decide whether a *where(ever)* form is an adverb of place or an adverb of direction. Directional adverbs are most often prepositional phrases in which the preposition circumscribes a direction, and such prepositions rarely take *wh* clauses as objects. Nevertheless, you can usually depend on the preceding verb to give you a clue as to the adverb's semantic type. In *I will stay where I am,* it's reasonable to assume that both the clause and the proform *where* are adverbs of place.

It is important to distinguish adverbial *wh* clauses from direct object *wh* clauses. In *I know **where you are going**,* the *wh* clause is a nominal clause functioning as a direct object and in *I will go **where you are going**,* the clause is a spatial adverbial clause. Within both clauses, however, the *wh* word is functioning as an adverb.

TEMPORAL ADVERBS

Temporal adverbial clauses are quite common in English and all three major semantic types can be expressed by clauses. As you will see, a number of very different clause types can communicate time frame.

Adverbs of Time (Point or Boundary)

Not surprisingly, the proform *when* can be used as a subordinator in an adverb of time clause. In the sentence *I will come **when I am called**,* when functions as an adverb of time within the clause, which itself functions as an adverb of time.

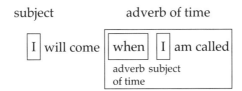

Here the proform *when* doesn't actually answer the question *when?* but, like the clause itself, stands for a time frame that is not specified.

Prepositions can take clauses as their objects, and *after* is often used as a subordinator in finite adverb of time clauses—*I will help you **after I finish the dishes**; Joan arrived **after Feryal left**. After* refers to an open time frame that begins subsequent to the event or action noted in the clause. The subordinator *as soon as* functions in much the same way. In *I will help you **as soon as I finish my lunch**, as soon as* marks a specific time frame, which occurs at the point when the event mentioned in the clause ends.

The preposition *until* usually occurs in adverbs of duration (*I will stay **until I am evicted***), but *until* can appear in an adverb of time clause when the preceding verb is negative—*He didn't help **until I insisted**; She didn't smile **until she saw the results**. In these sentences the events articulated in the clause represent the beginning of the time frame, i.e., the smiling begins when she sees the results.

The subordinator *while* is used in clauses in which the speaker wishes to communicate concurrent events—*Les cooked **while Kimberly mowed the lawn**; Michelle drove **while Scott slept**; I will scrub the floors **while you wash the windows***.

Adverbs of Frequency

Clausal adverbs of frequency are far less common than clausal time (point/boundary) adverbs. They exploit the subordinator *whenever* and a few subordinators containing the construction *as . . . as*.

*How often did the baby cry? The baby cried **whenever I came into the room**.*

*How often does Teddy drink wine? Teddy drinks wine **whenever he is eating dinner**.*

*How often do you go to Budapest? I go **as often as I can**.*

*How many times can we go to the salad bar? I'll go **as many times as they'll let me**.*

Adverbs of Duration

There are also a limited number of adverbial clauses that express duration. The preposition *since* can take a clausal object, and this construction is often used to indicate duration—*Phil has lived here **since he left his parent's house**; We have been friends **since we attended the same grammar school**. Sometimes *since* is modified by *ever*, which intensifies the notion of duration—*I have lived here* **ever since I was a kid**.

The phrase *as long as* is also used in adverbs of duration.

How long has Evelyn lived here? Evelyn has lived here **as long as I have known her**.

How long will you stay? I will stay **as long as they will have me**.

Note that adverbs of duration can co-occur with the perfect, since duration is implicit in this aspect.

Temporal Adverbs in Discourse

Because a clause expresses a proposition, a temporal adverbial clause allows a speaker to manipulate the time frame in complex ways. The following examples are from Sister Helen Prejean's autobiographical narrative *Dead Man Walking* (1994) and Elizabeth George's novel *In the Presence of the Enemy* (1997). (Boldface added.)

I had promised her that I would be waiting for her at the gate **when she came out**. (Prejean, p. 227)

He helped his wife up, and **as she tidied everything from her denim skirt to her greying hair**, he introduced himself. (George, p. 510)

"**After I gave them the statement** I asked the District Attorney investigator if he would help my Mother." (Prejean, p. 161)

"He's waiting **until he's settled completely into the new job**." (George, p. 444)

Word Order and Temporal Adverbial Clauses

While all temporal adverbial clauses can appear in the predicate, many also occur in sentence initial position.

When Ellen fell, *she broke two ribs.*

After I cooked the meal, *I cleaned up the kitchen.*

As soon as my old girlfriend arrived, *I left.*

Ever since she lost her job, *she has been morose.*

Every time he picks something up, *he drops it.*

Iconicity may be one reason that temporal clauses sometimes appear first in the sentence. In all the examples above, the event described in the subordinate clause precedes the event described in the main clause; in other words, the clause order reflects the temporal order of the events. While sentence initial clauses are subordinate, they are not embedded.

Summary of spatial and temporal adverb clauses

Adverbs of place	She lives **where the sun never sets in the summer**.
	The baby will stay **wherever you put him**.
Adverbs of direction	I will travel **wherever the train takes me**.
	She went **wherever she was sent**.
Adverbs of time (point/boundary)	Sasha left the room **when she heard the alarm**.
	I will leave **as soon as you give me an answer**.
	Adam arrived **after Eve had left**.
	He didn't sleep **until his son got home**.
Adverbs of duration	Roberta has been an athlete **as long as I've known her**.
	She has not spoken to me **since I told her off**.
	I have known her **ever since I was a child**.
Adverbs of frequency	Charles attends the opera **as often as he can**.
	I can hit the target **as many times as you can**.

ADVERBS OF MANNER

Adverbs of manner are usually lexical or phrasal rather than clausal, but prepositions sometimes take clause objects, which produce adverbs of this type. The preposition *like* often participates in adverb of manner constructions—*She acts **like she doesn't know the answer**. The child was crying **like she would never stop**. As* combined with *if* functions in much the same way—*He was acting **as if he were the boss**; Marta is talking **as if she knows where the report is**.* Prescriptivists usually reject *like* in favor of *as if*.

ADVERBS OF MEANS

Prepositions readily take *ING* clause objects, and most adverbial means clauses take this shape. *By* is the preposition most often used in such constructions.

*You can get to Boston **by taking the next bus**.*

*Erin angered her boss **by proposing that he be more supportive**.*

*Andres was shocked **by his friend('s) stealing a bicycle**.*

Interestingly, *without* can also participate in an adverb of means clause, but *with* cannot. *Without* clauses express <u>negative</u> means—*You should be able to open this* **without using a hammer**; *You can fix this* **without using any special tools;** *The kids settled their argument* **without resorting to violence.**

When the clause has no overt subject, which is often the case in such constructions, subject controlled equi pertains—*You can fix this without [you] using any special tools; The kids settled their argument without [the kids] resorting to violence.*

ADVERBS OF REASON/PURPOSE AND RESULT

A rather heterogeneous set of subordinators operate in adverbial clauses of reason/purpose and result. *Because* is the most frequently used subordinator in an adverb of reason clause—*I dropped the class* **because I didn't like the teacher**; *The engine blew up* **because he forgot to add oil.** *Because* is so closely associated with adverbs of reason that children, when asked why they did something, will often answer in a drawn out "Becauuuse."

So that is a subordinator that also is commonly found in adverbs of reason and purpose—*I loaned her my notes* **so that she wouldn't be embarrassed**; *I tripped him* **so that he would fall in front of the whole class.** *That* can be omitted, leaving *so* as the sole subordinator—*I whispered* **so they couldn't hear me.** *That* occasionally appears alone in adverbs of reason/purpose, although such constructions sound quite archaic—*Give* **that others may live.**

While the subordinator *since* is usually associated with adverbs of duration (*I've lived here since 1984*), *since* also functions as a subordinator in adverbs of reason. In these clauses, *since* has no temporal content—*I washed the car,* **since Jane had refused to do it**; *I invited him in,* **since I wanted to ask him some questions.**

Adverbs of result are closely related to adverbs of purpose but they underscore the final outcome, rather than the initial motivation. In *We did it to impress the judge*, purpose is highlighted; the sentence is silent on the issue of result. But in *I insulted Philip* **so he slugged me in the mouth** and *We did it* **without waking the baby**, it is the result that is being underscored. *Without* is often used to indicate negative results.

Infinitive clauses often function as adverbs of reason/purpose and result. The subordinator is the infinitive marker *to* alone or accompanied by the prepositional phrase *in order*—*They cheated* **to win**; *I yelled* **in order to restore order.** Infinitive clauses can express <u>potential</u> results and when they do, they frequently appear first in the sentence—**In order to fix this**, *you'll need new cables*; **To pass this course,** *she'll have to get a B on the midterm exam.* Strangely enough, the proform *why* never appears in adverb of reason clauses. In *I know* **why they are laughing**, *why* functions as an adverb of reason within a <u>nominal</u> clause.

Adverbial clauses of reason/purpose and result are extremely common in technical writing and how-to books. Consider these sentences from Sloane's *The Complete Book of Bicycling* (1988) and Hittleman's *Yoga* (1964). (Boldface added.)

Make sure the chain is long enough **so you can shift to the large, freewheel cog**. (Sloan, p. 308)

I recommend installing a chain guard . . . on your chainstay, **to prevent occasional chainrub from damaging its finish**. (Sloan, p. 309)

The point is to lower the legs and roll the trunk forward **so that the head does not leave the floor**. (Hittleman, p. 110)

Summary of manner, means, reason/purpose, and result clauses

Adverbs of Manner	Aldo dances **as if he were a professional**.
	She's acting **like she's feeling better**.
Adverbs of means	You can open this **by kicking it with your boot**.
	I can't fix this pipe **without using force**.
Adverbs of reason and purpose	The child stole the cookies **because she was hungry**.
	Tammy told those lies **to hurt her brother**.
	We planted a hedge **in order to have privacy**.
Adverbs of result	I left the dog alone too long **so she ate my slippers**.
	We removed the tile **without damaging the wall**.

DISJUNCTS AND CONJUNCTS

Disjuncts and conjuncts occasionally occur as clauses. Such clauses are subordinate but not embedded. As you saw in Chapter 4, disjuncts and conjuncts have no modifying relationship within the sentence. The fact that they stand apart is underscored by the pause that follows or precedes the clause.

Speaking frankly, I don't see how she can succeed.

To be brutally candid, I think Mickey will do a lousy job.

I really don't want this job, to be honest.

What is more, she even paid his bills.

What was even more aggravating, she refused to help us clean up the mess.

CONCESSIVE AND CONDITIONAL CLAUSES

The category *adverbial* has become a bit of a garbage can for grammarians. As you've already seen, it is impossible to assign formal criteria to adverbs, since there is very little distinctive adverbial morphology and it is not completely clear what sorts of semantic relations should be considered adverbial. Many grammarians consider sentence modification an adverbial function. **Concessive clauses** are among those that modify the entire sentence. They take many different shapes but in each of the following examples the proposition expressed by the matrix clause is surprising or unexpected in light of the proposition expressed by the subordinate clause.

He lived with his parents, ***even though the house was too small for three adults.***

She worked hard, ***even though they were paying her very little.***

No matter how hard I study, *I can't master statistics.*

I like her, ***although I hardly know her.***

He is still dating her, ***despite the fact that she is seeing someone else.***

Conditional clauses are often discussed in the context of adverbial clauses, but it is not at all clear that they are really adverbials. F. R. Palmer (1986, p. 188) notes that "Although conditional sentences are important in all languages, and although their logic has been thoroughly, if inconclusively, investigated by philosophers, our knowledge and understanding of them in the languages of the world is very poor." In the face of this discouraging prognosis, we will examine just a few of the most typical conditional clause types in English.

Conditional sentences are odd in that they contain two clauses, and in many cases both of the clauses are hypothetical, i.e., neither clause describes an actual event.

If Fred fails, his father will cut off his funds.

If Lisa should fall, you will be blamed.

If he showed up, I would leave.

Cut down this tree and I'll pay you 100 dollars.

Put your hands up or I'll shoot.

As you can see from the last two examples, conditional clauses need not contain *if.*

Conditional sentences vary in the extent of their "hypotheticalness." Consider the following examples. (The first comment in the brackets characterizes the verb in the *if* clause; the second comment characterizes the modal in the independent clause.)

(a) *If she gives me a gift, I will*   [present tense; present
    accept it.   modal]

(b) *If she gave me a gift, I would*   [past tense; past modal]
    accept it.

(c) *If she were to give me a gift,*   [subjunctive semi-auxiliary;
    I would accept it.   past modal]

A sentence in which both the matrix clause and the *if* clause contain present tense forms is less hypothetical than one in which the verbs are in the past tense or the subjunctive. The speaker who utters sentence (a) has more hope of receiving a gift than the speakers of sentences (b) and (c). Note that while both clauses in sentence (b) are in the past tense, the time frame is not past time. In conditionals, both past tense and subjunctive forms are used to intensify the hypothetical quality of the utterance.

The perfect has an interesting effect on *if clauses.* When a speaker uses the present perfect in an *if* clause, the hypothetical nature of the utterance is retained. In *If Leah has finished her homework, she can go the movies,* the speaker indicates not knowing whether or not Leah has finished her homework. But when a speaker exploits the past perfect in an *if* clause, the nature of the speculation changes. In *If Leah had finished her homework, she could have gone to the movies,* the speaker indicates that Leah did not finish her homework and thus did not go to the movies. In this case the speaker speculates on what would have happened if the situation that did pertain had not pertained. The following examples reflect the same semantic pattern.

If she had told me, I would have forgiven her. [She didn't tell me.]

If I hadn't been there, there would have been trouble. [I was there.]

I would have been ecstatic if my aunt had willed me that necklace. [My aunt didn't will me the necklace.]

Conditional and concessive clauses are subordinated but not embedded.

Summing Up

Recursion is a powerful linguistic tool. English speakers use subordinated and coordinated structures constantly. Examine any piece of text (aside from books for small children) and you will find many examples of both coordination and subordination. Sometimes embedded structures lie four and five deep.

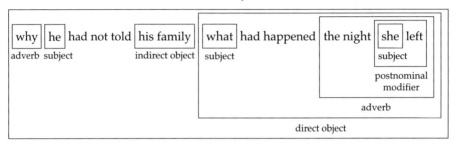

But as complex as embedded and coordinated structures may appear, when you look inside the clauses, you find the same basic structures that were explored in Chapters 1–4, i.e., subjects, direct objects, indirect objects, subject and object complements, adverbials, and adjectivals. All of this complexity is built up out of relatively simple structures. Furthermore, although there are a limited number of clause types in English, each can be used to perform a variety of these syntactic functions, as the following chart illustrates.

Like all languages, English has always exploited recursive processes, although Old English employed coordination far more than subordination. Our capacity to embed has increased dramatically over the centuries. Unfortunately, the terms and analyses that we inherited from classical Greek and Roman grammarians and their eighteenth-century English imitators have been inadequate to the task of describing these deeply complex structures. But even those modern syntacticians who have developed new models for explaining English clause structure find some of these constructions extremely problematic. There is still much to be learned about the nature of subordination in English, and the study of clause structure is still a highly contentious enterprise.

Function

Major clause types

	that clause	infinitive clause	*ING* clause	*wh* clause
subject	That Mr. Nguyen had left upset me.	To do well in school is important.	Riding a bike is easy.	What he did shocked me.
direct object	I know that it's wrong.	I want to attend graduation.	She likes walking in the rain.	I know what she said.
indirect object	———	———	———	Give whoever attends a souvenir.
predicate nominative	The plan is that he will leave first.	His solution is to act incompetent.	Her favorite activity is playing chess.	Life is what you make it.
object complement	———	———	———	Name the puppy whatever you like.
verb complement	He warned me that the stairs were bad.	She forced the child to confess.	I heard him yelling at the dog.	———
adjective complement	I am angry that she was selected.	Gene was anxious to help us.	Rory was upset about leaving home.*	I'm not sure who took your hammer.
adverbial	Give that others might eat.	She cheated to win.	You can start it by pushing this lever.*	You must come when you are called.
postnominal modifier	The fact that they had lied upset me.	Their plan to rob the bank was thwarted.	The student sitting in front is my son.	The folks who live there raise orchids.

*In these sentences the clause is actually the object of a preposition and the prepositional phrase performs the indicated function.

Notes

Introduction

1. Swift understood that the Romans had been in Britain but he believed (quite correctly) that Latin had very little impact on the Germanic tribes who settled there in 449.
2. Some linguists use the term *syntax* to refer only to structural relationships and the term *grammar* to refer to structural relationships plus morphology, i.e., root words and affixes. This distinction has weakened in recent years, and I will use the two terms interchangeably.

Chapter 1

1. Some linguists call any NP that is located in a place or perceived of as moving from one place to another a **theme**. This applies to direct object NPs as well as subject NPs—*The bread is in the cupboard; Joe put the bread in the cupboard*. I will not use this label, but you may encounter it in other books and articles about semantic roles.
2. Actually the dative forms never disappear completely. *Him* and *whom* derive from the Old English dative forms *him* and *hwæm*. The Old English accusative (direct object) forms were *hine* and *hwone*.

Chapter 3

1. Periphrastic constructions usually exploit very common lexical items like *be, have,* and *of*.
2. Thanks to my colleague Kemp Williams and his aunt Ms. Eddie Vance Pate. Ms. Pate is from southeast North Carolina.
3. The term *operator* means something very different in formal semantics, where it refers to processes like negation.

Chapter 5

1. Thanks to Ric Altobellis.
2. Be aware that some grammarians label any required nominal clause in the predicate a *verb complement*. In such grammars, the clauses that I have identified as *direct object, indirect object*, or *predicate nominative* clauses would simply be categorized as complements of the verb. While the term *verb complement* appropriately indicates that all these clauses are required by the verb, it ignores their kinship with a variety of simple NP constructions. I will, therefore, reserve the term *verb complement* for a particular construction, as you will see later.
3. Certain kinds of *wh* nominal clauses are considered by some grammarians to be *headless relative clauses, free relatives,* or *nominal relatives*. All of these labels refer to structures in which (theoretically) the NP head has been deleted in a relative clause construction and the relative clause then takes on a nominal function.

Glossary

abstract noun   A noun that expresses a quality that has no concrete physical reality, e.g., *fact, truth, idea.*

adjective complement   A phrase or clause that serves as a complement to a predicate adjective. *Linda was aware **of the problem**. Bonnie was upset **that all her guests were late**.*

adjunct   Technically, an optional element in a construction. In this textbook the term refers to adverbials of space, time, manner, means, reason/purpose, and result and to non-prenominal adjectives that occur in the predicate but do not follow copulas. *Gloria is playing **in the park**. Morris went to work **angry**.*

agent   The semantic role of an NP that is the willful doer of the action. ***Ryuji** devoured his lunch. The teacher was slapped by **an angry student**.*

anaphoric reference   When a determiner or pronoun refers back to something that has already been introduced into the discourse. *My cousin is a real success; **she** has three advanced degrees.*

Anglo-Saxon   See Old English.

appositive   An NP postnominal construction that provides additional information about the NP. *Andrea, **a point guard on our basketball team**, was recruited by a professional team.*

article   The determiners *the* and *a/an*. Traditionally *the* is called a *definite article* and *a/an* is called an *indefinite article*. Stressed and unstressed *some* are often considered articles, as well.

aspect   Works with tense to establish the time frame of an action, event, or state, but has other functions as well. (See *perfect* and *progressive*.)

attitude disjunct   An adverbial that allows a speaker to comment "editorially" on the content of the sentence. Usually sentence initial. ***Stupidly**, he left his wallet on the bus.*

bare infinitive   Infinitive form without *to. We saw Jonathan **fall**.*

benefactive   The semantic role of an NP that benefits from an action performed by the subject. This NP typically occurs with *for* and a monotransitive verb. *Marty fixed the roof **for Don**.*

cataphoric *it* Occupies the position of a clause that has been extraposed. ***It** is shocking that the commissioner embezzled those funds.*

causer The semantic role of an inanimate or animate subject NP that inadvertently causes something to happen to a direct object. ***Phyllis** accidentally tripped the boss. **The rain** ruined the rug.*

clause Any structure that contains its own verb. (See *matrix clause* and *subordinate clause*.)

closed class Any class of words that will not admit new members, e.g., modal auxiliaries.

cognate object A direct object that derives from the same lexical source as the verb. Can be used with a normally intransitive verb. *He dreamed a terrible dream last night.*

collective noun Noun that refers to a collection of individuals. Can be used with a singular or plural verb, depending on the intent of the speaker. *Our **team** is lousy this year. The **faculty** are angry about their raises.*

common noun Any noun that is not a proper noun, e.g., *motorcycle, bush, plate.*

comparative An inflected or periphrastic form by which an adjective or adverb compares one entity relative to another. *Is Groucho **taller** than Harpo? She works **more quickly** than her sister.*

complex transitive verb A verb that takes both a direct object and an object complement. *Blair **considers** his brother a loser. I **find** the professor's monologues tedious.*

compound A word that is made up of two previously independent lexical items. In compounds the first element typically carries the primary stress, e.g., *ráilroad, hót tub.*

concessive adverbial A phrase or clause containing a proposition that seems surprising or unexpected in light of the rest of the sentence. *He finished the marathon **despite a stress fracture**. I continually loan her books **even though she never returns them**.*

concrete noun A noun that refers to entities with a physical reality, e.g., *book, tree, woman, nail.*

conditional clause Sets up conditions under which the terms of the matrix clause will be met. ***If you help me**, I'll pay you. **Come any closer** and I'll scream.*

conjunct Words or phrases that join together pieces of discourse, e.g., *therefore, however, in addition.*

conjunction   A small category of function words (*and*, *or*, and *but*) that con-join like elements within the sentence or conjoin two or more sentences. *I'll have a hamburger **and** fries.*

control   Whereby a covert subject in a non-finite clause is the same as another NP in the higher clause. Covert NPs can be subject or object controlled. ***She** wants [**she**] to eat. Marge persuaded **Homer** [**Homer**] to leave.*

copula   A small class of verbs (some of which have little semantic content) that link the subject to its complement. A copula can express a current or resulting state. *Annette **is** unhappy. My parents **got** upset. She **looks** ill.*

co-referential   When two or more forms refer to the same real world entity. ***Teddy** scratched **himself**.*

correctness   A traditional doctrine that argues that there are correct and in-correct ways of speaking. (See *prescriptive grammar*.)

correlative   *Either* and *neither* when used with *or* and *nor* to express (usually) mutually exclusive options. *Benny is either sick or tired. I neither borrowed nor lost your book.*

covert structure   Any structure that is not expressed in the sentence but can be recovered from the grammatical or discourse context. *I want **[I]** to eat pizza tonight. **[You]** Sit down!*

created direct object   A direct object that is actually brought into existence by the actions of the subject. *Marconi invented **the radio**.*

dative case   The form carried by the indirect object (and some other struc-tures) in Old English and many other Indo-European languages.

deixis/deictic   Refers to forms the meanings of which are relative to the con-text in which they are uttered. First and second person pronouns, demon-stratives, and some adverbs are deictic. ***This** machine is no good. **I**'ll finish it **tomorrow**.*

demonstrative   A determiner or pronoun that reflects spatial (or sometimes temporal) deixis. ***These** apples are rotten. **This** is my room.*

denominal adjective   A noun form that functions as an adjective, e.g., *a **city** park*.

deontic modality   Constructions in which the speaker expresses volition or obligation and/or attempts to direct the behavior of another. *I **am going to** fix dinner now. She **should** be nicer to her parents. **Close** the door.*

derivational suffix   A suffix that derives one part of speech from another, e.g., the adjective *crabby* from the noun *crab*.

described subject   The subject of any copula the complement of which is de-scriptive. ***Carla** is short.*

descriptive grammar   Grammars that describe language as it is actually spoken.

determiner   A small class of function words (articles, demonstratives, interrogatives, and genitives) that precede both the noun and any adjectives in the NP. *A new woman has joined our research group.* *My brother is single.*

deverbal nouns   Nouns that are derived from verbs, e.g., *refusal, reaction, execution.*

directive   A construction in which a speaker attempts to influence the behavior of another. *Put that game away. Can you pass me the potatoes? I want you to leave.*

discourse   Any stretch of speech (or writing) longer than a sentence. A discourse can involve any number of speakers.

disjunct   A speaker comment construction. Except in the case of epistemic adverbs, disjuncts have little effect on the proposition. ***Honestly,*** *he is incompetent.* ***Amazingly,*** *she found the misplaced money.*

ditransitive verb   A verb that takes two objects, a direct object and an indirect object. *She **handed** me the gift.*

double genitive   A structure in which the genitive is marked both inflectionally and periphrastically, e.g., *a poem **of Kipling's**.*

downtoner   A modifying word or phrase that softens the meaning of the word or phrase it modifies, e.g., *They were **somewhat** angry. She is **kind of** a prima donna. I **sort of** insulted him.*

dual object plural   A non-count noun that refers to an entity composed of two identical halves that are connected, e.g., *trousers, binoculars, tweezers.*

dynamic verb   A verb that expresses an action or an event. Can typically co-occur with the progressive. (See *stative verb*). *Bonilla **ran** to first base. It is **snowing**.*

Early Modern English   English as it was spoken in Britain from 1500–1800.

echo question   A question that typically repeats something a previous speaker has said. It does not exhibit subject/operator inversion. *Dick said he wanted to go?*

edited English   Rules for formal writing.

embedding   The inclusion of one structure inside another. *I know **that Kim lied**.*

empty *it*   Usually the semantically empty subject in sentences that refer to weather or general ambience, e.g., ***It***'s *cold outside.* Occasionally it is a semantically empty direct object, e.g., *Let's call **it** a day.*

epistemic modality   The expression of possibility or probability. Can be communicated by auxiliaries, lexical verbs, and adverbs. *She **might** be late.* ***Maybe*** *it will snow tomorrow.*

equi When a covert NP is identical to a higher NP. *Selma wanted [Selma] to leave. We forced the suspect [the suspect] to confess.*

existential *there* A construction in which non-locative *there* is a subject and is used to point something out or introduce something into discourse. ***There** is girl in my neighborhood who raises pot-bellied pigs.*

experiencer An animate NP that has a non-volitional sensory or psychological experience. ***Tillie** heard the explosion. The meat smelled bad to **the cook**.*

factive A construction containing a direct object *that* clause, the content of which is presumed to be fact by the speaker. *It is strange that Lee is selling his truck.* (See *non-factive*.)

finite verb A verb phrase that expresses tense. *Guido **is sleeping**. I know that she **stole** it.*

gapping A structure in which the second of two coordinated clauses omits the verb. *Adriana loves Merlot and Joanne brandy.*

generic reference When an NP refers to all members of a class. ***The pronghorn antelope** is the fastest animal in North America.*

genitive Inflected or prepositional *of* constructions that express a variety of semantic relationships including possession, measurement, and part/whole, e.g., *Lilith's coat; the roof **of the car**.*

gerund Traditional label for a highly nominal *ING* form. *The **storming** of the castle will take place at dawn.*

given information (old information) Information that has already been introduced into the discourse.

gradability The scalar property that allows some adjectives and adverbs to take comparative and superlative forms and intensifiers. *She ran really fast. Walter is taller than Ben.*

grammaticality judgements Judgements about the relative acceptability of a given utterance. Ungrammatical sentences are typically marked with *, while marginally grammatical sentences are marked with ?? and odd sentences are marked with ?.

group genitive A construction in which a complex phrase receives the genitive morpheme, e.g., *[the Dean of Engineering]'s office.*

head The central element in a syntactic structure, e.g., *a tall, handsome **man**.*

heavy NP shift The process of moving a particularly long or complex NP or nominal clause to the end of the sentence. *Give **the woman standing next to your brother's car** the bag. / Give the bag to **the woman standing next to your brother's car**.*

homophones Two or more words that sound the same but have different meanings. They may or may not have the same spelling, e.g., *two/to/too* and *port* (wine) / *port* (harbor).

iconicity/iconic When the form of a word or structure is influenced by its function, e.g., repetitions of a word indicate more of the quality it represents. *Charles is **very, very** talented.*

idiom An expression the meaning of which cannot be extrapolated from its parts, e.g., *kick the bucket, bite the bullet.*

imperative A normally subjectless directive in which the covert subject is *you*, e.g., *Sit down.* Indefinite third person imperatives, second person imperatives with overt subjects, and first person plural imperatives also exist, e.g., *Nobody move! You leave him alone! Let's leave.*

inalienable possession A relationship in which the possessed is not normally separable from the possessor. Often used to refer to body parts and family members, e.g., ***Jake's** leg; **my** aunt.*

indefinite pronoun A determiner or pronoun that has an unspecified referent, e.g., *somebody, anything, nobody.*

indefinite *this* A non-deictic, non-anaphoric determiner that is used to introduce an NP into the discourse. ***This** guy walks up to me and starts punching me.*

independent clause Any clause that can stand alone. Any sentence is an independent clause.

indirect object The traditional label for the grammatical structure that expresses the recipient. It may appear as an NP directly after the verb or as a PP after the direct object. *I offered **them** some coffee. I loaned a book **to Frances**.*

infinitive A non-finite form of the verb that typically appears with *to*, e.g., *to eat, to work.* (See *bare infinitive.*)

inflectional suffix The suffixes taken by an individual lexical item that help define it as a grammatical category. These suffixes never change the part of speech, e.g., *books, walked, taller.*

instrument The semantic role of an inanimate NP that is being used as an instrument. *Tom fixed his computer with **a hammer**. **The key** opened the safe.*

intensifier A word or phrase that has little meaning of its own, but intensifies the meaning of the word it modifies, e.g., ***very** tall, **really** fast.*

interrogative Sentence types used in asking questions. *Is Rhoda sleeping? What are you doing?*

interrogative proforms *Wh* words and *how*. Used in constructing information seeking questions. ***Who** are you talking to? **Where** did Tina go?*

intransitive verb   A verb that does not normally take a direct object. *The kids* **slept**. *Michael* **sat** *on the couch*.

lexical verb   The final verb in the verb phrase. Usually has significant semantic content. *Pete* **sang**. *Sally has been* **digging** *a hole*.

lexicalization   The process whereby a syntactic/semantic difference is reflected in the lexicon, e.g., *look at* versus *see*; *in* versus *into*.

light transitive verb   A verb that takes its meaning from the following direct object. *Maurice* **took** *a bath. Helene* **had** *a smoke*.

limiter   Limits the hearer's attention to the word or phrase that follows and excludes other possibilities. *I* **just** *tapped his fender*. **Only** *Joel was selected*.

located subject   A subject that is located in space by its predicate. **Tirana** *is in Albania*. **Your sandwich** *is on the table*.

locative   Any structure that expresses location. Often but not always an adverb. *She lives* **in Quebec**. *They have climbed* **Mt. Everest**. **Tucson** *is hot*.

locative inversion   Constructions exhibiting operator/subject inversion in which the locative adverbial appears first in the sentence. Sometimes exclamatory. *Here comes Beatrice*.

main clause   The structure in which all other clauses are embedded. ***Jonah wants England to win the World Cup***.

main verb   The lexical verb in the main clause. *I* **know** *that Sam likes you*.

malefactive   Threats that exploit the same construction as benefactives. *I'll break your arm for you*.

markedness   When one form stands in contrast to another (to which it is semantically or structurally related) because it carries a morpheme the other lacks, e.g., *prince* versus *princess*, or because it is used in a more restricted set of constructions, e.g., *How old are you?* versus *How* **young** *are you?*

matrix clause   The structure in which another clause (or clauses) is embedded. It may be a main clause or a subordinate clause.

Middle English   The variety of English spoken in Britain from 1100–1500.

modal auxiliaries   A closed set of auxiliary verbs, all of which have unconventional morphology and all of which share a relatively small set of meanings, e.g., *will, should*.

modality   The expression of nonfacts, e.g., speculations, desires, directives. *It might rain. I wish I were tall. You must clean your room*.

monotransitive verb   A verb that takes only one object, a direct object, e.g., *eat, study*.

mood   Constructions in which modality is marked by special forms of the verb. The imperative and subjunctive are both marked for mood. *Be quiet. I wish I were rich.*

multi-word verb   Lexical verbs that contain a head plus one or more *particles.* In some cases the particle is movable and in others it is not. *Andrew put out the cat. I can't put up with this behavior.*

non-count noun   A noun that does not exhibit number contrast and cannot be counted without a partitive, e.g., *rice, milk, scissors.*

non-factive   Sentences in which a *that* clause is treated epistemically by the speaker. *I think that Violetta has finished the project. It's likely that it will rain tomorrow.*

non-finite verb   A verb phrase in which tense is not expressed. *Winning first prize was not important. Grandpa wants Heidi to come home.*

non-inherent adjective   Prenominal adjective that does not express a quality inherent in the noun it modifies, although it often express a quality inherent in a related noun, e.g., *an old friend; a big fool.*

non-restrictive relative clauses   *Wh* clauses that provide additional information about the NP. *Tim's sister, who lives in Liverpool, owns a bicycle shop.*

Norman invasion   The invasion of England in 1066 by French speakers from the Kingdom of Normandy in northern France.

noun phrase   A noun head and its modifiers, e.g., *a sweet kitten; a telegram from my brother.*

number   In English, refers to the contrast between singular and plural forms in nouns, pronouns, and verbs, e.g., *cat/cats, I/we, go/goes.*

object complement   An NP or adjective that follows a complex transitive verb and a direct object and has the same referent as the direct object or modifies the direct object. *They have made Dick an officer. The jury found my sister guilty.*

object genitive   A construction in which the genitive plays the semantic role of direct object within the NP. *Joy's promotion pleased her colleagues.*

Old English (Anglo Saxon)   English as it was spoken in Britain between c. 500–1100.

operator   The first auxiliary in the verb phrase. Used in the creation of negatives and questions. *Is Cecilia moving away? Liz didn't finish her lunch.*

part/whole genitive   Construction in which the genitive expresses the whole and the NP it modifies expresses the part, e.g., *the car's battery; the roof of the house.*

partitive   A measurement or quantity phrase that allows non-count nouns to be counted, e.g., *four pounds of hamburger; one carton of milk.*

passive voice   A construction that contains the auxiliary *be* or *get* plus a past participle. The subject is typically affected by the action of the verb. *Rocky* **got** *mugged last night. They* **were** *annoyed by the commotion.*

past participle   A form of the verb that participates in perfect and passive constructions. *The baby has* **fallen***. The roof was* **damaged** *by the storm.* Also used as an adjective, e.g., *the* **broken** *swing.*

patient   The semantic role of an NP that is affected by the action of the verb. *The fisherman caught* **three trout***.* **The tree** *toppled.* **The village** *was destroyed.*

perfect   A construction that contains the auxiliary *have* plus the past participle form of the following verb. Often expresses duration or current relevance. *Janice* **has** *lived there thirty years. I* **have** *just* **cut** *my leg.*

performative   A construction in which the actual utterance of the words constitutes an act with social and sometimes legal ramifications. *I sentence you to life imprisonment.*

periphrasis/periphrastic   A construction that exploits additional words rather than inflectional morphemes. *The top* **of the table** as opposed to *the table's top.*

personal pronoun   A pronoun that reflects person (first, second, and third), number, and subject, genitive, and (except for *it*) object case, e.g., *she, them, its.*

phrasal verb   See *multi-word verb.*

possessive genitive   A construction in which the genitive reflects the possessor or owner of the NP it modifies, e.g., **Brian's** *pickup truck;* **Judith's** *face.*

possessive reflexive pronouns   Constructions in which a genitive is always construed as referring back to the subject. *May won't help* **her own** *father. Patty blinked* **her** *eyes.*

postdeterminer   A small class of quantifying words that follow the determiner in the NP. *It was her* **fourth** *bologna sandwich. The* **two** *boys in the group dissented.*

predicate adjective   An adjective that follows a copula and modifies the subject. *Lucille is* **smart***.*

predicate nominative   An NP that follows a copula and has the same referent as the subject. *Shirley is* **a mechanical engineer***.*

prenominal adjective   An adjective that precedes the noun in the NP, e.g., *a* **big** *boat.*

prescriptive grammar   Language rules that focus on which forms and structures are "correct" and which are not. *Don't end a sentence with a preposition* is a classic prescriptive rule.

present participle   The {-ing} form of a verb. Participates in the progressive and also functions as a prenominal adjective. *I am* **eating** *now. I could hear a* **laughing** *child.*

preterit   Another term for *past tense*.

primary auxiliary   The semantically empty auxiliaries *be* and *have* (which are used in constructing the perfect, progressive, and passive) and periphrastic *do*.

proform   A small word that stands in for another lexical item or construction e.g., *she, where, which, why, everyone*.

progressive   A construction that contains the auxiliary *be* plus the present participle of the following verb. Typically communicates an ongoing, incomplete activity or short-term state. *Gus **is being** mean. I **am** read**ing** a comic book.*

pronoun   A proform that stands for an NP, e.g., *she, it, who, what*. Some pronouns have indefinite reference, e.g., *anyone, somebody, whoever*.

proper noun   A noun that has unique reference and no determiner or number contrast, e.g., *William Shakespeare, Saudi Arabia*.

pseudo passive   Constructions that are active in form but passive in meaning. *This fabric washes well.*

psych-verb   A verb expressing a psychological state, e.g., *want, consider, think*.

punctual verb   A verb that refers to an event of very brief duration, e.g., *blink, cough, punch*.

quantifier   A determiner, predeterminer, postdeterminer, pronoun, or NP that expresses quantity, e.g., *each, many, four, all, a lot of*.

quantifier float   The process by which some quantifying predeterminers can move into the verb phrase. ***All** the kids are yelling for ice cream. / The kids are **all** yelling for ice cream.*

reciprocals   Constructions in which two or more elements have the same relationship to each other. *Jenna resembles Nolan. Newt and Ed dislike each other. Huey, Dewey, and Louie chatted.*

recursion   The repetition of structures. Recursion can yield conjoined structures, e.g., *Lucy and Ricky* or embedded structures, e.g., *I know **that Arlene is mad**.*

reduced relative clause   A term sometimes used to describe postnominal modifiers that are not full relative clauses. They can be restrictive, as in *The cat **hiding under the couch** is my favorite* or non-restrictive as in *Jeff, **a software engineer**, is setting up my computer.* (See *appositive*.)

referent   The NP to which a pronoun refers. *I like **Mindy**. She is very generous.*

reflexive pronoun   A pronoun that has the same referent as a preceding NP in the same clause. Except in the case of *possessive reflexives*, a reflexive is a personal pronoun form plus {-self}, e.g., *himself, ourselves, myself*.

relative pronoun   The subordinator in a relative clause. Always has the same referent as the NP it modifies. *I know the woman **who** sold you that car.*

relative tense   Occurs when the tense of a non-finite clause is determined by the matrix clause. *I want to win* versus *I had wanted to win.*

restricted copula   A small class of copulas that occur with a limited number of subject complements. *The issue **loomed** large. The audience **fell** silent.*

restrictive relative clause   Clause that modifies the preceding NP, usually by restricting its possible referents. Subordinator is a *wh* proform or *that. All the trees **that Paulette planted** are doing well.*

resulting copula   Copula that reflects a change of state. *My brother **became** sleepy.*

scope of negation   Refers to those parts of the sentence actually affected by the negative particle.

semantic role   Delineates the role played by a lexical item, phrase, or clause in relationship to the verb, e.g., *agent, experiencer, adverb of direction.*

semi-auxiliaries   Multi-word constructions that express deontic and/or epistemic modality, as well as ability and habituality, e.g., *be going to, is certain to, used to.*

sensory copula   A copula that refers to one of our five senses. *That guy smells bad. Your daughter sounds hoarse.*

stative adjective   A predicate adjective that expresses an ongoing state. Co-occurs with a stative copula. *My great grandmother is very **old**.*

stative verb   Any verb, including a copula, that expresses an ongoing state. Typically does not co-occur with the progressive. *Claudia **is** tall. Melinda **enjoys** Tai Chi.*

style disjunct   Adverbial that indicates in what mode the speaker is speaking. ***Truthfully**, I can't stand the man. **Frankly**, I think my brother is incompetent.*

subject complement   An NP or adjective in the predicate that has the same referent as the subject or modifies the subject, i.e., a predicate adjective or predicate nominative. *The tree is **dead**. Yesim is a **physicist.*** A locative adverb after copula *be* is also considered a subject complement. *I am **in the garden**.*

subject dominant language   A language in which the subject of the main verb must be expressed, e.g., *English.*

subject genitive   A construction in which the genitive plays the semantic role of subject within the NP. *The **contractor's** shortcuts weakened the building.*

subjunctive   A set of distinctively marked verb forms that are used to express directives, volition, and hypothetical situations. *I demand that she leave. He wishes he **were** a bird.*

subordinate clause   Any clause that cannot stand alone. *I want **you to enjoy yourself. If you talk,** you'll have to leave.*

subordinator   A function word or morpheme that signals a subordinate clause. *I wanted Patricia **to** have the car. I hate eat**ing** with slobs.*

superlative   An inflected or periphrastic form used with adjectives and adverbs that expresses the final degree of comparison. *Joseba ran **fastest**; She is the **most annoying** person here.*

suppletive form   A form that has a different root from its base form, e.g., *go/went, good/better.*

tag question   A question that follows a statement and seeks confirmation of the truth of that statement. *The Yankees are winning, **aren't they?** You're not leaving, **are you?***

tense   A small set of inflectional suffixes and special forms that are used to establish time frame, among other functions. *The dog chewed up my slippers. Libby likes chocolate.*

topic   What the discourse is about. Topics represent *given information.*

transitive verb   Any verb that can take a direct object. *Tarzan **eats** sushi.*

verb complement   A clause that follows a direct object NP and complements the higher verb. *I warned Doris **that her friends would be upset**. I forced Marcus **to help me**.*

verb particle   The preposition-like words that occur in multi-word lexical verbs. Some particles move to a position after the direct object, e.g., *Jay put the cat **out*** and others are unmovable, e.g., *Virginia called **on** her cousins.*

volitional   Any construction that expresses wants, willingness, promises, or threats. *I wish I were rich. I won't tell anyone that. I'm going to ground you.*

References

Aijmer, Karin and Bengt Altenberg (Eds.). 1991. *English Corpus Linguistics*. London: Longman.

Ambrose, Stephen E. 1996. *Undaunted Courage: Meriwether Lewis, Thomas Jefferson, and the Opening of the American West.* New York: Simon and Schuster.

American Psychological Association. (1994). *Publication Manual of the American Psychological Association* (4th ed.). Washington, DC: Author.

Austin, J. L. 1962. *How to Do Things with Words*. Oxford: Clarendon Press.

Barry, Dave. 1997, April 27. Mr. Language on the butchered apostrophe. *The Denver Post, Empire Magazine,* 7.

Battistella, Edwin L. 1990. *Markedness: The Evaluative Superstructure of Language*. Albany: State University of New York Press.

Beach, Hugh. 1993. *A Year in Lapland.* Washington: Smithsonian Institution Press.

Beaman, Karen. 1984. Coordination and subordination revisited: syntactic complexity in spoken and written narrative discourse. In Tannen (ed.), 45–80.

Bernstein, Jeremy. 1997, June 12. The road to Lhasa. *The New York Review of Books*, 44:10, 45–49.

Berry, Chuck. 1959. *Back in the USA/Memphis Tennessee*. Chess Records 1729.

Boyce, Jim, et al. 1995. *Inside Windows 95*. Indianapolis: New Riders Publishing.

Brown, Penelope and Stephen C. Levinson. 1987. *Politeness: Some Universals in Language Usage.* Cambridge: Cambridge University Press.

Burke, James Lee. 1995. *Burning Angel.* New York: Hyperion.

Bybee, Joan, Revere Perkins, and William Pagliuca. 1994. *The Evolution of Grammar.* Chicago: University of Chicago Press.

Chandler, Raymond. 1971. *The Little Sister.* New York: Ballantine Books.

Chomsky, Noam. 1957. *Syntactic Structures.* The Hague: Mouton.

Cloran, Carmel. 1995. Defining and relating text segments: subject and theme in discourse. In Hasan and Fries, 361–403.

Collins, Peter. 1991. The modals of obligation and necessity in Australian English. In Aijmer and Altenberg, 145–165.

Comrie, Bernard. 1976. *Aspect.* Cambridge: Cambridge University Press.

Comrie, Bernard. 1985. *Tense.* Cambridge: Cambridge University Press.

Cornwall, Patricia. 1995. *From Potter's Field.* New York: Berkley Books.

Crystal, David. 1997a. *A Dictionary of Linguistics and Phonetics.* 4th ed. Oxford: Blackwell Publishers.

Crystal, David. 1997b. *The Cambridge Encyclopedia of Language.* 2nd ed. Cambridge: Cambridge University Press.

Culicover, Peter. 1988. Autonomy, predication, and thematic relations. In Wilkins, 37–60.

Dahl, H. 1979. *Word Frequencies of Spoken American English.* Essex, CT: Verbatim.

Dawkins, Richard. 1996. *The Blind Watchmaker: Why the Evidence of Evolution Reveals a Universe Without Design*. New York: W. W. Norton.

The Denver Post. 1997, May 6, D-1.

Dibdin, Michael. 1996. *Dead Lagoon*. New York: Vintage Crime/Black Lizard.

Dowty, David. 1986. Aspectual class and discourse. *Linguistics and Philosophy, 9*, 37–61.

Fillmore, Charles and Paul Kay. 1995. *Construction Grammar*. Stanford: Center for the Study of Language and Information.

Fox, Barbara. 1987. *Discourse Structure and Anaphora: Written and Conversational English*. Cambridge: Cambridge University Press.

Fox, Barbara and Paul J. Hopper. (Eds.). 1994. *Voice: Form and Function*. Amsterdam: John Benjamins.

Friedman, Kinky. 1996. *Gold Bless John Wayne*. New York: Bantam Books.

Fries, Peter H. 1995. Themes, methods of development, and texts. In Hasan and Fries, 317–359.

George, Elizabeth. 1997. *In the Presence of the Enemy*. New York: Bantam Paperback.

Gillagan, Gary. 1987. A cross linguistic approach to the Pro-Drop Parameter. Ph.D. dissertation: University of Southern California.

Givón, Talmy. 1979. *On Understanding Grammar*. Orlando, FL.: Academic Press.

Givón, Talmy. 1993a. *English Grammar: A Function-Based Introduction*, Vol 1. Amsterdam: John Benjamins.

Givón, Talmy. 1993b. *English Grammar: A Function-Based Introduction*, Vol. 2. Amsterdam: John Benjamins.

Givón, Talmy. 1995. *Functionalism and Grammar*. Amsterdam: John Benjamins.

Givón, Talmy and Lynne Yang. 1994. The rise of the English *GET* passive. In Fox and Hopper, 119–149.

Glassner, Andrew S. 1995. *Principles of Digital Image Synthesis*. San Francisco: Morgan Kaufmann.

Glaves, Paul. 1997, March. Steering head bearing adjustments. *BMW Owner's News*, 16–19.

Goldberg, Adele E. 1995. *Constructions: A Construction Grammar Approach to Argument Structure*. Chicago: University of Chicago Press.

Grob, Gerald N. and Robert N. Beck. 1963. The Declaration of Independence. *American Ideas*, Vol. I. 186–189. New York: The Free Press of Glencoe.

Grundel, Jeanette, Nancy Hedberg, and Ron Zacharski. 1993. Cognitive status and the form of referring expressions in discourse. *Language, 69*:2, 274–307.

Haiman, John (Ed.). 1985. *Iconicity in Syntax*. Amsterdam: John Benajmins.

Hall, James. 1993. *Hard Aground*. New York: Dell.

Harrison, G. B. (Ed.). 1952. *Shakespeare: The Complete Works*. New York: Harcourt, Brace, & World.

Hasan, Ruqaiya and Peter H. Fries (Eds.). 1995. *On Subject and Theme: A Discourse Functional Perspective*. Amsterdam: John Benjamins.

Hillerman, Tony. 1993. *Sacred Clowns*. New York: HarperCollins.

Hittleman, Richard L. 1964. *Yoga*. New York: Warner Books.

The Holy Bible. n.d. Authorized or King James Version. Chicago: John C. Winston.

The Holy Scriptures. 1917. Philadelphia: Jewish Publication Society of America.

Hopper, Paul and Sandra Thompson. 1980. Transitivity in grammar and discourse. *Language, 56*:2, 251–299.

Hopper, Paul and Sandra Thompson. 1984. The discourse basis for lexical categories in universal grammar. *Language, 60*:4, 703–752.

Hopper, Paul and Sandra Thompson. 1985. The iconicity of the universal categories 'noun' and 'verbs'. In Haiman, 151–183.

Hulme, Keri. 1983. *The Bone People.* New York: Penguin Books.

Hussey, Stanley. 1995. *The English Language: Structure and Development.* New York: Longman.

Ignatieff, Michael. 1997, June 12. The center of the earthquake. *The New York Review of Books,* 44:10, 31–33.

Joshi, Aravind K., Bonnie L. Webber, and Ivan A. Sag (Eds.). 1981. *Elements of Discourse Understanding.* Cambridge: Cambridge University Press.

Kidder, Tracy. 1985. *House.* Boston: Houghton Mifflin.

Kingsolver, Barbara. 1994. *Pigs in Heaven.* New York: HarperPerennial.

Klein–Andreu, Flora (Ed.). 1983. *Discourse: Perspectives on Syntax.* New York: Academic Press.

Kolata, Gina. 1997, December 3. The FDA OKs irradiation of red meat. *The Miami Herald,* 30A.

Lakoff, George. 1987. *Women, Fire and Dangerous Things.* Chicago: University of Chicago Press.

Lakoff, George and Mark Johnson. 1980. *Metaphors We Live By.* Chicago: University of Chicago Press.

Lambrecht, Knud. 1994. *Information Structure and Sentence Form.* Cambridge: Cambridge University Press.

Langacker, Ronald. 1987. *Foundations of Cognitive Grammar,* Vol. 1. Stanford: Stanford University Press.

Leonard, Elmore. 1996. *Out of Sight.* New York: Dell.

Levin, Beth. 1993. *English Verb Classes and Alternations.* Chicago: University of Chicago Press.

Levin, Beth and Steven Pinker (Eds.). 1992. *Lexical and Conceptual Semantics.* Oxford: Blackwell.

Lowth, Robert. 1767. *A Short Introduction to English Grammar with Critical Notes.* A new edition, corrected. London: A. Millar, T. Cadell, and J. Dodsley.

Lui, C.L. and James Layland. 1973. Scheduling Algorithms for Multiprogramming in a hard-real-time environment. *Journal of the Association for Computing Machinery,* 20:1, 46–61.

MacDonald, Ross. 1996. *Black Money.* New York: Vintage Crime/Black Lizard.

Martin, Rux, Patricia Jamieson, and Elizabeth Hiser. 1991. *The Eating Well Cookbook.* Charlotte, VT: Camden House.

McGinley, Patrick. 1982. *Goosefoot.* New York: E. P. Dutton.

Miller, George A. 1996. *The Science of Words.* New York: Scientific American Library.

Miller, George A. and Christiane Fellbaum. 1992. Semantic networks of English. In Levin and Pinker, 197–229.

Mindt, Dieter. 1991. Syntactic evidence for semantic distinctions in English. In Aijmer and Altenberg, 182–196.

Moore, Samuel and Thomas A. Knott. 1955. *The Elements of Old English.* (James R. Hulbert, rev. ed.). Ann Arbor, MI: George Wahr Publishing.

Mosley, Walter. 1997. *Gone Fishin'.* Baltimore: Black Classic Press.

Motorcyclist. 1997, April, 96.

Oates, Joyce Carol. 1997. *Will You Always Love Me?* New York: Plume/Penguin.

Palmer, F. R. 1986. *Mood and Modality.* Cambridge: Cambridge University Press.

Paretsky, Sara. 1995. *Windy City Blues: V. I. Warshawski Stories.* New York: Dell.

Parker, Robert. 1996. *Thin Air.* New York: Berkley.

Penn, Larry. 1997. Why don't a tow truck haul toes? *The Whiskey's Gone.* Cookie Man Music.

Pickthall, Marmaduke (transl.). 1992. *The Koran.* New York: Everyman's Library, Alfred A. Knopf.

Piraro, Dan. 1997, April 1. Cartoon distributed by Universal Press Syndicate. *The Denver Post,* 6E.

Prejean, Sister Helen. 1994. *Dead Man Walking.* New York: Vintage Books.

Prince, Ellen. 1981. On the reference of indefinite-*this* NPs. In Joshi, et. al., 231–250.

Proulx, E. Annie. 1993. *Shipping News.* New York: Touchstone.

Quirk, Randolph, Sidney Greenbaum, Geoffrey Leech, and Jan Svartvik. 1972. *A Grammar of Contemporary English.* London: Longman.

Scarry, Richard. 1992. *Huckle Cat's Busiest Day Ever!* New York. Random House.

Schiffrin, Deborah. 1987. *Discourse Markers.* Cambridge: Cambridge University Press.

Schwarzchild, Roger. 1996. *Pluralities.* Dordrecht, The Netherlands: Kluwer Academic Publishers.

Sloane Eugene A. 1988. *The Complete Book of Bicycling.* New York: Simon and Schuster.

Swift, Jonathan. 1957. A proposal for correcting the English tongue. In Herbert Davis (Ed.). *Jonathan Swift, Vol. 4: Polite Conversation, Etc.* Oxford: Blackwell.

Tannen, Deborah (Ed.). 1984a. *Coherence in Spoken and Written Discourse.* Norwood, NJ: Ablex Publishing.

Tannen, Deborah. 1984b. Spoken and written narrative in English and Greek. In Tannen 1984a, 21–41.

Ward, Benji. 1983. Reference and topic within and across discourse units. In Klein-Andreu, 91–116.

Weinberg, Steven. 1997, June 12. Before the Big Bang. *The New York Review of Books* 44:10, 16–20.

Wierzbicka, Anna. 1988a. *The Semantics of Grammar.* Amsterdam: John Benjamins.

Wierzbicka, Anna. 1988b. Oats and wheat: mass nouns, iconicity, and human categorization. In Wierzbicka 1988a, 499–560.

Wierzbicka, Anna. 1988c. Why can you *have a drink* when you can't *have an eat*? In Wierzbicka, 1988a, 293–357.

Wierzbicka, Anna. 1997. *Understanding Cultures Through Their Key Words.* Oxford: Oxford University Press.

Wilkins, Wendy (Ed.). 1988. *Syntax and Semantics Vol 21: Thematic Relations.* San Diego: Academic Press.

Visser, T. Th. (1978). *An Historical Syntax of the English Language.* Vol. 4. Leidin: E. J. Brill.

Index